Compromised Bodies

CONTEMPORARY ETHNOGRAPHY

Alma Gottlieb, Series Editor

A complete list of books in the series is available from
the publisher.

COMPROMISED BODIES

Cultural Imperialism, Agency, and the Ban
on "Female Genital Mutilation" in Senegal

Sarah O'Neill

PENN

UNIVERSITY OF PENNSYLVANIA PRESS

PHILADELPHIA

Published by
University of Pennsylvania Press
Philadelphia, Pennsylvania 19104–4112
www.pennpress.org

Printed in the United States of America on acid-free paper

10 9 8 7 6 5 4 3 2 1

A Cataloging-in-Publication record is available from the
Library of Congress.

Paperback ISBN 978-1-5128-2723-1
Hardcover ISBN 978-1-5128-2724-8
eBook ISBN 978-1-5128-2725-5

To Anaïs and Aly

CONTENTS

Contents

Introduction

S emme, Senegal. June 22, 2007. *An important day in the history of the opposition to the law against female circumcision in Fouta Toro—it is the morning of the second-ever public declaration of the "abandonment of excision and early/forced marriage" in this region. Since the national ban on excision was passed in 1999, numerous governmental and nongovernmental attempts to raise awareness about the law and the harmfulness of female genital cutting (FGC) have been strongly opposed by some religious leaders and their followers. Afraid of the power and political influence of the* marabouts *(religious leaders), most NGOs have given up raising awareness in Fouta Toro, deemed "the most difficult region" in terms of reaching the national target of complete abandonment of excision. Only the NGO Tostan has some forty to fifty education centers still running in the district of Matam. In Podor, the religious leaders' polemics have forced centers to close and have driven away public health education and literacy programs that mention excision.*

I have spent the night with Tostan facilitators and anti-excision activists, whom I have come to know well, on mats in the courtyard of a family who want to declare their renunciation of excision today. The compound is crowded with guests who have come from afar to witness this event. There is a nervous tension in the air. Is it going to work? Are they really going to achieve the feat of running this public declaration right through to the end? Are there going to be participants? Probably not that many—it is Ceedu, *the hottest period of the year, when temperatures climb to 48 degrees Celsius during the hottest hours of the day. The NGO facilitators I am with have been working very hard to prepare this event, raising awareness about excision, persuading people to invite their relatives from other villages to join their declaration so that more villages declare their renunciation of excision and early/forced marriage. But people are anxious not only that enough locals will participate, but that the event could be sabotaged by religious leaders saying that abandoning is anti-Islamic. Although government officials, the prefect, and the village chief will be present as well as health care professionals and midwives, who will explain why excision should be stopped, many locals consider that publicly renouncing it equates with publicly confessing one's abandonment of religion. Although the UNICEF representatives and "the white man's NGO," Tostan, are welcomed by those who aspire to change and development, they are condemned and despised by others who believe that they are trying to destroy Futanke culture and Islam.*

∗   ∗   ∗

This book explores why there has been such vehement opposition to the law criminalizing excision and NGO (nongovernmental organization) awareness-raising programs in Fouta Toro. According to recent figures (UNICEF, 2022), 25 percent of women and girls have undergone the practice in Senegal, a slim 3 percent decrease since 2005 (Demographic Health Survey Senegal 2005). Given sustained efforts to achieve the complete abandonment of the practice since the ban in 1999, and the millions of dollars that have flown into raising awareness campaigns about the law and harms of what is widely termed "female genital mutilation" (FGM), the progress is perceived to be meager and it is unlikely that the target of its complete abandonment by 2030 will be reached (UNICEF 2022).

To health professionals, NGO workers, and researchers like myself, living and working in rural communities, the complete abandonment target always seemed ambitious. When I began working on the subject in 2004, people in remote parts of Senegal were barely aware that a law criminalizing the practice existed. Furthermore, at the time many people hesitated to oppose a practice that had been recommended by religious leaders and was strongly associated with women's purity and honor. When I first started formulating research questions on the opposition to the ban on FGM, I wondered to what extent the passing of the bill had been a result of compliance with international standards of human rights by a government that was to a large extent in the hands of ethnic groups (Wolof, Serere) who do not practice FGC themselves and who might have had an interest in representing their country as advancing and meeting transnationally recognized standards of development. For the Futanke, however, the ban might have been read as undermining their ethnic and cultural integrity and attacking their beliefs by outlawing a practice they call a religious recommendation—but the Mourides Wolof in semiurban

Senegal do not. On closer inspection, however, I realized that it was more complicated—the divisions and differences between the Futanke who oppose the ban and development and the government run by pro-ban Wolof were blurred. To introduce the main actors in the national call for abandonment, those who oppose the law and the NGOs involved, in what follows I continue to explore the political role-play of the public declaration at Semme introduced above.

* * *

The NGO facilitators and anti-excision activists with whom I have spent the night take me to greet other local women, men, and children who have prepared theater sketches and dance performances. They have dressed colorfully in their best gowns (wutte) *and traditional dress* (cosaan). *Despite the nervous uncertainty in the air as to whether everything will go well, people are proud of what they have prepared for this important event, where local authorities and officials will come together to witness the women's resolution to stop practicing excision.*

At midday we approach the public space where the declaration is going to take place. There are tents and chairs for the representatives of each village to sit and hold up signs with the name of their village. I have come to know a lot of them well over the last six months in Fouta and they invite me to come and sit with them. However, in the end it is decided that I should sit on the stage with the officials and the other white people who are here to document this event for the NGO Tostan and UNICEF.

Radio presenters are getting their equipment set up, the microphones are being tested, and people are taking time to greet each other at length while traditional hodu *music is blaring through the loudspeakers. Eventually the authorities arrive. They slowly get out of two cars, dressed in beautiful gowns made of expensive Malian cloth, and approach the stage with solemn expressions on their faces. I can see the regional Tostan coordinator, a* Galluŋke/Maccudo *(the caste of former slaves). By his side is his assistant, a* Ceddo *(warrior), and the national Tostan coordinator, a* Cubballo *(fisherman) whose parents moved from Fouta Toro to Casamance before he was born. The Tostan coordinators are accompanied by some influential regional supervisors and other officials who I know must be the village chief, the prefect, and some influential marabouts. Traditional music is playing as they slowly ascend the stairs of the stage. The UNICEF representatives, whose presence is also important at the declarations, are already seated on the stage, one of them Senegalese, accompanied by a white colleague based in Senegal. Samba Sarr, my Pulaar teacher and a poet, has accompanied me to Semme. We move to the side of the stage to make space for the officials. He is hoping for reemployment by Tostan once the job of teaching me Pulaar is finished.*

So far everything is going well: the declaring villagers are in the shade of the awnings, there is an audience of at least five hundred people, the music is playing, the officials and toubabs (white people) are there, and no serious "poisoning" (bonnitde), as Tostan staff in Fouta call polemics against their activities, seems to be threatening the success of this event. The second-ever public declaration of the abandonment of excision in Fouta Toro is finally beginning, after many other planned and failed declarations that were boycotted by influential people or religious leaders.

*   *   *

The public declaration of Semme follows the model of the first declaration in 1998, when women in the village of Malicounda Bambara, near Mbour, came to a consensus to stop practicing excision after having taken part in the NGO Tostan's basic education and literacy program for some months. After the director of the NGO and UNICEF Senegal had heard what effect the program had had on these women, they were asked if they would be willing to make their resolution public. The women agreed and declared in front of the national media that they had stopped excision in their village. This event became nationally important and, as some say, a precursor to the law (see Chapter 1). Since this first declaration in Malicounda, Tostan has received funding from organizations (e.g., UNICEF and USAID) to conclude its two-year education program with a public declaration for those who want to make their abandonment of excision and early/forced marriage public. By 2008, more than 3,548 communities across Senegal had officially declared their abandonment of excision: at that point, Tostan's strategies became officially recommended in "the national plan for the abandonment of excision by 2015" proposed by the government and a committee in Dakar in 2008 (République du Senegal 2008).[1]

*   *   *

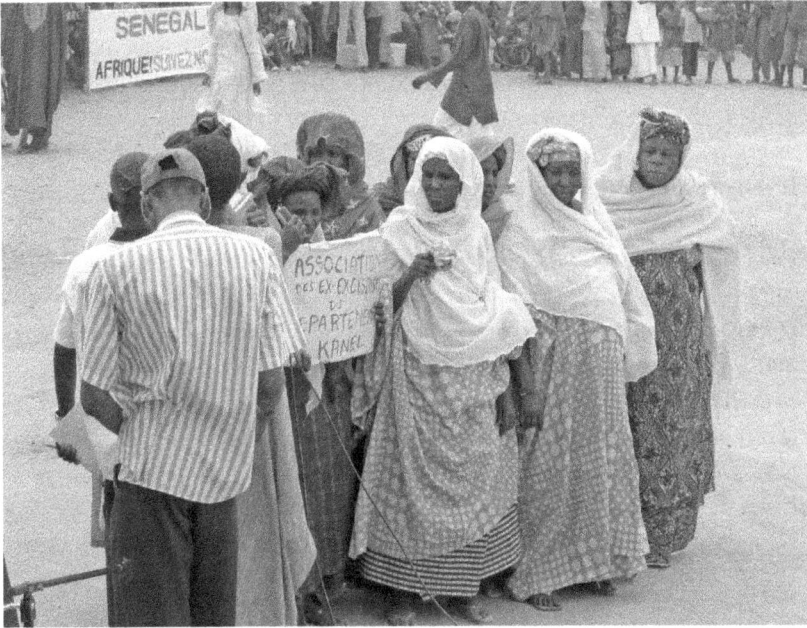

Figure 1. Association des ex-excisieuses du department de Kanel' declaring that they no longer practice their trade. Photograph by the author.

The declaration begins with various authorities making speeches, explaining that everyone has come together on this day to hear the villagers of Semme and sixty-nine other villages declare that they are no longer going to excise their daughters. Present are five excisers who have come to lay down their knives forever in the name of human rights.

Nurses and midwives have come to speak of the difficulties excision causes women in labor and to explain that unexcised women suffer less during childbirth. Participants of the Tostan classes have prepared a sketch about a girl who hemorrhages and dies after being excised. Two influential religious leaders vow that excision is not a religious obligation and is nowhere mentioned in the Qur'an. On the contrary, the Qur'an states that practices harmful to health are better abandoned. The woman's body is sacred and it should be protected from any practices that cause harm. This is important for everyone, I am told, because without the consent of the religious leaders it would be impossible for people to abandon the practice that is embraced as a prophetic recommendation or sunna. The prefect affirms that excision has been banned by Senegalese law and anyone caught practicing will be sentenced to between three months and five years of imprisonment. The speeches and sketches are interspaced with hodu music and dance performances. Individual women bear witness to the problems they have experienced through excision and encourage others who have suffered to be brave and speak out. Eventually, representatives of each of the seventy declaring villages slowly walk to the center of the square with signs showing the names of their villages. On the other side there are others who carry signs with symbols of human rights—the right to health, the right to vote, the right to a name, the right to nondiscrimination, the right to freedom of speech are important ones that people refer to when they explain their reasons for renouncing excision.

During these speeches and sketches, a schoolteacher who is sitting behind me on the stage says, "Ah! They are never going to abandon the practice. If it really is as harmful as they say, why has it been around for thousands of years? That is not possible!" My Pulaar teacher, who has half-heartedly been trying to convince his wife and his mother to stop excising their daughters for years

Figure 2. Villagers holding up signs with the names of their villages and declaring their abandonment of excision and early/forced marriage. Photograph by the author.

Figure 3. Women holding up Tostan's human rights learning tools: the right to work, the right to health, and so on. Photograph by the author.

without success, turns around and explains why the practice is harmful. The discussion is taking place rather loudly simultaneously with the ceremony below in the center of the square. The officials, who are sitting only a few seats away from us, pretend that they cannot hear the debate between these two men. They continue their polemics about the village of Semme now having abandoned excision together with sixty-nine other villages, even though the schoolteacher, who is a local, seems to think differently.

* * *

We have been introduced to traditional leaders, such as marabouts and village chiefs, who tend to be *Toorobbe*. Their views for or against excision are crucial with regard to whether people stop practicing it. Representatives of the state, like the prefect, have to represent the law. Midwives and health care assistants also play a central role. As employees of statutory health structures, they officially represent the state but have their own views about whether excision is a good thing. Excisers' and ex-excisers' stances also inform debates on whether to stop or continue the practice. Then, we have the ambiguous role of activists against the practice and facilitators, who are partly driven to raise awareness about the harmfulness of excision as a source of income, sometimes fervently convinced of the importance of their work, sometimes not so sure, and sometimes personally opposed to stopping the practice.

The public declaration at Semme indicates that FGC is the nexus at which tensions between the global and the local, secular and religious, human rights and community law, NGO policies and sectarianism, new elites and inter-caste relations all come together and cross over, intersecting at various levels. The debate around excision is a point at which these groups' conflicting views meet. It is one particular component of their relationships centered in and on the body.

Why is it that the physical body is at the center of these conflicts? Mauss (1973), Bourdieu (1977), Bordo (1993), Elias (1997), and others have shown how cultural features of belonging and identity, such as gender, sexuality, and social class, are embodied in comportment, dispositions and emotions, and movements. But beyond embodiment, the body is also part of our conceptual world. It is described, conceived, and imagined; it has needs and rights and it belongs. It is a marker of cultural identity that is read, critiqued, and judged differently by members of society depending on their positioning within the social hierarchy. Female circumcision is a practice that transforms not just the physical body but with it the social body. The body in its physical form is the site of political tension. It is not just the subject of these debates but also subject to changes that result from them. It is a locus of resistance to different forms of imperialism, to social and political movements that challenge existing social norms. But it can also be a pioneering agent of social change, a signifier of resistance to stagnant social structures and social norms that are perceived to be restrictive. The refusal to adjust the appearance of the body to socially acceptable standards has long been understood as a way of negating culturally dominant values. Whether this involves cutting one's hair or growing it long, tattooing or piercing one's body, or circumcision— the way in which the body is kept is a marker of social identity, a display of embodied values and concepts, of political orientations and of belonging to a particular group of people who share values and beliefs. Lambek and Strathern (1998), Boddy (1998), and others have shown that our understanding of embodiment can be muddled by a distinction between the "embodied body" and the imagined body. *Compromised Bodies* looks at both the female body as conceived of in human rights debates and Fulani discourses on the one hand and how these discourses are viscerally embodied, lived, and felt.

There is an interesting parallel between a woman being required to undergo intervention so that she can become a full member of society and a society being required to undergo intervention so that it can become a full part of international society. In both cases the body is saved from the "other," which is considered to be barbaric and uncivilized. The body is rendered appropriate; its integrity is restored and its dignity preserved. This book is concerned with how excision can be an act of protection against unwanted social change, how it can be seen as a form of defense against cultural imperialism. But I also look at how the abandonment movement can act as a refusal to adhere to Pulaar social structure and can represent a form of disobedience to the authority of those who have been leaders of this society since the Islamic revolution of the eighteenth and nineteenth centuries.

I am interested in what excision is for particular interest groups and how it constitutes relationships between people who disagree with each other's laws and oppose each other's politics—but also in how excision makes women and men. An understanding of how excision represents the moral foundations for female personhood and the honor of the family is crucial for grasping why many Futanke oppose the law. Honor is not an abstract entity: it requires a particular comportment, it grants safety, and loss of it brings sadness and grief.

Agency

Agency is a complex concept, much debated and critiqued. It has been argued that the concept of agency is particularly Western, emerging from philosophical notions linked to possessive individualism, assumed to be universal. Put simply, agency is closely related to intentionality, which means "to people's projects in the world and their ability to both formulate and enact them" (Ortner 2001:78). This often happens without breaking social conventions but by referring to cultural signifiers that are available. I disagree with the idea that agency is an inherently Western concept. Wardlow (2006), for instance, discusses the sexual agency of sexually promiscuous Huli women in Papua New Guinea, locally called passenger women. A woman's sexuality and reproductive capacity belong to her kin, particularly her male kin. In bridewealth transactions a woman belongs to her clan because she is an aspect of them. The withdrawal of her reproductive energies from the social body through sexual intercourse with men other than her husband is transgressive. "If a woman uses her sexuality autonomously—in premarital sex, in extramarital sex—it is considered a 'theft' of the woman by the other (male) party, and thus a theft of clan potency and potential clan wealth" (Wardlow 2006:16). Women's sexuality is subordinated to the larger project of social reproduction. Thus, promiscuous women refuse to be encompassed by the larger interest of their clan. By refusing marriage, running away from existing marriages, exchanging sex for money, they defy the interest of their clan. Sex becomes more about the consumption of bodily sensations rather than reproduction of the clan (Wardlow 2006).

However, agency is not always about resistance. Mahmood (2005) shows how pious Muslim women in Egypt exercise agency when making up their minds about which religious doctrine to choose from to justify their behaviors. From the outside their behavior may be misinterpreted as oppression due to lack of agency, yet well-informed choices are made within the bounds of what is socially acceptable and religiously endorsed.

Diabate (2020) argues with reference to Ahmadu (2017), Njambi (2004), and Hodzic (2016) that "there is a kind of agency in local African women fighting against, or endorsing, FGC, a long-established tradition that some deem harmful. This manifestation of agency both curtails and amplifies male power [. . .] resistant practices, both progressive and regressive, regarding FGC emerge in contexts caught between two putatively opposed orders, authenticity and foreign influences" (Diabate 2020:17). In *Making Gender*, Ortner suggests that the denial of the intentional subject misreads and works against the intellectual and political interests of women, minorities, and post-colonial and subaltern subjects (1996:8). *Compromised Bodies* explores the social environment in which people make choices about bodies, and how other people's intentions and choices about bodies elicit reactions. Some of these decisions are welcome and make people hopeful that the lives of their daughters will be better than their own, that they will have more possibilities and a better future. Some build up courage to speak out for change. Others are afraid of these decisions and the resulting changes and get angry. Their responses to discourses that disagree with their habitus are viscerally embodied reactions. The book explores the multiple ways in which people act and react to discourses, political decisions, and doctrines.

What Is Female Circumcision or FGM?

Female circumcision only began to be called female genital mutilation, or FGM, in the 1970s, when internationally organized campaigns became successful. Although campaigns against the practice have been around since the beginning of the twentieth century (Boddy 2007; Thomas 2000, 2003; Hodzic 2016), the League of Nations, and after 1946 the Economic and Social Council (ECOSOC) of the UN, refused to take it up as an agenda or to recommend legislation against it due to the conflicts that campaigns against the practice caused in the colonies of Sudan and Kenya (Abu-Salieh 2001:398). Yet, in Sudan (Boddy 2007) and Ghana (Hodzic 2016), activism to stop the practice continued. Boddy (2007:290) describes how British wives of colonial administrators, such as Lady Constance Huddleston, were passionately engaged in lobbying the government to bring pharaonic circumcision (Type III) to an end. Despite reservations from the colonial government, which was concerned that banning circumcision "would do more harm than good" (2007:290), it was eventually decided that to reduce the suffering of women, efforts would be made to substitute pharaonic circumcision with *sunna*—the removal of the clitoris (Types I and II). In 1946, a law banning pharaonic circumcision was passed. The law stated that "it is not unlawful circumcision to remove the free and protruding part of the clitoris with the assent of the woman, or, if she is subject to guardianship, of her guardian" (Boddy 2007:291). Abu-Salieh (2001) notes that at an international level, female circumcision came up for the first time in a conference held by the Société pour la sauvegarde de l'enfance in Geneva in 1931, when some European delegates pleaded for an end to these "barbaric customs." However, the majority did not share their views and the subject was dropped until the 1950s (2001:398). In 1952 ECOSOC recommended that its member states take action toward abolishing female circumcision. However, by 1959 it was decided at an international assembly of the World Health Organization (WHO) that no further action should be taken because "these ritual operations . . . are a result of social and cultural conceptions"[2] (Abu-Salieh 2001:398).

In 1976 the ECOSOC pushed the WHO to publish the Robert Cook report, which defined four types of FGM (Abu-Salieh 2001:398):[3]

Type I   Clitoridectomy: partial or total removal of the clitoris (a small, sensitive and erectile part of the female genitals) and, in very rare cases, only the prepuce (the fold of skin surrounding the clitoris).

Type II   Excision: partial or total removal of the clitoris and the labia minora, with or without excision of the labia majora (the labia are 'the lips' that surround the vagina).

Type III   Infibulation: narrowing of the vaginal opening through the creation of a covering seal. The seal is formed by cutting and repositioning the inner, or outer, labia, with or without removal of the clitoris.

Type IV   Other: all other harmful procedures to the female genitalia for non-medical purposes, e.g. pricking, piercing, incising, scraping and cauterizing the genital area.

Finally, in 1979, at a seminar on traditional practices affecting the health of women and children in Khartoum, Sudan, the WHO officially became committed to fighting against FGM. Feminist activist Fran Hosken, who had been carrying out research on where and how the genital operations were practiced, suggested that not getting involved in campaigning against the practice would lead to medicalization—the practice being carried out by health care professionals (also see Gruenbaum 2001). People would seek to improve the hygienic conditions in which the procedure is undertaken and try to reduce complications rather than stop practicing. The result would be that the "female sexuality" of "healthy girls" would continue to be "permanently impaired," with the "objective of altering females to make them submissive to males" (Hosken 1982:47). Furthermore, Hosken argued that female circumcision was not just an attack on female personhood and sexuality but also a "planned manipulation of the human personality or psyche" associated with the political control of men over women, "as for instance described by Huxley and Orwell" (Hosken 1982:47).

In 1991, the WHO recommended that the UN officially adopt the term *female genital mutilation*. "The extensive literature on the subject, the support of international organizations, and the emergence of local groups working against the continuation practices appear to suggest that an international consensus has been reached. The terminology used to refer to these surgeries has changed, and the clearly disapproving and powerfully evocative expression of 'female genital mutilation' has now all but replaced the possibly inaccurate, but less value-laden term of 'female circumcision'" (Obermeyer 1999:80). Although research since the 1980s has indicated that calling such practices mutilation was causing anger, noncompliance with policies aimed at stopping the practice, and psychological damage to women of minority groups who had undergone the practice in France and the United States, the term continues to be used by political groups, campaigners, and activists.[4]

Other organizations (e.g., Tostan) expressed preference for the use of the term *female genital cutting* (FGC) as it does not suggest that parents intentionally mutilate their daughters. In Senegal, the most frequently used term in French is the value-neutral term *excision*. In Pulaar the term is *haddinde*. In this book I use the three terms as they were used by my interlocutors.

Instead of saying "to eradicate FGC," which has radical connotations, or to "stop" or "end the practice," the official term used by NGOs and the Senegalese government is "to abandon" excision. This term implies leaving a practice that has unquestionably been carried out for generations due to the realization that it represents a threat to women's reproductive health or rights. The Pulaar word for abandonment of excision is *woppude*—to leave something. The same verb is used for *leave me alone*, for example, *woppu am* ("let go of my gown") or to leave or abandon someone—*a woppi kam?* ("have you abandoned me?")). Similar to the word "abandonment" in English, in Pulaar it has connotations of leaving something or someone that was cherished.

When I was in the field, I discovered that in the context of public declarations and NGO awareness-raising programs, the abandonment of excision came in a package with the renunciation of early and forced marriage. Early marriage was perceived to be between the ages of ten and eighteen. I frequently encountered girls of this age who were keen on marrying soon. So-called early marriage is therefore not necessarily against girls' consent or "forced." The law against early marriage, Article 111 of the family code, was passed nine months after the law against excision, Article 299.[5] I did not set out to study these, and in this book debates around early and forced marriage mainly come up in the context of how they are raised by interlocutors, such as NGO facilitators or participants in the Tostan program. For my interlocutors, excision was only indirectly associated with early marriage and not at all with forced marriage. A lot of people believed that excision, like early marriage, would prevent a girl from getting pregnant before wedlock. Stopping excision was not inextricably linked to stopping early and forced marriage. Some people wanted to renounce early marriage at a public declaration but could do so only by renouncing excision as well, because these things were "abandoned" together.

Prevalence of Excision in Senegal and Fouta Toro

Since 2005, the prevalence of FGC in Senegal has dropped from 28 percent to 25 percent. In 2005, 83 percent of excised women in Senegal had parts of their genitals, such as the clitoris and labia, removed. Twelve percent are said to also have undergone infibulation. In 2018, 58 percent of women declared having had parts of their genitals removed, and 7 percent declared having been closed (infibulated); 26 percent declared that they did not know what type of FGC they had undergone (Demographic Health Survey Senegal 2018:244).

For the regions of Fouta Toro where this research takes place, in 2005, 93 percent of women were excised in the region of Matam and 44 percent in the region of Saint Louis. In Matam 90.1 percent were said to have had genital tissue removed (resembling WHO Type II excision), 0.7 percent were said to have just been nipped (WHO Type IV FGM), and 8.7 percent said that they were closed (WHO Type III FGM). In the region of Saint Louis, 91 percent have had tissue removed (resembling WHO Type II excision), none were nipped (WHO Type IV FGM), and 7.9 percent had their vagina closed (WHO Type III FGM). As far as the age of excision is concerned, the 2005 Demographic Health Survey showed that 45.1 percent of girls in Matam and 43.2 percent in Saint Louis were cut in their early childhood ("dans la petite enfance"; Demographic Health Survey Senegal 2005:248). Later Demographic Health Surveys no longer allow for a comparison between different regions of Senegal and the results for Matam and Podor are presented together as "région du nord." In the 2019 Demographic Health Survey, 37.7 percent of women had undergone excision in the north, 97.5 percent of these under the age of five (ANSD 2019:227).

Although these figures and facts are the result of surveys and statistical analyses, in practice the identification of WHO FGM types is not straightforward at all, neither for doctors caring for women as part of their daily routine, nor for experts who have to note the type on medical certificates. FGM types are subject to debate and dispute. Decisions in court cases where migrants are accused of having performed FGM on their daughters in Europe and the United States are all about types identified or not identifiable by expert witnesses. Birgitta Essén, a Swedish gynecologist and expert witness for court cases in the United States, Ireland, and Denmark, has shown that many of the so-called experts consulted to examine supposedly cut girls have in fact very little experience examining children's genitalia or the vulvas of women who have undergone FGC more generally (Essén 2020).

To use the words of my Futanke interlocutors themselves, in Fouta Toro *sunna* is commonly practiced, which can be of Type 1, Type 2, or Type 4. Locals describe *sunna* as cutting "a third." This expression is often accompanied by a gesture whereby the thumbnail is pressed against the tip of the little finger. Others talk of some women being "completely closed" (*muumiraado*)[6] and needing to be opened before the first sexual intercourse. The procedure for complete closure has been described to me as completely cutting the visible parts of the clitoral glans and the labia and letting the blood coagulate and heal so that a scar forms on top, which closes the vulva. This seems to correspond with the occurrence of what the Demographic Health Surveys classify as Type III FGM in Fouta Toro. I have never heard of women being stitched or pinned up like in East Africa. However, in conversations with midwives and other health professionals working in Guinea and southern Senegal, I heard that there are cases of infibulated women needing an operation before sexual intercourse or childbirth. Keloid scars are also common. Senegalese midwives, nurses, and general practitioners are not trained to operate on keloid scars, and such cases are referred to the larger hospitals. According to health professionals I have spoken to, women tend to be incredibly embarrassed about keloid scars and often do not follow up on recommendations for referral to the larger urban centers.

Since Hosken's (1982) and other feminists' claims that female circumcision represents a "sexual mutilation" and impedes the ability to experience orgasm and sexual pleasure, there has been extensive discussion in anthropology about pleasure and orgasm (Abusharaf 2000; Shell-Duncan and Hernlund 2000; Skramstad 1990; El Dareer 1982; Dopico 2007; Shweder 2002; Ahmadu 2007, 2009; Lightfoot-Klein 1989). Most recently, Ahmadu (2007, 2009) and Dopico (2007) have argued, first of all, that the ways in which sexual pleasure is expressed by excised and unexcised women depends on the cultural context. Whereas some women might downplay the pleasure they experience when interrogated because of social and cultural norms of their society, Western women expect and are expected to have orgasms—so more of them do (Dopico 2007:231). Women who perceive orgasm during sex to be an important component of sexual life feel like failures if they do not achieve it, which may lead to loss of desire. Hence Dopico argues that "sexual response is a biopsychological phenomenon (Leiblum 2000) and, rather than envisioning an orderly, linear progression of desire, arousal, and orgasm, it can be more accurately understood as consisting both of sexual and non-sexual elements that affect each phase" (Dopico 2007:231). Ahmadu argues that the Westernized iconographic representation of the clitoris as the ultimate symbol of female sexual autonomy biases neurological research on our understanding of women's sexual response during orgasm (Ahmadu 2007:295). She asks, How do we know what a woman experiences when she is having orgasmic contractions monitored by a machine? And how do we know if a woman who is monitored to have more contractions than another experiences more pleasure (2007:299)? Ahmadu's ethnographic examples show that women's and men's sexual responses strongly depend on the cultural context and beliefs of what "the other's" (excised or unexcised) experiences are, which are often tainted by ideas of race and of physiological difference.

Throughout my fieldwork I found that women did not see themselves as sexually mutilated through FGC. Sex is not taboo, and women spend a lot of time talking and joking about sex and how to enhance pleasure through aphrodisiacs. Many women told me or insinuated that they experience immense pleasure when sleeping with their husbands. I did not speak to women about orgasms during fieldwork, mainly because there is no word for the experience other than pleasure (*mbelemma*). From later research on clitoral reconstructive surgery in Belgium, I know that some women who have undergone a Type II FGC do experience orgasm (O'Neill et al. 2021). Others do not.

I have never worked as an activist on FGC and have never told anyone to stop practicing FGC. As an anthropologist—and not a health professional, sexologist, or development agent—I have always stated that I do not feel in a position to tell anyone what to do. Instead I see my job as trying to understand and empathize with all views on the practice, even if I personally find them offensive. For instance, I found discourses on women not being able to control their sex drive and leading men to temptation more offensive than the actual genital modification itself. Nevertheless, when doing research on such controversial practices, it is irrelevant what I think and feel about such views. Emotions are a methodological tool to rethink concepts that are taken for granted and to dig deeper by asking better questions that help understand practices that are not intended to do harm but are considered in the interest of girls and women and society at large.

Introducing the Place and the People

The inhabitants of Fouta Toro divide their country into those zones north of the only tarmac road that crosses their country and those to the south of it. The zones northeast of the road are river land, where the Senegal River divides in two, creating the Ile Amorphile, or Hakkunde Maaje in Pulaar. The Ile Amorphile is to all intents and purposes an island, as it is a stretch of land completely surrounded by the two rivers and their many branches during the rainy season. The border of Mauritania is naturally defined by the north banks of the upper Senegal River. This zone, north-northeast of the road, is called Waalo. According to people's mental maps, it is where the Toucouleur or Tukuloor live, the sedentary Fulɓe of Fouta Toro. The Toucouleur have inhabited this land for over a millennium and defended it against foreign invasions (see also Robinson 1975a, 1975b; Wane 1969; Curtin 1971; Schmitz 1986, 1994).

The area south-southwest of the tarmac road is called Jeeri (Diery) and eventually, the further away you get from the road, it turns into the Ferlo, the grasslands where the nomadic herders graze their cattle. The landscape changes greatly throughout the year and the nomadic *Fulɓe* are constantly on the move, depending on how much grass is available for their cattle. The *Fulɓe* of the Jeeri, however, regularly come back to the road for trade, to sell milk and buy other goods, and some are settled there. Administratively, Fouta Toro is divided into the Départements de Podor, Matam, and Bakel with different *sous-préfectures*. The fieldwork took place in the Département de Podor and the Département de Matam. The Département de Podor also is divided into provinces: Dimat, Toro, Laaw, Yirlaaɓe, and Hebbiyaaɓe. These administrative categorizations were introduced by the French and do not conform to the mental and cultural landscape divisions between riverland and grassland, Waalo and Jeeri, but they are frequently used as they represent political constituencies that affect work and relationships between people.

In Pulaar the Fulani people are referred to either as Haalpulaar—which literally means those who speak Pulaar (*haalde*, to speak) or as Fulɓe. The expression Fulɓe does not refer to a homogenized group of people living in

Map 1. Fouta Toro in West Africa. Cartographer: Nicolas Nikis, ULB/Africa Museum Tervuren, Belgium.

one place but is a general term for a society that consists of multiple status groups (*kinɗe*) that differ greatly in their livelihoods. In local discourses in Senegal, people make a distinction between the *Peul*, who are thought to be nomadic cattle herders, and the *Toucouleur*, who are thought to be the sedentary inhabitants of Fouta Toro. The Haalpulaar'en themselves, however, do not refer to themselves in such a way in Pulaar and the origin of this distinction is said to be rooted in the French colonial administration. Dilley (2004) notes that the term Toucouleur became established in the French literature in the nineteenth century, though some lone voices, like the explorer Raffenel, spoke out against its use because it was based on wrong assumptions (Willis 1989; Dilley 2004).[7] The so-called Toucouleur consist of at least four noble status groups or *Rimɓe* (*Tooroɓɓe, Seɓɓe, Subalɓe, Jaawamɓe*) and six

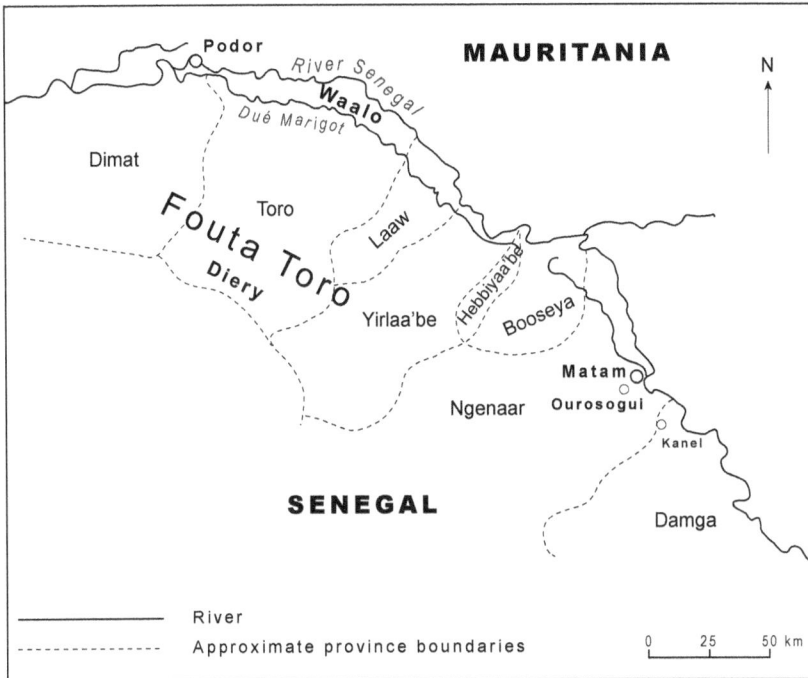

Map 2. Fouta Toro, northern Senegal. Cartographer: Nicolas Nikis, ULB/Africa Museum Tervuren, Belgium.

lower-rank status groups called *Ñeeñbe*, or men/women of skill (*Maabube, Waylube, Sakkeebe, Lawbe, Awlube, Wambaabe*), as well as categories of for- mer slaves: *Galluŋkoobe/Maccube (Soottibe, Halfaabe)*. The so-called nomadic Peul or Fulɓe who are also noble (*Rimbe*) make up just one category, whereas the term Toucouleur comprises ten local categories that are still used. In addition, the French distinguished between nobles whom they called *non-casté* (without caste) and the *casté*, who are the men/women of skill and the slaves. In Pulaar, however, the different status groups are all referred to as *kinde* (plural) or *hinnde* (singular), including slaves (*Galluŋkoobe/Maccube*). A distinction between those with caste[8] and those without does not exist in Pulaar but has been adopted in local discourse in the French language.

Throughout my research in Fouta Toro, I found that my interlocutors and people in general referred to themselves as *Futaŋkoobe*, or *Futanke* in French. Regardless of which status group they saw themselves as belonging to, when people spoke of their culture and their way of life, particularly with reference to foreign practices that they wanted to protect their society from, they very much identified with this term. I therefore frequently use Futanke when referring to local discourses on identity and ethnicity. Although I am aware that this local designation of ethnic and localized identity is made up of many status groups and peoples living in Fouta Toro, my intention is to explore who the Senegalese refer to when speaking of "the Futanke's opposition to the ban on FGM."

The majority of my fieldwork took place in a village I call Diawoury, which is located on the farthest corner of the Ile Amorphile, beside the upper river Senegal facing the border of Mauritania. However, when I was in need of a break from sandstorms and felt the lack of fruit and electricity, I stayed in a place I call Weendouly along the tarmac road.

Social Structure, Identity, and Belonging

When I started fieldwork in Fouta I had no idea whether or how social structure was related to opposition to the law or to willingness to renounce the practice of FGC. My choice of field site was not determined by caste. I have no interview material in which a so-called *casté*—man/woman of skill or slave (*Ñeeño* or *Galluŋke*)—admits to being oppressed, and most of them told me that there was no longer any difference between the castes. It took me a lot longer to understand the subtleties of how status groups or what locals call caste (*kinde*) affects people's behavior toward each other. It wasn't until the end of my fieldwork that I realized that caste is one of the pillars of the platform from which this battle for the preservation of excision is waged.

My Haalpulaar interlocutors used to define the so-called noble *Rimbe* status groups (see Table 1) the following way: the *Rimbe* depend on no one, follow no one, and do not have to obey anyone but their own elders and allied families (except for God and the state). This ideology is also reflected in their code of honor—it is shameful to make oneself dependent on someone else or ask for money or a favor without returning it.

How the status of these different categories emerged historically is discussed below. Each category prefers to marry endogamously; however, intermarriage is common, particularly with people of the same rank—for example, *Fulbe* and *Jaawambe*. It is also acceptable to marry a person from a category below (e.g., *Tooroodo* and *Jaawando* or *Fulbe* and *Subalbe*) but some families

Table 1. Haalpulaar'en social hierarchy following Wane (1969) and Tal Tamari (1991) and Dilley (2004). The table shows that not all authors ranked the status groups in the same order.

Rank

Highest	**Rimɓe—Noblemen and Noblewomen**
	Tooroɓɓe (Islamic clerics)
	Fulɓe (herders), *Seɓɓe* (warriors),
	    Jaawamɓe (councillors of the
	    Almaamy)
	Subalɓe (fishermen)	

	Ñeeñɓe - Men/Women of Skill Wane (1969: 33)	Tamari (1991: 228)
	Maabuɓe (weavers) *Wayilɓe* (blacksmiths, silversmiths)	*Wayiliɓe* (blacksmiths) *Maabuɓe* (weavers) *Wambaaɓe* (bards) *Awluɓe* (praise singers)
	Sakeeɓe (leatherworkers) *Lawɓe* (woodworkers) *Buurnaaɓe* (potters)	*Buurnaaɓe* (women potters)

lowest	**Former slaves**
	Galluŋke, Jeyaaɓe (old fashioned
	    term), *Maccuɓe* (politically
	    incorrect term)	

prefer not to. Intermarriage with a *Ñeeño* (man/woman of skill) or former slave (*Galluŋke*) is extremely rare and shunned by many.

According to my interlocutors, there is no rank among the *Ñeeñɓe* (men/women of skill) and everyone is proud of their family's occupational lore. Wane (1969) and Tal Tamari (1991), however, did rank these groups (Table 1).

Dilley (2000, 2004, 2009) demonstrates how each artisan is in some ways in touch with the spirit world of the elements he is crafting. For example, a blacksmith, who is constantly in contact with fire, associated with spirits and *jinne*, has to acquire the powers that enable him to handle red-hot metals (Dilley 2004:71). In a similar way, a woodcarver's skill does not merely rely on the carving of a piece of dead wood. On the contrary, the trees are a home to spirits and must be approached with caution, "for if the woodcutter does not follow the correct procedures, he will fall foul of their powers" (Dilley 2004:73). Whether caste occupation is practiced or not, it encompasses a skill in a trade that represents the pride and identity of its members because one's ancestors handled the same elements and the good and bad spirits connected to them.

Some *Ñeeñbe* also specialize in praise singing for noble families and remembering their genealogies. *Awlube* and *Wambaabe* are known as praise singers and musicians who honor and charm the *Rimbe* at occasions like baptisms, weddings, and funerals. If a *Gawlo* (singular of *Awlube*) sings of a noble's glorious family history, the latter feels obliged to reward him with money or goods for honoring their ancestors. If a *Dimo* (singular of *Rimbe*) is not generous with their bondsmen, they risk being given a bad reputation by the *Gawlo* singing about his lack of generosity. My teacher, Samba Sarr, told me that although the nobles are higher in rank and may hold politically important positions within the community, they are always worried about their reputation and what rumors may be spread about their ancestors by an angry *Neeño* praise singer. As *Ñeeñbe* praise singers hold the memory of historically important events and their noblemen's lineages, recounted on special occasions, weddings, funerals, and baptisms, they can be incredibly powerful. A *Ñeeño* can ask as much of the nobles as he wants without seeming rude or shameless—it is part of their occupation to honor the nobles and receive something in return. Even a *Ñeeño* who is richer than a noble does not break the code of honor by asking for gifts. I found that, as a result, nobles tended to avoid a *Ñeeño's* company in fear of being asked for things they do not have the means to give and thus having to embarrass themselves by saying no.

Wane (1969) distinguishes between two types of slaves (*Jeyaabe*): *Soottiibe* and *Halfaabe*. *Halfaabe* are slaves who were or are owned by a noble family. Although today many people refuse to be considered slaves, some older generations still take pride in serving their nobles. *Soottiibe* are slaves who bought their freedom and hence are no longer obliged to the noble castes. Most slaves were acquired during warfare with other peoples in West Africa and have family names that are not recognized as Pulaar but are, for example, Malinke (Coulibaly, Dramé, Cissoko, etc.). Other slave families have been with their nobles in Fouta Toro for centuries and have taken on their family names (Ba, Diallo, etc.) According to Dilley (2004: 29), the nobles (*Rimbe)* compose around 70 percent of Haalpulaar'en, those of servile origin and bondsmen

(*Jeyaaɓe*) about 20 percent, and the remaining 10 percent men/women of skill (*Ñeeñɓe*).

Even though in Senegalese law everyone is equal and has the right to be voted into leading positions, caste still determines who can become a leader. People say that this is slowly changing. When I first did fieldwork in 2007, it was unthinkable to have a Galluŋke or a Ñeeño as mayor of a town. When I returned and interviewed people in 2022, I was told that things had changed! The new mayor of "Weendouley" was now a former slave but he was said to be very competent and well educated, which was why he was elected. The traditional village chief is still a Kane—the family of the Almaamies, but the mayor is a former slave. Thus, contemporary politics are a power play in which the traditional authority of Toroodo leaders is necessary alongside the elected leaders of political parties who may be of any caste background.[9]

Yet, I was told in 2022 that it was incredibly difficult for someone of low rank to be holding a management position in an NGO like Tostan as this required engaging with religious leaders who will only take the word of another *Toroodo* on questions regarding religious practice—and excision was believed to be a religious recommendation.

Besides belonging to a social category (*kinde*), Islam is also inextricably interwoven with Futanke identity. Most people are tremendously proud that their land became one of the first Islamic states in West Africa. Being a Futanke thus means being a Muslim from the cradle of Islam in West Africa. Those who have knowledge of Islam, the *Toorobbe*, have power because they instruct and advise people on correct Islamic conduct and define what is non-Islamic.

Islam, Power, and Caste

The first known rulers of the Tekrur empire (*Tekuruur* in Pulaar), which was located in the area called Fouta Toro today, were of the Dia Ogo dynasty, from 850 until the tenth century CE. Al-Naqar (1969) cites the Arab historian al-Bakri:[10] "the city of Takrūr, is inhabited by *sudan* [i.e., blacks]. They were, like any other *sudan*, pagans worshipping Dakakir; the Dukur is their idol, until they were ruled by War-Jabi ibn Rabis who became a Muslim, established among them the laws of Islam, forced them to obey them and adorned their eyes by that" (Al-Naqar 1969:367). Al-Naqar shows how the generic Arabic term Takarīr came to be applied to all West African Muslims, derived from this ancient state of Tekrur. One common explanation for this is that fervent Muslims from the Tekrur empire became known in the Arab world while on pilgrimage to Mecca and Medina, as well as in Egypt (Al-Naqar 1969: 370).

After waging war against the pagans of the empire of Ghana in the 1050s in alliance with the Almoravids, the Tekrur empire (Mandinka dynasty of Mana) came under the domination of the empire of Ghana in the eleventh century, the empire of Mali in the thirteenth century, and the Djolof empire in the fourteenth century (Wane 1969). In 1512, *Fulɓe* herders led by Koli Tengela Ba overthrew the Mandinka rule of the empire of Mali and founded the Deniyanke dynasty (Wane 1969). From then on, Tekrur was called Fuuta Toro (*Fuuta* means land of the Fulɓe and Toro is the name of a province by the Senegal River). The Deniyanke were "pagans" who tolerated Islam in their empire and 250 years later (1776) were defeated by it through the emergence of the *Toorobɓe* and the empire of the Almaamies (Wane 1969; Robinson 1975; Curtin 1971, Schmitz 1985, 1998).

How did the *Toorobɓe* become the most powerful status group (*kinde*) in Fouta Toro? Robinson discusses the emergence of the Almamate of Fouta Toro in the sixteenth and seventeenth centuries. After regular raids from Moorish groups, particularly from Hassani tribes who supplemented their nomadic pastoralism with raiding and tribute collection (Curtin 1971: 12), many *Futankoobe*[11] aspired to the *zwaya*[12] idea of an Islamic state ruled by Sharia law. The rulers of Fouta at the time, the Deniyanke, were not able to protect the inhabitants of Fouta from regular attacks from the north and the south. A religious cleric called Nasir al-Din, who took the title of Imam, the constitutional equivalent of a caliph (commander of the faithful), and possessed *baraka*, the power to bless, attempted to impose Islamic government on Arab groups and the rulers of Fouta and the Wolof states (Robinson 1975b: 189). He opposed slave raiding and pillaging. This *zwaya* movement led by Nasir al-Din in the 1670s led to the emergence of the *Toorobɓe* of Fouta Toro, who longed for the Deniyanke dynasty to be replaced by an Islamic state in which fervent Muslims could be protected and live in peace (Robinson 1975b: 190). The Deniyanke rulers, who were *Fulɓe* herders with *Sebɓe* warriors, made fun of the first *Toorobɓe*, calling them "beggars of alms" in the seventeenth century. They raided, enslaved, or killed *Toorobɓe* as regularly as Moorish groups from the north did (Robinson 1975b). Wane argues that by the eighteenth century, the last Deniyanke rulers had lost power and jurisdiction in their vast empire and were rulers only in name. Suleyman

Baal brought an end to the "pagan hegemony" in 1776, and the first Almaamy Abdul Kader Kan was inaugurated by the *Toorobɓe* in 1778 to rule the Islamic state of Fouta Toro (Wane 1969). He accepted the oaths of allegiance of provincial and village chiefs throughout the whole kingdom. The Deniyanke negotiated virtual autonomy within the Almamate, and although they harbored resentment against the new regime, they withdrew to the eastern floodplains of the kingdom (Robinson 1975b: 199).

Initially the *Toorobɓe* were merely an association of fervent Muslims from different ethnic groups and caste backgrounds who were enthralled by Nasir al-Din's idea of an Islamic state, which would bring an end to existing insecurity. With the first Almaamy Abdul Kader Kan, however, the Futanke stopped paying the annual tribute of five kilograms of gold to the Moorish groups (Wane 1966: 13). The reign of the Almaamies was brought to an end by the French in 1891. Wane says that it was not until they recruited "armed Moorish assassins that the turbulent nationalism was brought to complete silence" (Wane 1969: 15). But the political and social position of the *Toorobɓe* as leaders of Futanke society was not ended when they were defeated militarily by the French, and they continue to be the superior status group to the present day.

The Futanke Way of Life, Pulaaku, and Honor

The notion of *Pulaaku*, the way of the Fulani or "Fulaniness," was used by my interlocutors to refer to a code of honor and behavior when interacting with others. It is also commonly referred to in the literature on the Fulani (Riesman 1974; Stenning 1959; Ly 1938).

According to Stenning (1959: 55), *Pulaaku* includes a code of behavior that is tied to the language but incorporates a whole range of rights and duties particular to the *Pullo*. In Pulaar, the traits that define *Pulaaku* are *muñal*—endurance/patience, self-discipline; *hakkille*—intelligence or forethought and managing one's own; *gacce*—literally "shame," meaning modesty and respect; and *tinnaade* or *cagataagal*—bravery, courage. For my interlocutors, the *Pulaaku* code of honor had the same significance.

According to my interlocuters, *muñal* means enduring preordained vicissitudes of life. *Muñal* is needed, for example, to describe withstanding pain, heat, or longing to be reunited with a loved one. In her ethnography on transnational marriages in Senegal, Hannaford also describes *muuñ* as an important virtue among Senegalese wives (2017: 56). *Muuñ* (the Wollof spelling) means having the ability to suffer and endure without complaining. "A woman's ability to *muuñ* is essential to the longevity of her marriage" (Hannaford 2017: 56). *Muuñ* also reflects religious piety and the faith that Allah will allow you to put up with whatever trials He puts you through (2017:56). The word *hakkille* conveys a blending of prudence and shrewdness in livelihood management and face-to-face encounters. *Gacce* is commonly translated as shame[13]. It involves both restraint and self-control in daily social interaction and a lacking in weakness when facing adversity (*semteende* for Riesman [1974]). In her ethnography on Bedouins in Egypt in the 1980s, Abu-Lughod extensively discusses the difficulty of translating and conveying the meaning of *hasham*—shame. She argues that *hasham* is closely tied to the concept of *'agl*, the social sense of self-control of honorable persons (Abu-Lughod 2016:108). Hillewaert (2020) explores the notion of *heshima* (respectability) among the Muslim upper-class residents of Lamu, Kenya, where the virtue of heshima is claimed as a sign of social status embodied in "sophistication" and "civilized" behaviors. The concept is "contingent on 'having others as contrastive foils, *washenzi* (savages), the unwashed, those fresh off the boat and unfamiliar with coastal norms, Kiswahili and Muslim *umma* (Bissell 2018:59)" (Hillewaert 2020:55). I find these related concepts incredibly useful when thinking about the meaning of *gacce* (shame) among the Fulani. In essence, *gacce* represents resistance to weakness or to nonconformity to the code of *Pulaaku*. *O alaa gacce* means "he has no shame." A *Pullo*, whether male or female, must know of the social constraints on behavior and be able to avoid contravening them in all situations. Not being able to do so is perceived as a weakness and a sign of being inferior, lacking civilization and self-control. Riesman also states that a true *Pullo* is in total control of his emotions and impulses (Riesman 1974). *Cagataagal* means bravery in the sense of both the courage of a warrior and the hard work of any person. It is often used to congratulate someone for their valor and accomplishments.

In addition to the Pulaar terms described above, Ly argues that the Pulaar code of honor constitutes not only respect for others, courage, honesty, generosity but also pride at being a member of one's group—caste and family. An honorable person always has his name and his family in mind when interacting with others, bearing in mind that bad behavior will reflect badly on their name (Ly 1938:47). Ly also says that someone who does not fulfill their duties toward others is not a person: "Ne pas remplir ses obligations de sociabilité c'est n'être pas Homme" (Ly 1938:58). Dignity for the Haalpulaar'en is therefore strongly linked to fulfilling one's obligations toward others and behaving according to the codes of honor of one's society (see also Strathern 1990, 2004). Joking relations are a control mechanism against breaking this code of honor, being different, and not meeting people's expectations.

The Fieldwork, Methods, and Research Constraints and Opportunities

My interest in Fouta Toro dates back to my first visit to Senegal in 2001, when I was a Student Volunteer Abroad in Guediawaye, a suburb of Dakar. We were twelve European volunteers between the ages of nineteen and twenty-two, guided by a French political science student, who had been there the previous year and decided to set up a project whereby we were to teach English to suburban kids in the morning and play with them in the afternoon. Most of us spoke hardly any French at all and, rather than our group of volunteers contributing to what we thought of as the "development" of this run-down suburb ourselves, it was the members of the UNESCO club in Guediawaye who spent most of their time looking after us. The group of young men and women in their late twenties were from different ethnic backgrounds, some Serere, some Wolof, some Diola, but the core of the club was run by Haalpulaar'en who were born in Fouta Toro and lived with relatives in Guediawaye. Grateful for having been able to attend French state schools, they were all keen to promote education among the youngsters in Guediawaye.

The project was challenging for the volunteers from the University of Glasgow and for the Senegalese volunteers, but we had long discussions about many issues I had been studying in sociology and anthropology—modernity, tradition, development, gender, human rights. The difficulty of achieving what we had imagined as development, and the enormous generosity and warmheartedness of our hosts, as well as long conversations with friends from Fouta Toro, had an enormous impact on me and I came back from Senegal mesmerized. I wanted to know more about this place and the many issues that turned out to be so complex, so I organized another Student Volunteers Abroad project to take place in 2003. At the same time, I collected data for my dissertation in anthropology. On this trip I stayed with the family of one of the Senegalese volunteers I had met during my previous stay. There was little space in her home in Guediawaye and I ended up sharing a bed with

Rosa and her sister's three-year-old daughter while Maimouna slept on the floor. The household was lively and turbulent and, absorbing every bit of it, I did not mind the lack of personal space or privacy.

In 2005 I returned to Senegal to prepare for my PhD research and spent another five months living with this family in Guediawaye. I was working with ENDA Graf, a Senegalese NGO. I had arranged for the Student Volunteers Abroad to work with *talibe* in the suburbs of Thiaroye, Madina Gounass, and Yeumbeul. This time I had come alone, which encouraged my Senegalese friends to watch out for me and make sure I was okay. Already familiar with the complexities of working with marabouts and *talibe*, assisting at meetings with women's groups, at health care centers, and in hospitals broadened my understanding of health and development issues that people living in the suburbs faced on a day-to-day basis. As my PhD research was going to be on female circumcision, I had many informal discussions, carefully testing the ground to see how people talked about the practice without being intrusive. I also organized some focus groups on female circumcision with NGO workers at ENDA Graf.

That summer I went to meet with NGOs that worked on FGC in Dakar. I interviewed Madame Sidibe Ndiaye of COSEPRAT, one of the first NGOs to campaign against excision in Senegal. I also arranged a meeting with Molly Melching of Tostan, the most prominent NGO working on FGC at the time. Molly Melching was accompanied by a French volunteer, Sabine Panet, who was working on her *mémoire* on FGC for her *maitrise* in development studies at the Sorbonne. After hours of fruitful discussion and exchange I decided to accompany Sabine to Casamance in the south of Senegal to interview villagers about their decision to stop excision and why they decided to publicly declare this resolution. We collected rich interview material and I was asked to return to Senegal in 2006 to research the success of the public declaration in Salemata, a remote region in Kedougou, for Tostan and UNICEF with Sabine Panet.

Before my fieldwork in Fouta Toro, I had therefore spent extended periods of time in Senegal. I had lived with people and built relationships of trust and friendship over extended periods of time, worked for Senegalese development institutions and international NGOs, interviewed people in rural and urban settings, and established social networks that became useful during fieldwork.

My fieldwork in Fouta Toro, however, represented a completely new and extremely challenging phase of research. I had visited friends' families in

Fouta on various occasions before my fieldwork started and went to the Tostan Fouta coordination at the beginning of 2007 in the context of a research project to improve Tostan's strategies in the four regions with the highest prevalence of FGC. However, my ethnographic research on opposition to the law against excision required me to move away from development institutions and to learn Pulaar. Settling into rural life in one of the hottest regions of Senegal, where the average temperatures are between 30 and 45 degrees Celsius during the day for most of the year, and there is no electricity or running water, was not just physically but also psychologically challenging.

I was put in touch with someone from Diawoury on the Ile Amorphile who would be able to teach me Pulaar. As I knew that I would learn a lot faster in an environment that was 100 percent Pulaar, I moved there in February 2007.

It was dark when the bush taxi dropped me off in Weendouly, where I had arranged to meet my teacher. From there we continued our journey to Diawoury—through Weendouly down to the river on a horse cart, crossing the river in a narrow canoe in the dark, and then on to another horse cart, which took us across the Ile Amorphile for another hour's ride to Diawoury. Although I had traveled through regions without electricity before, my senses were unaccustomed to the dark. When we arrived in Samba's home at midnight we ate meat from a bowl with the family under the stars. I was exhausted.

The next weeks were spent learning Pulaar grammar every morning from nine till lunchtime. People came to greet me at length, and neighbors sent bowls of food to welcome me to the village. Some had never seen a white person close up. Children were screaming and following me wherever I went; they laughed at my gestures and imitated my movements, ridiculing my sense of dress, which I tried to balance between dressing appropriately to meet people's expectations and being unable to bear the heat in the requisite long cloths and gowns. I learned the greetings in Pulaar quickly, but apart from that I could hardly communicate with anyone, because very few people spoke French. As soon as the children got used to me, they came into my room and started asking me things I could not understand. When I tried out the new words I had just learned, they looked at me with big eyes and said, "*Mbiydaa* [What did you say]?" I suddenly understood that they had conjugated the verb to say *wiyde* in its reflexive form to ask a question. As I had no other choice I learned the basics fast.

Language was not the only challenge, but also being taken seriously as a person. Initially I was not allowed to go out by myself in case something happened to me. My hands were as soft as a baby's, the women remarked, and I was not allowed to help fetch water, or do any other physical work. My feet were softer than the children's hands, I was told—I was not allowed to go searching for firewood with the older children. There were snakes and scorpions in the bush under the branches and a bite can be fatal. Eventually I gained more autonomy and spent the late afternoons by the river with the children or the three schoolteachers, who soon became my closest friends as I could communicate with them in French, not the child-like language I was forced to speak with my family. My family, however, objected to me seeing them after dusk. After all I was an unmarried woman and it was not appropriate for me to go out at night. They were my guardians and I was their guest—my behavior reflected on their honor, they explained. Once I had a conversation with a woman in which I talked about boyfriends. Afterward I was asked if I was not ashamed to talk openly about these things. Did I want to represent myself as a shameless woman?

As Diawoury borders Mauritania, the mobile phone network was terrible. At times it was possible to make phone calls only in the afternoon. When the battery was empty the phone had to be sent to someone else's house to be charged with solar power, which took two days. There was no Internet—I had to travel 160 kilometers to Ourosogui to check my emails. There was nothing to buy in Diawoury apart from dried biscuits and no mineral water—I got used to the well water very quickly. Batteries for my torch were sent from Weendouly. There was no fruit to purchase either. Every so often I crossed the river with the children and walked for three miles along the Senegal River to a mango plantation, where we spent all afternoon in the shady forest feasting on the fruit, and we took as much home as we could carry. No matter how much we brought back, the twenty members of the household and the many neighbors who had been so generous to me made them vanish very quickly. It was so hot that candles bent sideways when I tried to write in my room in the dark. I therefore did most of my writing in the mornings before my lessons.

Although being a complete alien may seem a disadvantage, it also had its benefits. Besides linguistic skills, I was taught codes of behavior, morality, and honor. People were not intimidated by me as a researcher; most women did not even understand what "research" (*wittooji*) was. I was an unmarried girl (*mboomri*) who had come to stay for a long time to learn Pulaar and write a book about Futanke customs. I was constantly instructed on how to do things correctly and told why they needed to be done a certain way. This process of learning, observing, and listening carefully was invaluable to my understanding of conceptions of purity, honor, and shame, gender roles, and gendered spaces. It was a process of embodied learning of sociability, boundaries, and moral codes of behavior.

My Pulaar teacher occasionally went to a local radio station to read his poetry on a popular Pulaar-language radio program called *Finaa tawaa Fulɓe* (*Pulaar Traditions*, or literally, "What the Fulɓe find when they wake up").[14] We decided that when I was able to read Pulaar correctly and communicate enough, I should accompany him to read some poetry. In May 2007 we therefore took a horse cart to cross the Ile Amorphil to the radio station. I was going to read a poem called "*Mbayniigu*"—which means *separation* or *goodbye*. The radio presenter introduced me as Saara Sy, a *tuubaako* (white person) who had come to learn Pulaar language and customs with Samba Sarr from Diawoury. After I read the poem, the presenter asked me in Pulaar to read it again. Afterward, people from all over the Ile Amorphile called to tell me how pleased they were that I had come all the way to Fouta to learn about their way of life. One man promised to give me a horse and horse cart if I came to visit him in his village. When we returned to Diawoury the following day, people cheered wherever we passed: "Saara Sy, *min mbeltiima*" ("Sarah Sy, we are so pleased"). Some laughed and joked, imitating my pronunciation; others congratulated me and told me I was brave. Some people from neighboring villages walked to Diawoury for hours to see me. I became known as the white person who had come to live in Fouta to learn about their culture.

As I knew that no NGO had been to Diawoury to raise awareness about FGC, I initially did not try to discuss excision or the governmental ban with people. This was first of all because I was not able to have a complex conversation with women in Pulaar and, second, for ethical reasons and for my personal safety. I felt that I needed to understand how people felt about the practice before asking questions in a region that has vehemently opposed the ban. I therefore focused on collecting data about everyday habits, things that were important to my interlocutors and the boundaries I kept accidentally crossing out of ignorance of their social and moral codes of behavior.

I occasionally left Diawoury to do research elsewhere. I found out what kinds of activities relevant to my research interests were going on at the Tostan Ourosogui coordination. In May 2007 researchers of the Sigrid Rausing project were staying at the Tostan Fouta coordination office to type up the data from questionnaires that I had helped to design before going to the field. With these researchers as well as the Tostan staff in Ourosogui, I was more openly able to discuss excision, why people practiced it and refused to comply with the NGOs and the governmental ban. These discussions provided me with different data about excision. The Tostan Fouta staff were all local men and women who had stopped practicing excision out of personal conviction. However, despite being on the side of the government, most of their families and relatives continued with the practice; they were deeply aware of how important excision was to them and why it was immensely hard to take the decision to stop practicing in one's family. Long conversations with the Tostan supervisors and facilitators of different caste backgrounds (*Toorobbe, Fulbe, Subalbe, Galluŋkoobe/Maccube, Maabube*), some of whom I became very close to, also provided me with data about the opposition to the law and the NGOs. They frequently told me about their everyday struggles at work and their encounters with marabouts and village chiefs, whose tolerance of the NGO they had to negotiate. Most of the data collected among the Tostan staff was through participant observation and semistructured interviews, some of which were recorded.

In May 2007 a public declaration of the abandonment of excision was to take place, but it failed, because the village demanded USD 5,000 from UNICEF to pay the costs. For ten days with the help of a research assistant I interviewed people in the villages that were to declare. We wanted to find out how people felt about the fact that their declaration had failed. We spoke to village chiefs, marabouts, and schoolteachers, as well as people who had nothing to do with the declaration.

In December 2007 I interviewed villagers who had participated at the public declaration of Semme. This was six months after the public declaration had taken place. I also conducted interviews in Sinthiou Sebbe in February 2008. Most of these interviews were recorded or noted down in great detail with the help of a research assistant. I also interviewed eighteen excisers and ex-excisers between December 2007 and February 2008 in different places (Semme, Ndouloumadji, Weendouly, Diawoury, etc.). I waited until the end of my fieldwork so that my grasp of Pulaar was good enough to communicate with them myself to some extent, or to understand how the translator interpreted what had been said. I knew some but not all of the excisers before the interview. In January 2008 I interviewed four members of the ex-exciser association in Thilogne and the president of this association in Ngouloumadji. This was also done with the help of a research assistant.

In between these research trips I went back to Diawoury. My interlocutors there were hardly aware of what I did when I left Diawoury. One thing, however, did change my status completely in Diawoury and during other interviews I did in Fouta Toro. After seven months of living in Fouta I became religiously attached in marriage (*humaneede*) to a Pulaar man. Besides making me free to come and go as I wished without causing any scandals and discontent, this meant I was no longer addressed like a child but as a woman. This, however, also brought disadvantages. People expected me to behave like a married woman. They explained what duties I had toward my husband and local women made a great effort to explain to me and help me with the customary preparations of the bedroom and the household and told me to cover my head. The fact that my husband did not expect me to do any of this and in fact helped me with the work caused confusion. Many women worried and were very critical at times. Although this was immensely confusing for me, it gave me a deeper understanding of women's roles in the household and their expectations.

Ethics—Informed Consent, Confidentiality, and Reciprocity

My fieldwork took place in three different spheres. The first was Diawoury, the second was Tostan Fouta and Tostan Senegal, and the third was villages that had declared and that were to participate at public declarations. My approach with regard to how I addressed my research subjects, interlocutors, and interviewees differed depending on the context.

In Diawoury I spent most of my time doing participant observation and taking notes on conversations with interlocutors. For confidentiality purposes I have changed their names in this book. When I judged the subject of conversation to be very personal or sensitive I changed identifying information. The questions I asked people in Diawoury depended on how familiar they were with my research and what kind of information they provided me with. I paid my Pulaar teacher a monthly salary while he was teaching me and showed my gratitude by regularly giving presents to his wife, his mother, and his sisters-in-law as well as the children. These presents mainly consisted of cloth, clothes, photos, and sometimes small sums of money that were appropriate to local standards. I gave plenty of photos to other inhabitants of Diawoury, and occasionally other presents depending on the occasion. I rarely gave anyone anything specifically for giving me information because I did not want people to seek my company for money. Only on one occasion did I agree to buy half a goat for my teacher's older sister in return for magical incantations (*cefi*), the traditional occupational knowledge (*gandal*) of the *Subalbe* of things related to water (see Dilley 2004; Wane 1966). I conducted a few lengthy recorded interviews with long-term interlocutors toward the end of my fieldwork. After informing them of what I wanted to talk about and before the interview started, they verbally gave informed consent—it would have been inappropriate to ask for written consent.

At Tostan, people knew what I was working on. I formally interviewed ten Tostan staff who were working in or had worked in Fouta Toro; prior to the interview they gave their informed consent. Most of these interviews took place after many informal and personal conversations with them throughout my fieldwork. The interviews were semistructured and focused on their work for the NGO, their motivations, the opposition to the law, and problems they had experienced. The names of most interlocutors and places have been changed to preserve their anonymity. Some Tostan staff accompanied me to villages that had participated in the program and acted as research assistants, helping me to find research subjects and translating. I mostly remunerated them for their services, especially if they helped me for extended periods of time.

The interviews I carried out in villages that had publicly renounced excision were mostly semistructured with verbal informed consent, at times recorded if the interviewee agreed to this; otherwise I took detailed notes with the help of my research assistants. Here I followed question guides that I had prepared beforehand, sometimes adding new questions if they came up, sometimes leaving questions out if I sensed that the interviewee was uncomfortable. The questions were designed in a way that was considered sensitive and inoffensive by Tostan staff and other local people whose opinion I asked. I never asked any direct questions in this context, for example, "Do you personally have problems because of your excision?" or "Have any of the girls you excised died as a result of hemorrhage?" because this would have been inappropriate. Apart from the president of the ex-exciser association, who would not have agreed to be interviewed otherwise, I never paid any of my interviewees as this is not done in Senegal. If I felt that people were avoiding me because they did not want to be interviewed or their answers were short because they felt uncomfortable, I did not insist but looked for other research subjects instead. I always made an effort to dress according to the local style to make people feel more at ease with me despite being white, greeting them politely at length in Pulaar and showing them as much respect as I could according to local standards. I often joked and chatted with people in the household so that they felt comfortable with me and became curious as to why I had come to see them. When I met these interviewees again during my fieldwork, they were often warmhearted and kind, asking me when I would come back to visit them.

Growing Up, Growing Older, and Returning

Decolonial critics of anthropology have strongly questioned what insight young, white, and highly educated people are really able to gain living in an unknown place for a year and a half, with rudimentary language skills. I think that this critique is incredibly important and a reminder of the epistemological limitations of our work. Yet, anthropologists have also shown the value of observing the transition from being an outsider to slowly becoming an insider and of describing certain aspects of social life that an insider would not necessarily pay attention to because it is taken for granted (Abu Lughod 1999, 2008; Narayan 1993). Social class, gender, and age also strongly influence what people may be willing to reveal to us or how.

I returned to Fouta in 2009 to visit friends. The idea was not to do research but to see my friends. In 2013 I brought my three-year-old son to Fouta Toro. My Pulaar was becoming more fluent, possibly because I used my Pulaar language skills while doing fieldwork on malaria in rural Gambia for my postdoc job. For many, this visit marked a status change as I was now a mother, no longer a young toubab who has come to get the information she needs and never returns. Many people who were not even related to me now perceived me as an in-law and searched for kinship ties and rather than perceiving me as an adopted daughter or friend. The bond of the relationship became much stronger, meaningfully tying me to their social world.

Between 2013 and 2015 I did not really work on FGC but worked on lots of other issues related to medical anthropology and tropical medicine. In 2014 an activist colleague in Belgium, where I had moved, enthusiastically put me on her grant application to coordinate research on African men's views on FGM in Belgium, the UK, and the Netherlands. Once we got the grant, my role was to design and coordinate this research with researchers employed by the NGOs. My knowledge and experience of FGC in Fouta Toro provided me with in-depth insight into migrants' views in Europe and also with the sensitivity to talk about it in a way that did not offend people. The results of the study were strongly publicized online, and I presented the results at the House of Commons in the UK, at the Belgian Parliament, in front of experts on FGC at various international conferences, and at UNICEF in Switzerland. Because of the publicity on social media this study became quite well known among scholars working on FGC in Europe. I became known as a person who works on men and FGM—rather than my PhD fieldwork in Fouta Toro—although the long-term fieldwork experience had helped me formulate sensitive issues in a way that made sense to activists and softened their radical approaches to end the practice. In 2017 I became a consultant for the European Institute for Gender Equality (EIGE), where I coordinated the qualitative research of their girls at risk estimation. EIGE liked how I responded to difficult questions that EU bureaucrats do not have the answers to, and they recruited me again in 2019. I also became a WHO consultant working on the social consequences of FGM, which involved a literature review, and I traveled to Guinea to support researchers there with their analysis of data on the medicalization of FGM. I thoroughly enjoyed these professional experiences, sleeping in expensive hotels and meeting the elites, very different from fieldwork sleeping in rural villages without electricity and running water.

My friends and in-laws in Fouta were unaware of this work I was doing; it was of no particular interest to them, in a language they did not understand (English). Hannaford (2017) has shown that Senegalese families are often not interested in what someone actually does in life and where the income of transnational migrants come from. This was the case for my friends, too; my professional life did not matter to them and was of no relevance. Many of the anti-excision activists I met in Fouta sensitized against the practice for a living, so even if I had been an activist it would not have mattered to them. I returned in 2019 with my daughter and my son. Building on the Pulaar I had learned more than ten years earlier, I was able to converse with villagers easily and fluently. My son went to the local village school for one month and my daughter traveled with me to Diawoury. The small girls who were my friends in 2007 were grown up, took turns in cooking lunch and doing housework for their mothers, and were almost ready to marry. Relationships with my host family in Diawoury were warmhearted, and we reminisced about my first stay and all the things I had said and done wrong when I first arrived. When I returned in 2022 by myself to collect some more data from activists and NGO workers, they also remembered me as the person they had met fifteen years earlier. They were not aware of all the other work I had done since and it was not important to them. My children were far more interesting to them than my professional life and status.

Although I never formally worked for Tostan, and never signed a contract, and I volunteered mostly when it suited me, I noticed with surprise in 2022 that people remembered me as "one of the old ones who has done so much for Tostan." When I asked what it was that I had done for Tostan, I was told "it doesn't really matter what you did, Tostan is a team, it's a movement and you were part of the movement no matter whether you are a driver or a cleaner or a cook, what matters is that you were there!" In her ethnography on NGO program and FGC in Ghana, Hodzic (2017) suggests that "researchers are routinely interpellated as potential benefactors or patrons, as are volunteers, tourists, and other who come through the region." She argues that the desire of the "humanitarian hero"—as an individual "who takes on the task of saving African lives is not only a Western projection but a joint construction of Ghana and the global North" (2017:129). Hodzic describes that she was acutely aware of the fact that she as a Western anthropologist may have been seen as yet another person who arrived, asked what women wanted, and then failed to return with a project that would resolve their problems. I very much relate to this analysis as my role and raison d'être in the field was often blurred by people's interpretations of what they thought I had come to accomplish.

Fowler and Hardesty (1994), Howell and Talle (2012), and Johnson and Searles (2021) highlight the importance of long-term fieldwork in response to postcolonial critiques of anthropology and the traditional fieldwork model developed during earlier colonial anthropology. I want to argue that returning strengthens interpersonal relationships with people so that the bond becomes far deeper than research and reaches beyond differences in race and status. A continuous relationship also provides more in-depth perspectives on social and economic changes that affect people's lives over time.

Time and Change

What has changed over the last twenty years? Mobile phones, the Internet, and social media have changed social life in the Global North as well as in the Global South. I have described how I had to travel a long way to check my emails in 2007. In 2019 and 2022 I could check email on my mobile phone, keep in touch with family all over the world via WhatsApp, and stay connected with interlocutors very easily after leaving. During visits to Senegal between 2000 and 2010, I was often asked to take photos of people, which I later printed out and then gave to my Senegalese friends in Dakar and Fouta as presents, just like many other Euro-American researchers at the time. The photos I took of my friends' parents in Diawoury in 2007 were greatly cherished, especially after some of them had passed away. What struck me returning to the field in 2019 and 2022 was that the camera was often pointed at me. For instance, when I traveled to Velingara Ferlo in 2022 to observe the public declaration of the abandonment of excision, many people filmed the event with their own mobile phones. On the videos of the event, you often see five or six arms filming at the same time. I was staying with Tostan facilitators in Velingara Ferlo, while the Tostan staff I had been traveling with, accountants belonging to the Dakar-based Senegalese elites, spent the night in an air-conditioned hotel 110 kilometers away in Lingère. On my first night in Velingara Ferlo, the DJ who had been hired for the public declaration set up his gear for a little girl's birthday party in the house where I was staying. While we were dancing in a lit-up space with all the children, the adults I was dancing with got their mobile phones out and filmed everyone around them. Similarly, the night before the declaration, Tostan had set up an event called "la veille" with music and contemporary dance performances for young people. The evening was animated by artists with drums organizing fun dance competitions for entertainment. As I saw teenagers running to the center to dance, my friends tapped me on the shoulder and told me that I should dance too. I refused at first and preferred to watch from the back. It was just a whole load of fun and I could see that many of the dancers running to the center to perform were not particularly skilled, so slowly I changed my mind, thinking that I would not do much worse than them. Suddenly Kumba, one of the highly educated Tostan staff from the coast, had arrived at the site from her air-conditioned hotel. She put her arms around my neck and said, "Sarah, let's go and dance!" with a big smile. So, I got up from my plastic chair and said, "Okay, I will dance with you." I grabbed the hand of another friend I had known for fifteen years and the three of us danced our way to the center stage. The audience started cheering and laughing. I was the only white person there and we have the reputation of being terrible dancers. I did some Senegalese dance moves to the beat of the drums and, to my surprise, my two friends got their mobile phones out and pointed them at me. Looking around I noticed more people coming toward the center pointing their mobile phones at me with huge smiles on their faces. Our little dance performance lasted almost two minutes and we ran back to our seats under the awnings. Other people ran to the center to show off their dance moves. People were really pleased, telling me that I danced well. I felt that this sense of people pointing cameras at you whenever you're doing something fun was new. It was certainly not like that fifteen years ago.

Another remarkable change that struck me twenty years after my first visit to Senegal was how the sense of dress had changed. In 2001 it was uncommon to see Senegalese women dressed in trousers even in Dakar. Although by 2007 it was more common in urban areas like Dakar, in Fouta respectable girls did not wear jeans. I remember trying to persuade my friend Fama Ly to wear a pair of my trousers and she was in stitches with laughter. I wore jeans during the cold season in 2007, which was tolerated because it was cool and windy, and I was a foreigner. In 2022 it was very fashionable for teenage girls to wear jeans. However, I did not see married village women wearing trousers; they preferred wearing traditional Senegalese gowns made of wax cloth. However, among the NGO staff from the coast whom I had traveled to Fouta with there were women who regularly wore jeans at meetings in villages and when relaxing in the evening around dinnertime.

COVID in Fouta

Writing in the middle of the COVID pandemic, I have to add a few words on how this affected social life in rural Fouta. During the first lockdown in Belgium in February and March 2020, we were incredibly worried about friends and family in Fouta Toro. Senegalese people from Fouta whom I know living in diaspora sent WhatsApp messages warning villagers to stop shaking hands, to wash their hands regularly, to stop using public transport, and to avoid large social gatherings, including at the mosque. Some migrants in diaspora started collecting funds for food, soap, and other basic necessities because it was assumed that soon shops would close and cars would stop circulating as during lockdown in Europe. Senegalese with family in Fouta were incredibly worried that lack of access to basic goods might lead to famine and malnutrition in addition to the risk of COVID. The response, however, was hesitant. Those working in trade and transport said that they had to continue making a living and could not stop working because of a disease. Villagers did not stop sharing bowls of food or drinking-water cups, nor did they stop greeting each other. The most shocking suggestion was that people should stop going to the mosque, and I believe that this was what eventually turned villagers against the COVID regulations. Many said that COVID did not exist, that it had been invented by the Westerners to stop people practicing their religion, and that the intention was to turn families against each other to make livelihoods more individualistic.

When I visited Fouta in 2022, locals asked me how the pandemic had affected my family in Europe, and I told them that the last two years had been very difficult, especially for older people who were sometimes completely isolated during lockdown. They listened attentively with compassionate looks on their faces, and I often received the response, "Yes it exists, it's a real disease." Yet, no one I met in September 2022 had met anyone who got seriously sick or died because of COVID. In the villages very little had changed. People still shook hands when greeting, food was still shared from a bowl among family members and guests, and the water reservoir was still kept under the tree where people could help themselves by drinking from a cup that was cleaned once in a while (every couple of days). At the public declaration in Velingara Ferlo, masks were distributed, and the response was, "Yes, COVID is real, it does exist." The constant verbal reaffirmation that COVID is "real" is interesting in medical anthropology as it shows that the biomedical concept (*gandal tuubakoobe*) of COVID was not universally accepted as a sickness that can cause morbidity and mortality, but rather for many it remained an abstract concept with no heuristic proof of existence. Among the officials invited to the delegation and NGO workers, those who were vaccinated did not put masks on, some wore their masks for a little while, while others merely strapped one around the chin to show that they were complying with health regulations.

An Outline of the Chapters

Chapter 1 looks at the circumstances under which the law against FGM was passed in 1999 and how the opposition from Fouta Toro surfaced. The legislation was the result of a number of events that led to a national call for abandonment by politicians, activists, and the national media. Based on archival research, I address how national, nongovernmental, and independent media discourses were produced in reaction to the law and how different responses to the ban reflect concerns regarding the gendered female body. Leading up to the national ban, Senegalese newspaper articles showed varying perspectives. Some described the unexcised female body as lacking femininity and as vulnerable to the threats from "Western imperialism," here seen to devalue womanhood by omitting a practice that preserves dignity and protects from evil. Others viewed the ban on FGM as protecting and liberating women from "harmful traditional practices" that deprive them of their right to "physical integrity." From the latter perspective, the law was an event of liberation from "custom" and a victory for women's rights, and a step toward the highest standards of health and physical integrity. Opposition to the law and to NGO activities was triggered in 1999 by publication of *Preuves Eclatantes au Sujet de la Pratique Recommandable de l'Excision des Jeunes Filles* (Striking Proofs for the Recommendable Practice of Excision of Young Girls) by religious leader Thierno Mountaga Tall. This booklet became a reference for regional religious leaders who were consulted about whether to endorse FGC.

Chapter 2 moves on to how the body is gendered through excision and circumcision. I show that, in contrast to Mande subgroups in Senegambia and West Africa, excision in Fouta Toro is not important in the context of initiation and coming of age. Rather, it is about making female gender by removing the external genitalia reminiscent of a boy's penis. As the literature on FGC among Mande subgroups (Ahmadu 2000, 2005; Ahmadu and Shweder 2009; Griaule 1948) and Boddy for Sudan (1989) suggest, excision renders the ambiguously androgynous unexcised body unambiguously female. The excised woman is "pure," "virginal," and socially appropriate. The process of becoming a woman, however, is not completed until she marries. For boys, on the other hand, there are initiation ceremonies, although circumcision is also frequently performed with little fanfare. The chapter shows how female excision and male circumcision respectively create the physical foundations for gendered personhood. Through encounters with three different cutters, I show that the way in which excision is practiced depends on the exciser's family tradition and occupational lore. I argue that so-called tradition is a term that accords value to a practice because of the relationship it represents between those who have passed it on and those who have taken it up. Tradition does not mean that a practice has never changed, but that it is reinvented and accorded value by each generation anew. The body as born accrues value in being culturally transformed by practices inherited from the previous generation. Female gender is hence made by connecting the physical body to the social body of the previous generation in a way that, according to Fulani, renders it safe.

Chapter 3 engages with local conceptions of bodily control as an asset of Futanke civilization. I discuss how the control of desire contributes to the maintenance of social harmony in Futanke society—an image resembling Hobbes's idea of a society without law and order and in complete disarray without the commonwealth. I show that, according to local discourses, excision helps women control their own sexual desire when their husbands are away making a living for the family. As Yanagisako and Delaney (1995) among others have shown, cultural concepts become especially powerful when they are naturalized, made to appear normal and inevitable. In Fouta Toro, desire, as in an individual's personal quest for sexual satisfaction, is not considered positive—on the contrary, I show that behavior seeking personal gratification is deemed barbaric and uncivilized. I suggest that moral personhood is thus intrinsically linked to the ability to control one's body and one's desires; a respected person, whether male or female, goes through the hardships of life showing that they can restrain their personal needs for the common good of the larger body of family and kin. The chapter argues that prioritizing the needs of the social body over those of a person's physical body begins with socialization during childhood. Girls and boys are taught from a young age the necessity of serving and obeying elders rather than pursuing their personal interests and passions—which in turn provides them with the certainty that they can rely on others' help if in need. However, being able to rely on the support of relations—whether those related through kinship or through solidarity within or between age sets—is a form of social security that requires strict submission to the rules. Those who refuse to participate in this social arrangement are not considered moral persons and are said to be "not like us" or not Futanke or Pulaar. A person who does not adhere to this moral code of behavior is therefore outside the boundaries of what the Haalpulaar of Fouta Toro identify with. They see other ethnic groups as less in control of their desires and thus less moral and civilized than themselves. Contemplating a society without excision conjures up fears of perversion and temptation, of women not behaving in an appropriate manner, dressing and dancing differently, and getting carried away with pleasure.

Chapter 4 engages with the sexual body and the boundaries of what is considered appropriate and inappropriate. Despite the measures to control sexual desire previously discussed, pleasure is fostered and encouraged in the legitimate realm of marriage. Excised women do not consider themselves and are not considered mutilated, sexually handicapped, or unable to experience pleasure. I show that sex in itself is not taboo, dirty, or shameful. On the contrary, some women enjoy making themselves desirable and performing pleasure-enhancing customs with aphrodisiacs. Nevertheless, there are aspects of sexuality that are considered inappropriate, dirty, and repulsive. For unmarried women, the use of pleasure-enhancing utensils would be shameful. Extramarital sex is shrouded in silence, the stuff of which myths and gossip are made but which is not openly practiced. It is thought inappropriate to interact with people if they have not rendered themselves pure through ablutions after sex. Uncircumcised men and unexcised women are perceived to be unclean because of the accumulation of impurity around the parts of their genitals that have not been cut. I argue that many Futanke men and women perceive uncut genitals as not just dirty but also ambiguous due to their androgynous status—being neither male nor female. Following Mary Douglas, the ethnography shows that ambiguity is potentially embarrassing and dangerous. On the one hand, such images are associated with fear of the unknown and the unsafe; on the other, the fact that an uncut woman is imputed to be malodorous and impure points toward moral and social inferiority. An unexcised woman is not just potentially loose, unable to control her desire, but also dirty, dangerous, and repugnant. With reference to Douglas (1966), the chapter argues that excision creates social order by curtailing the unbridled desire that threatens to arise in women if they are not cut. The demise of Futanke society is largely associated with pregnancy before marriage and illegitimate children. Illegitimate sex (childbirth before marriage or illegitimate children) brings social chaos. I argue that the visceral sense of revulsion that people feel toward unexcised women and their imagined impurity is an embodied reaction to the fears around what might become of society if women no longer manage to control their sexual desires.

Chapter 5 explores the conflicting voices in which the Futanke speak about the ban on FGM and nongovernmental intervention. Those who oppose the law and foreign influence see these as threatening the physical and social body. The first part of the chapter reconstructs versions of what happened during two so-called events of resistance to the NGOs and the law by describing my interviews with NGO officials who were directly involved in the events of Aere Lao and Ourosogui. The interviewees claim that although some religious leaders raised their voices against the ban on FGC, many people wanted to know more about the potential health consequences of the practice and their rights as guaranteed by the state. The opposition to governmental and nongovernmental intervention thus does not emerge from a unified group in Fouta Toro. Contrary to the picture painted by those who are against the ban, there is no clear-cut division with the Futanke on one side and the state as corrupted by the "white people" on the other bringing in subtle forms of cultural colonialism disguised as development through NGOs. The second and third parts of this chapter demonstrate that dissent over the NGOs' abandonment movement is a symptom of a conflict in leadership and decision-making processes as well as disobedience and generational conflict. I argue that the public outcry and pain about an attack on their culture and religious faith emerges mainly from *Toorobbe*, the religious clerics and leaders in most villages in Fouta Toro. Governmental and nongovernmental intervention on excision unsettles Futanke social, moral and political order by undermining the religious clerics' authority in a domain where they are not used to being challenged: the so-called religious recommendation of female circumcision. Although statutory law theoretically grants non-*Tooroodo* individuals of lower caste background rights to positions of leadership in local politics, in practice it is extremely challenging for a non-*Tooroodo* to be listened to and followed to the same degree as a *Tooroodo* leader. The opposition to the law and the NGOs is an act of defense against changes in morality that challenge the *Toorobbe* leaders' moral authority and political power. Many nobles perceive the Futanke way of life to be threatened and seriously challenged through these interventions and associated social change. Whereas they fear the foreign influence of NGOs and believe the Senegalese state to be corrupt, local people, including NGO workers and state representatives, fear the marabouts' spiritual power as well.

Chapter 6 discusses the female body as protected by the law and saved from the sickness and disease inflicted by the practice of excision. I introduce women who are not afraid to break social conventions, who collaborate with the NGOs and go out to raise awareness about the health problems excision can cause. Their support of these campaigns is often based on personal experiences with the practice. These women often seek the NGOs' help and justify speaking out against excision by referring to the Senegalese state and to human rights. For them, human rights are a vehicle for renouncing the practice despite social conventions that suggest they continue. Engle Merry (2006) suggested that so-called indigenous women are often pushed by NGOs to formulate their personal issues in terms of the violation of human rights. She argues that their orientation to human rights models is often temporary. This, however, seems misplaced in the case of Fouta Toro. Although some women and men feel pressured to publicly declare their abandonment of FGC, many Futanke women perceive the international human rights agreements as protecting their bodies and rights. I contend that those who have personally experienced difficulties because of their own excision, but find it hard to stop practicing, see the rights framework provided by transnational institutions and the state as a way to stymie oppressive structures in their own society. It provides them with an ideology that gives courage (*cuusal*) to publicly discuss their health problems and speak out against excision. Although local women felt that this transnational ideology had come from somewhere else, it was used as a vehicle for speaking out against excision despite religious leaders' opposition to the ban, and to speak up for ideals that they believed many communities had agreed to abide by. The fact that others in Senegal had declared their abandonment of excision before and that they were supported by an international community gave them strength to challenge local leaders' opposition to the abandonment of excision. The chapter argues that human rights ideologies are not necessarily top-down and prescribed by "middle-level women" and "transnational elites" (Engle Merry 2006) but, in this case, provide a lever that could alter social structure. It allows those who have traditionally had no say in Fouta Toro due to their social status (*ñeeñɓe*) to make decisions without their noble patrons' approval and to become leaders of local development movements. The fact that lower-status groups are provided with possibilities of leadership and social mobility through this movement means that those *Tooroɓɓe* who feel threatened by social change and are concerned about women's chastity are sidelined. For those who defy *Tooroɓɓe,* the image of the female body has shifted from being part of a kin group with a localized form of identity to being an individual possessor of rights subject to international standards of health.

=========

The Event

L'événement qui survient est un moment, un fragment de réalité perçu qui n'a pas d'autre unité que le nom qu'on lui donne. Son arrivée dans le temps (c'est en ce sens qu'il est le point focal autour duquel se déterminant un avant et un après) est immédiatement mise en partage par ceux qui le reçoivent, le voient, en entendent parler, l'annoncent puis le gardent en mémoire. Fabricant et fabriqué, constructeur et construit, il est d'emblée un morceau de temps et d'action mis en morceaux, en partage comme en discussion.

(The event that occurs is a moment, a fragment of perceived reality that has no other unity than the name we give it. Its arrival in time (in this sense it is the focal point around which a before and after are determined) is immediately shared by those who receive it, see it, hear about it, announce it, and then remember it. Fabricator and fabrication, constructor and construction, it is from the outset a piece of time and action put into pieces, shared and discussed.)

A. Farge, "Qu'est-ce qu'un événement?" *Terrain, revue d'ethnologie de l'Europe* (2002)

CHAPTER 1

Events, Representations, and the Beginning of the End of Excision in Senegal

This chapter is about the banning of excision in Senegal in 1999. NGOs, the government, and the international press consider that the ban led to reactions that are often described as "the backlash in Fouta Toro" or "the resistance." From this perspective, the passing of the law was an event of liberation from "custom" and a victory for women's rights and the highest standards of health and physical integrity. I will show how the passing of the legislation was constructed as having been the result of a number of events that led to a national call for abandonment by politicians, activists, and the national media. Abdou Diouf's speech, given at a human rights conference held in Dakar just over a year before the law against excision was passed, indicates important elements that framed the justifications for passing the law:

> Finally, let us fight vigorously against excision. A law is without doubt necessary to mark the government's commitment in this domain. But above all we need to convince the populations that this practice constitutes a threat for women's health—governmental and non-governmental organisations included. Excision frequently causes haemorrhages, infections and deaths during child-birth. Today this custom is no longer justified.
>
> In this respect, the example of Malicounda deserves being cited here. In this Senegalese village the women have become aware of the dangers of the practice and engaged in a dialogue with their husbands, the imam and the village chief. Through a collective decision the community decided that excision will never again be practised in their village.

> Today I formally appeal that this "oath of Malicounda" propa-
> gates through the whole of Senegal. I request that a great debate
> about excision should be organised in each village so that everyone
> becomes aware that the time has come to change these ancient
> practices.[1]

I want to draw attention to a number of things Abdou Diouf mentioned in his speech, which frame the context in which the passing of the law was justified by those in power and the experiences of my interlocuters in Senegal. President Diouf appeals for a "vigorous fight" against excision on a national level and the need for a law. First, intervention against excision was encouraged by the government, which pleaded for NGOs to be involved in convincing the population to abandon the practice. Second, Diouf's speech justifies the government's position against the practice in terms of an improvement of women's health. Such discourses of the abandonment of excision in the name of "women's health" continue today and have provided an ideology justifying abandonment. Third, Diouf constructs an opposition between the past, and the practice of harmful customs, and a vision of the modern Senegalese state, where such customs are no longer justified. These echoes of modernity and tradition, whether perceived as negative or positive, played a crucial role, not only during the period leading up to the passing of the law, but also in debates about women's bodies and cultural propriety in the resistance movement in Fouta Toro. Finally, Diouf refers to an event that is perceived by many as having initiated the social change with regard to excision in Senegal—the oath of Malicounda, when in July 1997, thirty-five women publicly renounced their practice of excision after having followed Tostan's education program. I will show how the story of the Malicounda declaration has been told and used for particular purposes in debates about the national call for abandonment of FGC.

I look at the ban on excision in Senegal and NGOs' intervention as an event that crisscrossed several institutions and redefined women's bodies in different ways. It would be too simplistic to see the passing of the law and activism against excision merely in terms of an imposition by the state onto the population, or merely as an act of liberation. Anthropology is no longer about the ethnographer's experience in one place, for the local and the global are intertwined, especially in questions of advocacy and law. In this case, the event of the law moved across boundaries of law courts, the parliament and ministers' decisions, the international community, village "communities," the family, bureaucracy, advocacy, and funding proposals and influenced how people feel, think, redefine, challenge, and silence women's bodies, morality, and honor.

Following Das (1996), I am interested in how transformations in space propel people's lives into unprecedented terrains—how particular events set new modes of action into being, which redefine notions of tradition and codes of honor and purity, for example (Das 1996:6). These transformations in space are brought into being by the ways in which political actors represent events in different documents for different purposes, and in this way redefine how bodies and lives may be perceived (Das 1996; Fortun 2001; Latour 2005; Kapferer 2010).

This book concerns itself with women's bodies and how the law influenced how people perceived the body as a result of FGC being outlawed. It is not a book about laws, governmental politics, and how the public reacted to the mediatization of the event. However, these are immediately relevant to how women's bodies were perceived and how existing moral standards were challenged through different authorities. I am concerned with the law and NGO intervention in the light of its impact on people's perceptions of women's bodies and honor in Fouta Toro. The information provided about women's activism against excision in Dakar and the activities of NGOs should therefore not be seen as a discussion of these actors in themselves. It is relevant with regard to how these groups influenced national and global policies that challenged my informants' views of morality, justice, the state, and women's reproductive behavior.

Events, however, do not just affect the way in which people rethink themselves and their rights; they are also made for particular purposes. With reference to Farge (2002), Handelman (1990), Kapferer (2010), and other authors, I argue that incidents involving NGOs and the government were made public in a way that turned these occasions into important "events" in the making of the law and human rights. Some events, unheard of and insignificant for many, have been retrospectively seen as having fabricated social movements and having led to the passing of the law. I show how the national call for abandonment was fabricated in a way that complied with transnational standards of human rights and development agendas with reference to newspaper articles and NGO documentation. The Malicounda declaration, for example, has been used in discursive practices that nourished politicians' public speeches to abide by international human rights and public health standards. Abdou Diouf's call "for further governmental and non-governmental commitment to convince populations to stop the practice" (*Le Soleil*, November 21, 1997) provides an example for this. For others, however, the Malicounda declaration was a nonevent (Farge 2002), and the passing of the law became an event only because of the emotional upheaval and anger it caused.

How Activism for a Law Against Excision Was Perceived and Experienced: An Introduction

For many, the passing of the law against excision was the logical consequence of years of activism for women's rights in Senegal. Women's rights were first institutionally recognized in 1972 in the Family Code, which granted equal rights to inheritance, legally recognized marriage status, divorce, and private property.

Various interlocuters of mine, who have worked closely with the government on feminist issues, told me that female ministers working in the Secretariat for the Promotion of Women (Secretariat pour la Promotion de la Femme) in the Senegalese government strongly believed in promoting women's rights and healthy behavior based on evidence, which had been provided by the WHO since 1972.[2] Some of these politically active women participated at the International Women's Conferences, for example in Beijing (1995), where the harmfulness of FGC was hotly debated. These women consider the moral and legal support provided by international organizations of authority (e.g., WHO, UNICEF, and UNIFEM) to be positive. Dr. Abibou Camara, a Senegalese sociologist I met in Dakar on various occasions in 2008 and 2009 while he was supervising a qualitative study on FGC for the WHO, explained to me that the female presence in the Senegalese government, as well as women's activism, created a favorable climate for passing a law against excision. In addition, only 28 percent of the population was recorded as practicing excision. The majority ethnic groups in Senegal (Wolof, 43 percent;, Serere, 15 percent), who make up 58 percent of the population, do not tend to excise either in initiation rites or for religious reasons. In addition, Camara reasoned that the most dominant religious brotherhoods in Senegal, the Mourides and the Tijannes (Cruise O'Brien 1971, Sanneh 1997) did not officially take a position on the practice. These factors influenced the parliamentarians to vote for a law against excision. When it was made public that a village near the city of Mbour had abandoned excision after having followed the NGO Tostan's basic education program, there was even more of an incentive to help women protect their bodies by outlawing the practice in the name of a right to physical integrity and a right to the highest standards of health. Camara concludes that, in governmental, NGO, and activist circles in Dakar, the passing of the law against FGC is seen as having been a result of favorable social, juridical, and cultural conditions, as well as the fruit of their hard work and activism.[3] Although this view was confirmed in conversations with figureheads of the movement against female circumcision in Senegal, like Melching and Madame Sidibe Ndiaye, none of these individuals belong to ethnic groups that practice excision, nor do they follow religious leaders who recommend the practice.

For others, however, the law against FGC represented a threat to their freedom to practice their customs and religion. Excision is understood to be a hadith, a recommendation of the Prophet Mohammed.[4] In this view it was inconceivable that the Senegalese government should pass a law that prohibits following a religious recommendation. Some protested that the harmful consequences propounded by these international organizations did not exist. Furthermore, in their view, there were many other practices far more harmful and against religion that should be outlawed before banning a practice that was recommended by the Prophet. Sex tourism and homosexuality were commonly cited as examples of harmful practices. Instead of furthering women's rights, the law on excision (Article 299) was perceived as a form of cultural colonialism imposed by "the white people" in the disguise of an international community.

A number of NGO-led events are considered to have been crucial to the national call for abandonment. The next section will provide an overview of the NGOs involved in raising awareness against FGC in Senegal. It is beyond the scope of this book to go into their activities in detail—and it is difficult to say to what extent their presence really had an effect on the passing of the law or to what extent the success was constructed by the newspapers.

Movements Against FGC in Senegal

Campaigns and "sensitisation"[5] activities against FGC had been taking place in Senegal since the beginning of the 1980s. A review is available in L'Abandon *de l'Excision* (UNICEF Senegal 1999), which I draw on. Some associations focused on raising awareness through conferences that were supported and funded by international organizations in Dakar, which formed networks and lobbied the government in the 1990s. Other organizations focused on raising awareness and on sensitization at a grassroots level through basic education programs in rural areas (see UNICEF Senegal 1999). In the 1980s and 1990s, Tostan and ASBEF were the only NGOs intervening against female circumcision in Fouta Toro.

Although many of the sensitization activities were funded by international development agencies, I disagree with the idea that NGO intervention is merely an imposition of the international community onto the Senegalese population. This position would deny that individuals act according to their personal convictions, presenting a rather monolithic, determinist view according to which individuals are completely guided by overarching systems of power. Instead, I favor approaches that aim to get to the bottom of why actors are motivated to participate in and lead activities that are supported and funded by "international development agents" (Fortun 2001).

Tostan

Tostan is considered one of the most prominent actors in the movement toward ending excision in Senegal for a number of reasons. First, Tostan is present in all regions of Senegal and has continuously received funding from international agencies such as UNICEF and USAID since its establishment. Second, Tostan's strategy was officially recognized as "a pertinent approach" (République du Sénégal 2008:5) with regard to "FGC abandonment," in the national action plan to reach complete abandonment of excision in Senegal by 2015.

The NGO was founded in 1991 by an American expatriate who had been involved in basic education and development associations in Senegal since 1976. Initially, Tostan's education program did not aim to persuade villagers to stop FGC—this was more of an unexpected side effect (Gillespie and Melching 2010; Tostan 1999). The objectives of the first versions of the program were to improve women's literacy in local languages, as well as to promote self-development through adapted educational materials.

After human rights modules were added to the program in 1995, thirty-five participants decided to end the practice of excision in the village of Malicounda Bambara. This first declaration in Malicounda has been depicted by the NGO and some Senegalese newspapers as having initiated a process whereby more than four thousand communities officially declared their abandonment of excision by 2010 (Kandala and Shell-Duncan 2019) with the help of Tostan and its funders. The effect of the Tostan program has been studied by various researchers and organizations. Diop et al. (2004) found in their evaluation that women and men became aware of the adverse health effects of FGC[6] after having undergone the program, and that the willingness to continue practicing FGC on their daughters went down by 50 percent on average.[7] In a long-term evaluation, UNICEF (2008) found that the Tostan program certainly had an effect on attitudes toward FGC and abandonment. The villages evaluated in the 2008 study had participated in some of the very first declarations in the country (the Diabougou declaration, eleven villages, in February 1998, and the Medina Cherif declaration, with eighteen villages in June 1998). The study found that although "there are still a few resistors who say they will never abandon the practice" (UNICEF 2008:26), "the abandonment of FGM/C is a reality confirmed by the majority of the people in the villages surveyed." Although the "progress" seemed promising before 2010 and UNICEF and other funders invested intensively in these public declarations, the 2010/2011 Demographic Health Survey revealed that the national prevalence had gone down by only 2 percent (Kandala and Shell-Duncan 2019). Many funders and policymakers were surprised and felt that the programs had not met expectations. Kandala and Shell-Duncan (2019) give a more in-depth overview of the geographical changes and age trends in girls who are not cut. Despite the positive evaluations cited, Tostan has faced considerable opposition not just from international funders but also from local leaders.

Although the founder of the program is an American, in Senegal the NGO is run almost exclusively by Senegalese staff. It is important to stress that Tostan is more than an international NGO intervening in the rural regions of Senegal. Its ideology of human rights, democracy, and public health promotion is one to which Senegalese staff and volunteers subscribe. The NGO is perhaps more appropriately described as a social movement or directed ideological social group than merely a foreign-led NGO sensitizing against "harmful" practices.

In the following section we shall see how Tostan unintentionally became one of the main actors in the national call for abandonment through the Malicounda declaration.

Malicounda Bambara and Public Debates About the Imminent Criminalization of FGC

From 1995 to 1997, the village of Malicounda Bambara[8] participated in a revised version of the Tostan program, which included new human rights modules. The following illustrates how the participants came to the resolution to stop FGC through a participatory process. I will eventually show how the mediatization of this process influenced the MPs when passing the law in the National Assembly in January 1999. The following should not be read as a historicizing account of how one event led to another but as fragments of a reality that was perceived and retold in different ways by different actors (Fortun 2001; Latour 2005).

Malicounda Bambara: The Decision-Making Process Retold

In July 1996, the women of Malicounda studied an education module in which the adverse health effects of FGC are discussed. According to the facilitator's manual, the participants of the program are supposed to perform a role-play telling of a girl who goes through the circumcision rite, is excised, hemorrhages, and dies. The volunteers for this role-play are asked to make the theater as vivid as possible, using real circumcision songs and crying loudly, as one does when a death is announced in the village (Tostan 1999: 34). As this session follows others in which participants discuss the development of the body and reproductive health, the women had become accustomed to discussing sensitive subjects in class that were previously taboo. The facilitator, who was based in Malicounda, explained how participants initially reacted to discussing FGC:

> The women were hesitant to do a theatre adapted from the story at first.
> We kept the same name as in the story—Poolel—which is a Pulaar
> name and didn't directly implicate the Bambaras in this tragedy, which
> may have helped. The women did the story as theatre but refused to
> discuss it afterwards. I kept asking them the questions that accompany

the session [in the teaching manual] and no one would answer. The discussions in Sessions 1 through 13 were normally lively and animated. "Why were they refusing to answer the questions?" I thought. "Is it because I am Wolof and have not practised FGC?" So I did the session again and again. Three times. The third time they finally started talking timidly, and then more and more women spoke up. They admitted that it was an ancient practice that they followed because it was tradition and expected of them by the men and religious leaders. Nonetheless, their human rights helped them to understand that they have the right to the highest standard of health. They also have the right to express themselves and give their opinion. They hadn't known all this before and had never discussed it together. Finally, we ended up talking and talking about it together often. The women decided to talk to their "Ndeye Dikke" [adopted sisters][9] and their husbands about the dangerous health consequences. They also thought it important to get advice from the Imam and the village chief on the issue. They were surprised when they discovered that many fellow villagers supported an effort to end FGC. (Tostan 1999:45)

This is how the women of Malicounda Bambara decided to stop practicing excision according to the early Tostan documentation (Tostan 1999). From the facilitator's perspective, the NGO did not impose this decision on participants—it was the result of a participatory process (Nelson and Wright 1994). The taboo on discussing excision was not lifted through a top-down process in which a teacher crudely depicted the problems of excision, but through discussion which allowed participants to question a previously unchallenged social norm. The facilitator argues that the women were "empowered" (also see Nussbaum 2000) by the discussion facilitated by the Tostan program.

As I did not have the chance to interview the women of Malicounda myself,[10] I refer to the documentation of the decision-making process by Tostan staff who recorded the participants' initial reasoning for stopping the practice. A lot of this material was then put together in *Breakthrough in Senegal: Ending Female Genital Cutting* (Tostan 1999). Besides giving a perspective on how the women of Malicounda came to this decision before it was picked up by and debated in the national media, it provides "expert" accounts (Marcus and Holmes 2005) of those who had been more deeply involved with these women than could be accomplished by a journalist or researcher during a short visit. However, it is important to bear in mind that the Tostan documentation was designed to present potential funders with a success story of how the abandonment process worked in Malicounda and hence a guarantee of how it would work in other places. Stern (2010) shows in her article on funding proposals for a town in the Cobalt region of Canada that stories are often fabricated in particular ways to apply for funding. The history of a place is relative according to who is intended to hear it and for what purposes. There is a body of literature that critiques so-called development (Escobar 1995; Nelson and Wright 1994; Mosse 2005; De Sardan 2005) and NGOs' representations of how their goals targeted in action plans are achieved (e.g., Green 2000, 2003, 2007). Green argues that satisfying the funders' requirements, dealing with the bureaucracy of NGOs and representing oneself as a benefactor are often more central to daily routines of NGO staff than actually responding to the needs and desires of the targeted population.

After studying Tostan and public declarations since 2005, I found that many informants of mine retold what happened in similar ways. My aim is not to judge whether the stories told are "true" or are mere stories to attract funding and justify banning excision in Senegal, but to look at what so-called events are doing in forming a ban and the opposition to it. The Malicounda women's decision to renounce excision and their press declarations are seen, by international players such as Tostan, UNICEF, the national and international press, etc., to have led to the ban of excision in Senegal.

According to Tostan documentation (Tostan 1999), by June 1997 participants of the Tostan program had convinced enough people of the harmfulness of excision that no public circumcision ceremonies were held during the rainy season in the village. It is noted that a participant of the Tostan classes testified that, "Everyone was aware that there was a movement to end the practice in the village. If any woman did cut her daughter, she did it in secret for the first time, knowing that she would be subject to public disapproval" (Tostan 1999:45).

The director of the NGO at the time, Molly Melching, was initially unaware that participants had stopped excision because of what they had learned in class. The primary intention of the program had not been to convince communities to stop FGC but to provide them with general learning tools and information for personal development and the development of their communities. In June 1997, Melching was called by the coordinator, who informed her that the women of Malicounda Bambara had stopped excision in their village (Tostan 1999:45). Surprised, Melching and the head of training visited Malicounda to hear firsthand what the women had to say for themselves. Initially,

Molly and the Tostan staff were hesitant to approach the subject of FGC openly, as they were aware of the sensitivity around the issue and did not want to raise any topics women might feel uneasy talking about (Tostan 1999: 46). However, they were immediately told that "we have decided to end 'the tradition' in our village" (1999:46). Excision had been discussed so much that it was no longer a delicate subject, according to Melching.

Melching noted how the women explained their initial decision in a report, which she sent to UNICEF (Tostan 1999:46). Here, participants formulated their rights in response to the program that echoed the discourse of the WHO agendas the government was dealing with. Coincidentally, the WHO had held a conference in Dakar three months before the Malicounda decision, in March 1997, in which Senegal had agreed with twenty-seven other African countries to adopt an action plan on strategies for the abandonment of excision. I suggest that the Malicounda women's discourses sustained the human rights ideologies the government was trying to reinstate in Senegal to prove to the international community (WHO, UN, World Bank, etc.) that Senegal was complying with the desired human rights standards.

I quote in illustration: "We started thinking and talking about things in class that we had never before discussed, things that had always been 'taboo,' you might say. [...] we learned about germs and the spread of disease and that made us think a lot about some of our traditions that might be dangerous for our children. [...] the Tostan program gave us a certain amount of confidence that we had never had before. Confidence that we could change things if we wanted to" (Tostan 1999:46). This passage shows how the program was perceived as an agent of change. The Malicounda women's experiences were seen as evidence that the program would empower communities to break oppressive social conventions in favor of the development agendas the government and NGOs had been prioritizing.

Another Tostan participant in Malicounda said:

> We studied Human Rights [...] in Module 7 on Women's health and particularly the right to health. We learned that this right implies the freedom of each woman to decide for herself what she does with her body. She also has the right to preserve her body as it is, without mutilation or changes. This was a revelation for us since it was in contradiction with one of our oldest traditions: the circumcision of

female children. In fact, in our traditions, it is unthinkable not to circumcise girls—why? She would be the laughing stock of the community and could never find a husband! It was so important that we were told that an uncircumcised woman was "dirty" and not fit to prepare and serve food to those who study the Koran! Yet, we have always been uneasy about the disadvantages linked to circumcision. Many of us suffered greatly during sexual relations with our husbands and during childbirth. Many got infections or haemorrhaged after the operation. (Tostan 1999:46–47)

This woman spoke of how they experienced the practice as important before—how it was impossible to question the practice despite the discomfort some were experiencing. Of course, the realization of their "human right" to stop the practice happened to be in the interest of what the WHO was pleading for a conjunction of human rights and health.

During the meeting an older woman who had been listening added the following:

We old women were the ones who insisted that all the girls in the community be circumcised! Even when the parents were against it, we'd go take the child and do it when they weren't around. But I'm in this class and I learned about Human Rights. Did you know that every man and every woman have the right to marry and live their lives according to their own beliefs? When I found that out, I realised I could no longer impose my will on my children and grandchildren. (Tostan 1999:47)

This woman's account brings the generational aspect into consideration. Whereas the elders are known to have authority and their decisions bear more weight in decision-making processes than the younger generations', this old woman voices a rejection of this "right" of the elders in favor of "human rights." What is particularly striking about these accounts is the realization of an individual's rights in contrast to what is perceived as the obligations of tradition and a community's laws (Das 1996). In all three accounts the women speak of the convention that could not be broken or was continued without question. However, what they had learned in the Tostan program changed their views of the unbreakable convention. In Das's sense, the education program was the trigger that brought new modes of action into being and redefined "traditional categories such as codes of purity and honour, the meaning of martyrdom, and the construction of a heroic life, for example" (Das 1995:6). I argue that the Malicounda women's discussion of excision became an "event," which was eventually amplified as an event of national importance. However, initially it was a merely a local dispute during which FGC was questioned in a debate among women, men, and local leaders. In this process of decision making, the excised body moved from being pure, chaste, and proper to a proprietor of human rights, subject to violation, mutilation, and vulnerable to disease and discomfort.

According to Tostan (1999), the women's final stage before making their decision to stop the practice publicly was the imam's view. After discussing excised women's health problems in the classes and deciding that these health risks corresponded to what they had experienced themselves, the women went to seek the imam's advice on this issue (Tostan 1999). The imam Serigne Amadou Touré told them that the Qur'an did not oblige them to practice this rite, and personally he was against it. He explained that he did not want his daughters to be excised. When he found out that his first daughter had undergone the operation without his knowledge, he told his wife not to let it happen again. His other daughters were not excised. The women were surprised about this as they had assumed that excision was recommended by religion. The participants told Melching that the information they had acquired through the program and the imam's stance toward the practice gave them powerful arguments and the courage to tell others about their newly formed convictions (Tostan 1999).

Fortified by the certitude that they were not violating holy law, there were no longer any constraints to their desire to renouncing the practice, according to the Tostan rhetoric (Tostan 1999). In Chapters 5 and 6 I discuss the role of religious and traditional authorities in more detail with reference to my own ethnography in Fouta Toro. As we shall see, religious leaders' opposition to the abandonment of excision does occur and can be an impediment to stopping the practice. Although this decision-making process was an event of local importance, it was a nonevent for others in Senegal.

How the Women's Decision to Stop Excising Became the Beginning of the End

To complete the account of how the nation found out about the Malicounda women's decision to abandon, I will continue to follow Melching's account of how she brought the news to UNICEF and the national press (Tostan 1999; Gillespie and Melching 2010).

Molly Melching sent the report of her interview with the women of Malicounda to the UNICEF representative in Dakar, and they discussed the surprising effect the program had had on the women's decision to abandon excision. Mr. Sonhy, the UNICEF representative, suggested sending twenty Senegalese journalists to the village. Melching was initially hesitant but Sobhy reasoned, "if these women are strong enough to make this incredible decision on their own, they are strong enough to defend their position before twenty journalists" (Tostan 1999:49). When Melching told the women that UNICEF wanted to bring journalists to their village, they were excited and said, "Yes! We have good news to share with everyone. Why not discuss it? This will be an opportunity for us to explain why we made the decision" (Tostan 1999:49; Gillespie and Melching 2010).

According to Tostan, the villagers prepared for the arrival of the journalists. They asked for more information about human rights articles to be in a position to defend their views. They rehearsed their play and invited the religious leaders and the village chief to come to the event. In *Breakthrough in Senegal: Ending Female Genital Cutting* (Tostan 1999), the media coverage of the event was considered to be extremely positive. Representatives from the Ministry of Health and the Ministry of the Woman, the Child and the Family were present and congratulated them on their decision. Radio interviews in the national languages were broadcast during the following weeks: the news on television showed film clips of the women and their play and an interview with the religious leader (Tostan 1999:49).

Events of National Importance for the Ban on FGC—Media Representations

Besides governmental and nongovernmental representations of how the Malicounda declaration became the beginning of the end of excision in Senegal, newspapers played a crucial role in the making of a national debate on excision and the need for a law. In what follows, we shall see how the progovernment and independent newspapers *Le Soleil, Le Matin, Nouvel Horizon,* and *Dakar Soir* depicted the Malicounda event and others. I discuss how modern Senegal is envisioned through these reports and for what purposes. Subsequently I will show how these events of national importance were ridiculed and minimized by the critical newspaper *Walfadjiri* to illustrate its stance against the anti-FGC movement. The selected articles are from 1997 to 1999, the period when FGC was subject to public debate.

The national press reported on the Malicounda event in the following ways:[11]

Le Soleil (governmental newspaper)
August 2 and 3, 1997
"Malicounda Bambara: the women renounce excision."[12]
"In a male chauvinist environment that is still ruled by tradition the women of Malicounda have come to the courageous decision to abandon excision. And to make their decision public, they have invited the national press to their village last Thursday with UNICEF as an intermediary. The women participated in a prodigious education programme that was put into being by Tostan/UNICEF/Government of Senegal."

Le Matin (a center right daily newspaper, which tends to have a less critical stance and more commercial interests)
August 4, 1997
"The oath of Malicounda 'No more excision!'"
"The women of Malicounda Bambara, a village situated a few kilometres away from Mbour, have decided to put an end to the sexual mutilation of girls. Supported by UNICEF and Tostan, an NGO interested in the rights of women, they have lifted a taboo. A report."[13] This article describes the ceremony in great detail and glorifies "the conservative and tradition-abiding Bambara women and their decision to give up 'an ancient tradition.'"

<u>*Nouvel Horizon*</u> (read mainly by people who consider themselves to be intellectuals, including schoolteachers, for example)
August 8, 1997
"La fin de l'excision à Malicounda."[14]
The article emphasizes the importance of "education" for an abandonment of "this ancient and deeply ingrained custom." It argues that without sufficient educational support (by government and NGOs) it is impossible to outlaw the practice.

Dakar Soir
August 9–15, 1997
"Malicounda Bambara. The women demystify excision."
The article argues that the women of Malicounda declared
because they do not want their daughters to suffer the same
problems they have had to go through. It is therefore "normal"
that they have decided to defy this "deeply ingrained tradition" to
protect their girls' bodies. Again, the article describes in great
detail how the women came to their decision to renounce
excision.

Le Soleil (governmental newspaper)
August 28, 1997
"Malicounda Bambara——The descendants of Malians well integrated"[15]; "The world is collapsing."[16]
These articles depict "the event" of the declaration as a proof of
the collapse of ancient traditions in a quickly changing Senegalese society. An emphasis is placed on how education programs
brought about this change in attitude toward "a Bambara custom" that has been associated with the preservation of female
integrity.

These articles convey how this event was represented as a break from tradition and the beginning of a new era in Senegal—a future that is depicted as
more modern and as guided by international standards of human rights
instead of holding on to backward traditions of a past era. The governmental newspaper *Le Soleil* in particular used this declaration to sustain the
idea that education and human rights are associated with development and
modernity. This place, modern Senegal, is depicted as free from oppressive
customs, injustice, poverty and "the imprisonment of traditions," but offers
physical integrity, democracy, and justice through a set of standards agreed
on by a so-called transnational community.

It was through the mediatization of the Malicounda declaration that
the women's decision to stop excising became an event of national and
international importance that was argued about across Senegal and outside. Handelman (1990:15) argues that public events are locations of communication that convey versions of social order in relatively coherent ways
to an audience. He says that in contrast to the general "flow of mundane

living," which may be uncertain in terms of direction and outcome, public events are put together to communicate comparatively well-honed messages (Handelman 1990:15). In this way, the Malicounda women's decision was reproduced through the national media in a way that depicted Senegal as moving away from harmful traditions, changing in the ways prescribed by the UN, and abiding by the international standards recommended by the WHO. The fact that Hillary Clinton visited the women of Malicounda, to hear about their resolution and to congratulate them for having the courage to end the practice, underlined that this event was not just significant for the inhabitants of Malicounda but of interest across the world.

For many, what was happening in Malicounda was very much congruent with other events that were going on in Senegal at the time, for example, the WHO conference held in April 1997, at which twenty-seven African nations developed an action plan to eliminate sexual mutilations.

Another event that is frequently referred to as significant in the history of activism against FGC was a conference held at the University of Dakar July 12 and 13, 1997. The aim was to discuss the religious point of view on sexual mutilations. At this conference, various scholars and Islamologues discussed the religious recommendations of the Prophet Mohammed (hadiths) and eventually came to a consensus that mutilations of the body are not recommended by Islam but are cultural traditions. The Qur'an itself does not mention the practice, but recommends the preservation of women's health. This event has been referred to as "the marabouts' declaration" by some informants,[17] as many perceived this intellectual and religious debate to prove that excision was not a religious obligation.

Below I have assembled some newspaper articles discussing public debates and important events that were going on around about the same time as the Malicounda declaration. These events are also considered crucial by activists, NGOs, ministers, and the national press to the passing of the law against excision two years later.

Le Matin
July 14, 1997
"Female Genital Mutilation in Senegal. The hidden face of the female drama."[18]
After an account of the discussions during the conference on FGM and religion at the University of Dakar, the article asks how an end

can be brought to sexual mutilations in Senegal. There is no easy answer to this question as the practice is not yet penalized by law. The populations are very attached to their cultural traditions and are not aware of the dangers of the practice. Furthermore, mothers wish to protect their children and future mothers. Due to the patriarchal system women are virtually absent in the decision-making process in the rural areas as well as being marginalized in the Family Code.

Le Matin
August 4, 1997
The religious point of view: "Excision is recommendable, not obligatory"[19]
The article discusses whether this practice, which is practiced by some ethnic groups in Senegal but not others, is in fact recommended by Islam. Dr. Taha, WHO specialist in hygiene, explains the difficulty of the situation in the following way: "It is likely that part of the confusion that appeared around the subject of the religious interpretation comes from generalising what applies to male circumcision to women. Although there is a general consensus about the fact that circumcision was one of the commandments that God gave to Ibrahima (Abraham), there was no clear indication as far as female circumcision is concerned."[20] Furthermore, the doctor argues that the Prophet Mohammed's often cited hadith that recommends "to reduce but not destroy" (the clitoris through cutting) has been found to be of unreliable and inauthentic sources. Some Islamic theologians recommend partial removal of the clitoris and justify their point of view by saying that it "embellishes" the woman. Nevertheless, one fact remains uncontested: historians agree that the practice of excision existed long before the arrival of Islam and other monotheistic religions, according to a professor of Sharia Law at Kuwait City University.

Nouvel Horizon
August 8, 1997
"Mutilations sexuelles féminines" explains that there are few countries in Africa where excision is punishable. Senegal is not an exception as there is no law in the Penal Code that punishes any form

of female genital mutilation. However, according to Madame Maty Diaw, legal councilor of the Ministry of the Woman, the Child and the Family, excision is currently considered to be an act of violence toward women. The problem is that mothers cutting their daughters do not do so with malicious intentions or to mutilate their children but because they wish the best for them and want them to be well integrated into a society that demands these practices. As mothers are not performing a crime to harm their daughters, this act is not punishable at present. However, the National Plan of the Woman 1996–2001 recommends introducing a law punishing excision, as well as encouraging and introducing education and sensitization programs to change people's mentality about these practices—which cannot be changed from one day to the next.

The Point de Vue
December 23–29, 1997
There is need for a law. It is stronger than tradition.[21]

The selected articles show how the debate about excision in Senegal revolved around its harmfulness and recommendations from the international community on the one hand, and on what grounds it is legitimate to stop the practice on the other. While the debates were at times initiated by activists, they also sought to inform the reader about the Islamic stance on excision and whether stopping the practice is legitimate from a religious point of view. Furthermore, the articles problematize the fact that although excision has been discouraged by the WHO on the basis of its harmfulness, the practice is not penalized, and question whether criminalization of the practice would be an effective way of getting communities to stop.

Farge's (2002) analysis of what makes an event significant to history making is relevant to the passing of this law. She bases her analysis on the premise that an event is not much more than a moment that occurs—a fragment of reality that is perceived and has not much more unity than the name it is given (Farge 2002:2). This fragment of time is perceived, understood, shared, and discussed by its recipients. An event is fabricated and fabricates (Farge 2002:3). She argues that the event is a moment of illusion of what was there in the past and what is to come in the future. In this way, the event can be significant in defining a vision of the future for those who experience it. One speaks of an event by characterizing it with regard to an expectation of something that is to come. It is announced in view of the good or bad news that is expected to occur (Farge 2002:4).[22]

An event, however, is not just relevant to those who witness it and who make it an event in their memories through assembling moments understood as the past, present, and future. It also gains historical and national importance through historians and the national media (Bensa and Fassin 2002). Historians seize on and make sense of the event, and reify it in ways that affect how it is remembered by those who come after (Farge 2002:6).

For many activists, politicians, journalists, and NGO workers, the Malicounda event marked the potential beginning of the end of a past that they had lived and struggled to change in one way or another. It represented a vision of something new—a transformation to modernity.

However, no matter how the event is represented by the historian or the national media, it may remain a nonevent for some. It may be too insignificant for some to register in their minds. They may not remember it years later because its significance did not concern them personally. For example, a lot of my informants in Fouta Toro, who were not associated with Tostan, had never heard of the Malicounda declaration, although it was probably featured in radio broadcasts. For them, this event of national importance was not significant enough to remember. Other informants in Dakar who were not involved in development work and activism against FGC had never heard of these important events either, or if they had, they could not remember them. What registers in people's minds as of national importance, therefore, depends on how relevant something is to their lives and how involved they are in the issue. Farge also looks at how a nonevent can become an event because of the emotional reactions it provokes—it may be that the happiness and euphoria of some simultaneously produce the anger, outrage, or sadness of others (Farge 2002:5). As we will see later on, some of Tostan's sensitization activities against excision have been ingrained in a lot of Haalpulaar'en minds across the whole of Senegal—because they caused so much anger and upheaval although they were not intended to do so. One of these events, that neither Tostan nor the national press documented as significant, is still referred to as *les événements de Aere Lao*. This was an occasion where Tostan had organized a meeting at which people were to publicly discuss excision and human rights in the presence of ministers and international agencies such as UNICEF. Locally renowned marabouts were strongly opposed (see Chapter 5).

The daily newspaper *Walfadjiri*, which always seeks to critique governmental actions, did not write about the Malicounda event. While other newspapers called for a need for a law against excision, *Walfadjiri* published various articles in 1998 that showed overt opposition to the idea of a law and ridiculed governmental and nongovernmental activities to get populations to stop the practice.

Walfadjiri
July 10, 1998
The excisers have not put their razor blades away,[23] arguing that although the women of Malicounda Bambara declared their abandonment of the practice, excision is still widely practiced in the neighboring communities and the statistics have shown that the rate of excision has not decreased in the department of Mbour.

Walfadjiri
December 31, 1998
"Kedougou: 120 excised girls waiting . . . about 10 days ago hundreds of girls were excised in this department. The penalisation of female genital mutilations is received without great illusion [*sic*] because the preliminary sensitisation work was rushed or indeed non-existent."[24] The article explains that even though the government has decided to ban female circumcision, it is extremely unlikely that the whole population will stop practicing if sensitization has not yet reached the remote parts of the country. It is argued that the government should give people time before criminalizing the practice as not enough groundwork has been done. Teachers "in the bush" testify as to their doubts: they ask themselves if the government is serious about the criminalization and sensitization against excision because for diseases like polio great funds for projects were released. Efforts to raise awareness about excision seem minimal in comparison.

Walfadjiri
December 31, 1998
Interdiction and Penalisation. They want to humiliate us.[25] "There are many ethnicities in the department and many different ways of practising excision. But the same line of defence is taken everywhere." This article demonstrates again that despite penalization by the government, the practice is far from being abandoned in Kedougou. The law is seen as shaming people's customs rather than as a reminder of the right to health and physical integrity.

As we can see, *Walfadjiri* recorded different events as "significant." Governmental attempts to discourage excision by establishing potential penalties are not taken seriously but are instead depicted as another potential failure like the many other governmental efforts to promote development in remote regions like Kedougou. In addition, the articles indicate that the debates going on in the city among governmental organizations and NGOs are far from the lived realities in "isolated"[26] rural parts of Senegal. According to *Walfadjiri*, this law and the Malicounda declaration represented not modernity and the right to personal integrity but, on the contrary, a form of cultural colonialism imposed indirectly by "the White people." The article below depicts this form of cultural colonialism vividly and intelligently, referring to the Senegalese intellectual tradition of *Négritude*.[27]

Walfadjiri

January 6, 1999

Criminalise paedophilia, not excision. The article begins by pointing out that Senegal is a popular destination for sex tourism and particularly pedophilia, and that sexual exploitation of children and adolescents for prostitution and pornography has reached an unimaginable level.[28] These practices should be banned and become a matter of public concern and not the religious practice of female circumcision. International concerns about female circumcision are misplaced and not everything that is supported by Westerners and the international community is appropriate and relevant. The article defends excision as a practice of "civilisation," as the Egyptian pharaohs attached the practice to the idea of divine androgyny and argues that the renowned Senegalese scholar Cheikh Anta Diop discovered that circumcision was introduced to the Semites through contact with the Black world. Circumcision is meaningful because it is integrated into general explanations of how the universe is constituted among Black people. One particular example of this is the cosmology of the Dogon (Griaule 1970). In this cosmology, male circumcision must be accompanied by excision—to remove the feminine from the man and what is masculine from the woman (Diop 1979). The author reminds us that Senegal is up to 90 percent Muslim and Islam dominates social life in Senegal. It is therefore impossible to criminalize a practice without enquiring into the exact position of Islam toward it. Does Islam recommend or tolerate excision? Niang, the author, states that the practice is not mentioned in the Koran but it was reported that the Prophet addressed the excisers of the female slaves of Medina in the following way: "Excise lightly and don't cut the clitoris completely. This way you allow the woman to experience some pleasure, to have a radiant face and to give some pleasure to her husband."[29] The Sharia classes excision as a practice of propriety/etiquette (*sunna* or *fitria*) that brings human nature to perfection—like circumcision, like cutting one's fingernails, depilating, shaving one's pubic hair.[30] The *Rissala*[31] says that circumcision of boys is a traditional obligation, whereas excision of women is merely an honorable practice (*khifad*).[32] The author of the article questions whether the health risks really are as grave as the press and the government presents them to be. If it really is a harmful practice, he argues, why has it persisted throughout the last few millennia? Is it right and legitimate to criminalize a cultural act, an act of civilization? Does the Senegalese government not prepare to pass this law to comply with Western opinions, to imitate the West? If it is criminalized for this reason (to imitate the West) against the practices of ancient civilization, then this law goes against common sense. Niang reminds the deputies who are about to make a decision on the law, that the law is the expression of the common will of the people and hopes that the deputies will abstain from voting for such a law. Instead, he recommends, pedophilia should be criminalized first.

Besides introducing us to arguments for a preservation of the practice and reasons for the opposition to the law, this article shows that the oft-cited assumption that excision is preserved out of ignorance is misleading. On the contrary, the argument for the preservation of the practice is laden with symbolism revolving around civilization and sophistication associated with highly regarded "ancient" peoples such as the Egyptians, the Semites, and the Dogon. Furthermore, excision is valued as enhancing the morality and social etiquette of society by relating it to the origins of the Islamic community and to practices that were common during the time of the Prophet Mohammed and personally endorsed by him. Instead of representing a shift from tradition to modernity, from ignorance to education, and from "victims of unquestioned customs" to autonomous, free-thinking citizens, the law against excision is seen as undermining civilization and as representing a threat to the cultural autonomy of Africans. The influence of the West is seen as culturally and morally inferior—excision, it is argued, is not a barbaric practice depriving women of their right to physical integrity, but rather it enhances their status and respect in the community in agreement with religiously sanctioned principles. The West, however, is thought of as merely having brought corruption and a breakdown of culture, community, and civilization—as the reference to sex tourism and prostitution shows.[33]

So far I have argued that the call for national abandonment and the law in Senegal resulted from a fabrication of a number of events, such as the Malicounda declaration and feminist activism in Dakar, and the representation of these events in the national press. I have also shown how these were nonevents to others, and I looked at the assumptions underlying propaganda against the law in leftist newspapers like *Walfadjiri*. The next part of this chapter looks at the debates in the National Assembly on the day the law was voted in—which in turn provoked resistance to the law and the NGOs in Fouta Toro.

Debates in the National Assembly and Voting for the Law Against FGC

The official proposal for modifying the Penal Code gave the following rationale for penalizing FGC:

> Female Genital Mutilations, although part of traditional practices and customs, constitute intolerable violations of the physical and psychological integrity as well as the health of many women and young girls. These practices are no longer relevant in the new socio-cultural dynamic of Senegal. Their legal abolition as indicated in Article 299 of the penal code takes this into account and also the respect of international conventions ratified by Senegal, especially convention 1979 on the Elimination of all Forms of Discrimination towards Women and the convention of 1990 regarding Children's Rights. (From the government's official proposal, in Tostan 1999:69)

According to Molly Melching, a group of parliamentarians sought Tostan's advice concerning the impending law to be debated by the National Assembly at the beginning of January 1999 (Tostan 1999:69). As Tostan had experience with villagers who stopped excision, they wanted to hear more about how to approach the abandonment. Melching sent some ministers to meet the women of Malicounda to discuss their reasons for renouncing excision and how they felt about the passing of a law. Tostan was not in favor of a law penalizing the practice, in contrast to other activists such as Madame Sidibe Ndiaye of COSEPRAT, who was a promoter of the new law.

The day before the law was passed, on January 12, 1999, a delegation of villagers from Malicounda and Diabougou and Medina Cherif, as well as other women's groups who had fought for abolition of FGC for many years, met with members of Parliament in Dakar. The villagers expressed their views that the government should take a firm stand against the practice by voting for a law. However, they unanimously requested a delay in its application. They were concerned about other members of their ethnic group who had not benefited from the education program and "did not know about the health risks involved in the cutting" (Tostan 1999: 70).

The parliamentary debate on the amendment of the law in the National Assembly on January 13 has been depicted in a number of documents, but unfortunately I could not obtain a complete recorded version of the event.

According to Melching (Tostan 1999), the event took place in the following way: Mata Sy Diallo of the women's parliamentary group began the debate and spoke of the dangers of FGC. She thanked the villagers who had testified in front of the committee and spoke of their warnings that sufficient education is needed before the application of the law. The famous and influential Tijanne leader Thierno Mountaga Tall, a Pulaar marabout and El Hadj Omar's grandson,[34] had distributed a carefully put together document for the parliamentarians on the same day. It was called *Striking Proofs Concerning the Recommendable Practice of Excision of Young Girls*[35] (Tall 1999) and contained information about the religious importance of excision. On the grounds of Tall's arguments for the practice and against the proposed law, many parliamentarians raised concerns about outlawing excision during the debate. Some said that they could not vote for the law because they did not want to criminalize their relatives for respecting tradition and religion.

According to Tall's document, in which he explains different Islamic scholars' positions on what the Prophet and his companions thought of excision,[36] the purpose of cutting the clitoris (khifad) is to protect women from excess of sensuality.[37] "Excessive sensuality" could tempt a woman to commit despicable acts, Tall argues. As nowadays most husbands travel and stay away from their spouses for long periods of time, the Prophet's warning against excessive sensuality is even more relevant than it was in the past. What Tall means is that the desire for sensuality might tempt a woman to commit adultery rather than waiting for her husband to come home.[38] "The wisdom of excision lies in the fact that the woman can abstain from sex for longer and thus guard her honor" (Tall 1999:15). The *Al-Fawz Wa An-Najah* states that "Virtuous women obey [their husbands] and protect what needs to be protected during the absence of their husbands, with the protection of Allah" (Tall 1999:15). Furthermore, "If the woman accomplishes her five prayers a day, lawfully, fasts her month [of Ramadan], protects her sex [exclusively for her husband] and obeys her husband, she is asked through which door she wishes to enter paradise," as the Prophet promised in a hadith.

Tall reminds the Muslim Senegalese citizen that the teachings of the Prophet as well as those of his wise followers should not be abandoned for foreign Western pretensions that are unfounded and false. He raises the rhetorical question of whether a Muslim has the right to abandon what has been legally approved (Sharia) to follow a Muslim who cannot justify his opinion or, even worse, to follow the advice of a non-Muslim (1999:16). Tall concludes his document with the following remarks. To prohibit Muslims from practicing the recommendations of their religion and their customs is a sinful act and an injustice that retards human rights. He reminds the reader that breaching human rights is condemned according to the constitution of the country—it is the right of every citizen to practice their religion and their beliefs without hindrance or harassment. Furthermore, the discussion about excision and circumcision is religious and customary in nature and a secular state should not get involved. If the state intervenes on this question, he says, why does it not intervene on worse crimes such as prostitution or the consumption of alcohol and tobacco? For there is no doubt about the fact that these practices are harmful to people's health, as has been proved by modern medicine, he says. In the name of religion he therefore appeals for medicalization of the practice instead of criminalization (Tall 1999).

This document strongly influenced the views of those parliamentarians who adhere to the *Tijaniyya* brotherhood (Cruise O'Brien 1988; Brenner 1988; etc.), and particularly Haalpulaar'en, who felt loyalty toward the most influential religious leader from Fouta Toro. Due to Tall's reputation as a renowned and influential religious leader it was very difficult for some parliamentarians, who had kinship ties or were morally obliged to this figure of authority, to speak out against his recommendations. The effect of this pamphlet is depicted in an article on the debate in the National Assembly in the governmental newspaper *Le Soleil*.

Le Soleil
January 15, 1999
"THE VOTES AT THE NATIONAL ASSEMBLY. Excision is
forbidden. The end of the first session at the national assembly.
Excisers risk a prison sentence of between 6 months and 5 years."[39]
"It is impossible to turn a cultural practice into an offence for it
cannot stop the act," argued the Member of Parliament Cheikh
Saad Bouh Fall. "The motivations for the project of passing this law
are unacceptable," said Abdou Fall, and Yoro Deh added to this
that: "The penalty of six months to five years of imprisonment
foreseen in the new Article 299 is excessive." Ibrahima Fall argued
that "The project of the law is precipitated. We did not expect this
now. We wanted a penal code on family planning first that incorporates all these questions in a more general way." The event of Malicounda was discussed in detail and it was said that abandonment
was achieved there because of the beneficial social environment
provided by the education project and NGOs' development efforts.
However this change in opinion was not possible in other places, it
was said. Some Members of Parliament, such as Cheikh Abdoulaye
Dieye, referring to Thierno Mountaga Tall's declaration condemn-
ing the law for religious reasons, went as far as saying: "My religion
forbids me to vote for this law against excision." Furthermore, the
possibility of medicalising the practice was discussed. Dieye
suggested that this would guarantee "the girls' aesthetic charm
without the harmful consequences." Babacar Baptiste Dioh countered this: "No! There is no charm, nor anything aesthetic about a
mutilation." Doudou Wade defended Dieye's point of view: "Excision is a religious problem. To attack it would mean challenging
[remettre en cause] Article 19 of the Constitution." Jean Paul Dias
reinforced their arguments saying that "To criminalise excision
means to criminalise a custom."

Despite the contradictory views voiced during this "long and difficult debate,"[40] the majority finally voted for the law against excision (Article 299) at
11:20 p.m. In the end the female parliamentarians, themselves being from ethnic groups that practice excision, seemed to be the greatest defenders of the
law and were extremely critical of the practice—whereas the men were hesitant

to vote for its criminalization, according to Melching (of the NGO Tostan) and Ndiaye (of the NGO COSEPRAT). Some were afraid of passing such a law and wanted to protect their relatives and members of their ethnic groups from penalty, but surely also to avoid criticism from their own relatives and the people whom they were supposed to represent. However, it was agreed that without education and social mobilization, it would be impossible to get people to accept the new law and stop practicing, thus that its application should be postponed. Instead, national strategies for the abandonment of excision would be developed.

Conclusion

In this chapter, I have discussed the movements that preceded the ban on excision in Senegal and how the legislation came to be passed. I have explained which organizations were involved in campaigning against the practice since the beginning of the 1980s, and how Tostan's basic education program was perceived to have led to the Malicounda declaration, which became an event of national importance. I have also discussed how different events of national importance were fabricated in ways that made many people perceive a need for a law and a national call for abandonment. However, in contrast to these views, there were others who did not register these events (Farge 2002) as important and who defied the law on the eve of the debate at the National Assembly. I argue that the passing of the law and related activities represent events that dramatically changed the ways in which women's bodies and their honor, morality, and purity were perceived, legitimized, and silenced in Das's sense (1996). From this vantage point we will continue to explore throughout this book how the law challenged perceptions of women's bodies and the authority of the state. This is particularly relevant in the region of Fouta Toro as it has been called "the most difficult area," or "the area with the most overt opposition" to the law and NGO intervention by governmental and international organizations.

The Events of Opposition to the Law and Nongovernmental Intervention in Fouta Toro

was told about these events by Tostan staff, health care professionals, and politicians who lived in or had worked in Fouta Toro. The reader will learn more about some of these incidents in Chapters 5 and 6 and will meet some of the key actors. This list of events should not be considered exhaustive; it is intended to indicate what kinds of incidents constituted "events of opposition" for Futanke who worked for NGOs aiming to achieve an acceptance of the law, as well as for others who opposed governmental attempts to bring an end to the practice.

1992	Tostan opens basic education centers in Fouta Toro focusing mainly on literacy, problem resolution, hygiene, health, management of resources, finance, and feasibility studies, not on reproductive health, human rights, etc. The program is popular and there is little resistance.
1997	A new Tostan program is introduced with changed modules commencing with reproductive health, the harmfulness of excision, and women's rights. A lot of people seem to find this shocking in Fouta Toro, and the program has difficulties continuing—some centers shut down. The Tostan coordination is set up in Ourosogui. The great marabout Thierno Aliou tells the team that he does not want them to talk about excision. The team agrees to this. There are some *sandar*

(small marabouts) in Ourosogui who organize discussion groups about the harmfulness of excision.

1998

In August, the women of Malicounda Bambara near Thiès publicly declare their abandonment of excision and early marriage after following Tostan's program.

1999

On January 13, after much debate and controversy, the National Assembly passes a law criminalizing the practice of excision in Senegal. The influential religious leader Thierno Mountaga Tall distributes a pamphlet arguing that excision is a religious recommendation according to the hadiths and speaks out against the law. This document creates a lot of upheaval and frustration about the law in Fouta Toro.

2000

"Les événements de Aere Lao." On November 4, the NGO Tostan plans to hold a meeting in Aere Lao, Fouta Toro, to discuss human rights, excision, and early and forced marriage with the population. Parliamentarians are invited to come to this meeting to explain the law to the religious leaders and the population. Various women for the abandonment of excision are present to publicly discuss the issue with local women. However, the activities are blocked by religious leaders who threaten the heads of the NGO and religiously condemn them for publicly questioning the practice of excision. A week later the marabout loses two legs due to diabetic shock. These incidents are widely seen as being linked.

2003

Tire burning incident. The NGO Tostan plans another meeting to discuss the harmfulness of excision with the local population in Ourosogui. They are accompanied by a German delegation of funders and UNICEF. However, the delegation is kept in the hotel and threatened by locals who order them not to discuss excision with the population. The foreign visitors are refused access to the local hospital. Tires are burned outside the hotel.

2003

The village of Sinthiou Sebbe and twelve other villages publicly declare their abandonment of excision and early and forced marriage with the help of Tostan. The declaration is funded by UNICEF.

2004

Tostan offered education classes in Podor. A group of marabouts claimed that girls were stripped naked in front of the students in the classes. The prefect of Ndioum called for a meeting with Malik (a marabout who works for Tostan) to discuss the accusations made against Tostan. Malik brought the Qur'an to the meeting with the marabouts and asked them to show the section in the Qur'an that recommends the practice. There is no such passage in the Qur'an. Malik then cited various passages in the Qur'an that aim to preserve women's health with reference to human rights and the respect of the law. The marabouts eventually agreed to let the program continue and the allegations were dropped.

2004

The villagers of Gassambiri want to organize a public declaration in their village but the local authorities refuse to go to Gassambiri for reasons related to what is called *ñaagunde Alla Jabaande*, which is translated into French as *prière divine acceptée*.[1] It is believed that since colonial times, the village has been protected by a spiritual force that kills any governmental administrator who enters the village to recruit men to go to war (i.e., World War II).

Enthusiastic "casted people"[2] of the village of Polel organize a public declaration, but a returned emigrant from the leading Tooroodo status group wants to take over the leadership. Tostan refuses because the organizing committee of the declaration is already in place with democratically elected casted people in the leading positions. The Tooroodo then blocks continuation of activities and the organization of the declaration fails.

| 2005 | In November, Sinthiou Sebbe hosts another public declaration of seventy-six villages in Fouta Toro who followed Tostan's education program and want to abandon excision. The great marabout of Doumga Wouro Alpha—Thierno Mohamadou Lamine Ly—tells the marabout of Sinthiou Sebbe to stop the declaration as it is un-Islamic. The marabout of Sinthiou Sebbe disagrees, arguing that excision is not mentioned in the Qur'an and by law, everyone is free to practice their religion as they wish, and therefore his followers in Sinthiou Sebbe can declare their abandonment of excision if they wish. |

| 2006 | Two marabouts (sandar), who collaborated with Tostan in 1997 on raising awareness in discussion groups on FGC in Ourosogui, start spreading rumors that Tostan is a white man's NGO that intends to destroy Islam and Futanke culture. Both marabouts died prematurely. By some, their deaths are interpreted as a punishment for having spread these rumors. |

| 2007 | In January, the influential religious leader Thierno Mountaga Tall dies. The question arises among NGO workers and activists as to what will happen now that the most vehement opposer is no longer alive. |

| 2007 | A public declaration of the abandonment of excision is planned to take place on May 6 in Daande Lao. However, the organizing committee of the declaration asks for 5 million CFA from UNICEF for the festivities. UNICEF refuses and the declaration does not take place. |

| 2007 | In June, seventy villages declare their abandonment of excision in Semme. The declaration is considered a success by Tostan and UNICEF. |

| 2007 | In June, Thierno Mountaga Tall's son tours the maraboutic villages after his mourning period of three |

months, three weeks, and three days has ended. He holds meetings that are attended by many influential religious leaders and the local population to speak of his father's death and answer questions about religious issues. As his father's son, he takes on his father's authority, is listened to and respected. At this meeting in Semme he is asked about his stance on excision. He replies that the most important thing is harmony among Muslims, that the practice is a religious recommendation, but it is up to individuals to decide for themselves whether they want to practice. Tostan considers this a success because he does not oppose the abandonment of excision like his father. In Semme, however, many local men reproach their wives for having taken part in the public declaration of their abandonment of excision and forbid them to continue working with Tostan.

2007   In October, fifty UNICEF-funded centers open in the district of Podor, which has previously shown a lot of opposition to Tostan.

2008   In the region of Kanel there was a village called Barkatu that followed the Tostan program. At first there were fifty participants. After a while the maraboutic family discouraged people from following the classes because Tostan calls into question a religious practice—excision. Participants stop coming and there were only between three and six participants left. When the great marabout of Madina Gounass (in Kolda), Thierno Ahmed Tidiane Ba, tours the maraboutic villages in Fouta to respond to questions regarding religious practice, the marabout of Barkatu asks him to talk about excision on three different occasions. The great marabout ignored the question the first and the second time. On the third occasion he responded, "this is the third time you are asking me and each time you asked I did not respond. No response is also a response. How dare you ask me a third time?" He did not endorse excision as a religious recommendation and did not speak negatively of Tostan. According to Tostan staff, from that point onward more than one hundred people followed the education classes in Barkatu.

2009 In May, an exciser is arrested in Matam after the activist organization Raddho (Rencontre Africaine pour la Défense des Droits de l'Homme) announced on the radio that a girl was excised. This creates enormous unrest in Fouta from religious leaders, who write a press declaration in response. A lot of NGO education programs are forced to close down by religious leaders all over Fouta. Tostan holds a meeting with a large delegation of marabouts in Ndioum to explain that they had nothing to do with the arrest of the excisers and that its job is merely to run an education program that people are free to attend if they wish. Tostan insist that by law everyone has the right to learn if they want. The marabouts reluctantly let the education classes continue.

2010 The assistant coordinator of Tostan based in Ndioum has a lot of discussions with the marabout Thierno Hassirou (a member of El Hadj Oumar Tall's family) on excision and whether it is a religious recommendation. After many meetings and hours of discussion, the marabout finally agrees that the practice is not in the Qur'an but that it is a custom (*aada*); however he does not want to publicly take position on excision. Tostan organizes a big sensitization event and shows a film in which women explain why they have stopped practicing. Thierno Hassirou critiques Tostan, saying, "you must not force people to abandon. Let those who want to abandon and respect the choices of those who want to continue." Thierno Hassirou is also recorded on TV telling the president, Abdoulaye Wade, to drop the law against FGC because it is a religious and cultural practice. I have no information on whether the president responded.

2010   In October, sixty-six villages declare their abandonment of FGC in the department of Podor.

2011   In June, forty-one villages declare in Ranérou Ferlo.

2014   In December, 121 villages declare in Velingara Ferlo.

2016   The midwife posted in Doumga Wouro Alpha, originally Wolof, regularly holds discussion groups there on reproductive health and the harmfulness of the practice. Sometimes the participants of the discussion groups are told not by their husbands not to attend because the midwife is against excision. One day, a radio advertisement announces that the midwife is scheduled to speak about excision on the radio in Matam. When the great marabout hears this, he sends his son to tell the midwife that she cannot discuss excision on the radio; otherwise, she has to leave the village. Intimidated by his threat and scared of this powerful marabout's spiritual power, she stops discussing excision and reproductive health with women in Doumga Wouro Alpha and on the local radio.

2017   In February, forty-five villages declare in Younoufere.

2017   In May, sixty villages declare in Hamady Ounaré.

2017   In Lougere Thiolly, people suddenly stop coming to the education classes. When the facilitator inquires into the reasons, he is referred to an image of the human right to freedom of religious belief. The image depicts a mosque and a church. Rumors start spreading that soon the mosque will be torn down and a church will be constructed in its place. After long discussions on the importance of respecting other people's religious beliefs and religious practice, the "poisoning" finally stops.

2017	In December, fifty villages declare in Gamadji Sahre.
2018	In May, fifty villages declare in Diongto.
2018	In December, fifty villages declare in Lougere Thiolly.
2018	After two months of the Tostan classes running in Fourdu two facilitators, who are originally from the village, are told that the lessons are against the religion and it is decided in a meeting of elders that if the facilitators die, they will not be buried in the village. Finally, the facilitators get support from others who see the benefit of the lessons and the classes are allowed to continue. In June 2021, fifty villages declare the abandonment of excision in Fourdu.
2021	A declaration is planned at great length in Agnam Goly. One week before the declaration there are disagreements between various village leaders who do not adhere to the same party and have different political objectives. Although some are extremely keen to abandon, others refuse because they were not sufficiently included by villagers who do not adhere to the same political party. The declaration is then planned in another village called Napadji, but the president of the women's group, who is also the daughter of the village chief, is for the continuation of excision. Eventually the declaration is held in the Cubalo (fisherman) village Aly Woury.
2022	In September, fifty villages declare in Maure 1, Velingara Ferlo.

As we can see, what constituted an event of opposition for people affected revolved mainly around nongovernmental intervention in Fouta Toro. Tostan is one of the main actors, but there were other organizations like UNICEF, GTZ, Raddho, and health care providers. Beside the law, the agendas of these organizations and their funders played a great role in what issues are prioritized despite the opposition. Some Futanke complied with these organizations because of the resources made available to them, rather than because of the agenda to stop excision in their villages. On the side of the opposers, religious leaders played a great role, like Thierno Mountaga Tall and his relatives (Thierno Hassirou), but also Thierno Ahmed Tidiane Ba of Madina Gousass (in Kolda) and Thierno Mohamadou Lamine Ly from Thierno Wouro Alpha who led rebellions against the law courts in Matam after the arrest of the exciser and continues to publicly defy government officials on excision today. Their opinion on the subject of excision is crucial.

Furthermore, there are conflicts between casted people who want to abandon FGC and Tooroɓɓe leaders who refuse to let public declarations take place in their villages. As well as the Tooroɓɓe's political influence, people also fear their power in the realms of the spiritual—as we can see, magical or spiritual power plays a role in the village of Gassambiri, where governmental authorities refuse to go. Besides international organizations, which are nonnegligible employers in Fouta Toro, the influence and status of emigrants' views on these issues also play a great role. An emigrant's approval or disapproval of the activities going on in a village can overturn the decision to comply with an NGO by stopping excision.

These actors and their reactions to the ban on excision will be explored further throughout the following chapters. I show that the law was an event that changed people's lives because of the political reactions it stirred up. These events also challenged the ways in which excised women perceive their bodies and redefine their identity.

CHAPTER 2

Making Gender

Changing Traditions and the Procedures
of Cutting

It's late morning in April 2007, and the dry heat is bringing those who have time to rest indoors. I am lying across Fatoumata's bed looking at her family photos. Five of her daughters are in the room with us, huddled together on a mat on the floor excitedly picking out pictures of their father, their parents' wedding, and other family members. They are screaming with excitement, arguing about which photos to show me next. Fatoumata is patiently sitting next to me, pleased that I am looking at all the pictures in detail. There is one photo of her oldest son, Ahmadu, who is now sixteen, dressed in a white robe and wearing a white hat. He is with three other boys, looking very solemn. "What is this?" I ask.

I had only just arrived in the Diawoury a couple of weeks ago, and my Pulaar is not good enough to communicate with Fatoumata directly. Her twelve-year-old daughter answers in French: "That was Ahmadu's circumcision."

I say, "Ah, circumcision. This is how they dress up? That is a very nice picture."

"Yes, circumcision is very painful. That is why the boys wear the white robes and are kept together in a house while it is healing. It takes a long time to heal. It is very painful." Kadia translates for me, while her smaller sisters on the floor are fighting over the pictures.

"Ahh, I see. Where do they stay?"

"Just in an empty house, with an older boy who looks after them. The neighbors send them food, they eat special food to give them strength." She tries to remember what the name for the food is in French.

"Ah, okay. And what about the girls. Do you do the same things for girls?"

She turns to ask her mother, Fatoumata, and then translates: "They [girls] are just taken over to the exciser and *tack*, it is cut away. It's not so bad [*c'est pas grave*], they cry a bit and then it's over after one day, it's all healed up and fine."

To confirm, her mother Fatoumata looks at me with a smile, smooths the bedsheet with her hand, and says, "*Hay dara. Muusani* [It's nothing. It doesn't hurt]." In contrast, Kadia explains: "The boys have more problems with their circumcision to heal than the girls. With the girls, the little thing that looks like a *ñebbe*, you know? It's like a little bean. It is cut, *tack*, they cry a bit, and then it is all over. But the boys can't wash for weeks and are all kept together."

The rhetoric of governmental and nongovernmental intervention against female genital cutting bases its appeal for abandonment on the assumption that the practice is harmful. Throughout my time in Fouta, I met many women and men who shared the belief that male circumcision is a lot more traumatic and painful than female circumcision, which is why boys need a period of seclusion after circumcision whereas girls do not (also see Johnson 2020). In my fieldwork village, Diawoury, the men were barely aware of when exactly their daughters were excised. Many men I met across Fouta explained this to me in a similar way: "With girls, you cannot know when they are excised. It's women's business. Your own daughter can be taken away for excision one evening and the next day you don't even realize that she was excised the previous night" (Abou Ba in Toulde).

Roy Dilley notes, too: "While male circumcision and initiation is the focus of much communal activity, female excision, involving clitoridectomy and sometimes infibulation, is done much more privately behind closed doors and with little public ceremony" (Dilley 2004: 119). Some of my interlocutors explained that excision does not need the celebration and time of seclusion that boys need after circumcision because it is not "a big deal" and is much less problematic than male circumcision.

Just as Ahmadu (2000, 2009), Dellenborg (2004), and Hernlund (2000, 2003) argue for Mande subgroups in the Gambia, Casamance, and Sierra Leone, excision in Fouta Toro is considered to be something that women take care of; men do not get involved or need to be informed of the details. However, in contrast to the respective literature, in Fouta Toro excision is not practiced during initiation at all and never has been, according to my interlocuters' views and other evidence.

On reading recent West African ethnography on female circumcision, one might expect that initiation and coming of age would be strongly associated with the practice in Fouta Toro as well. Furthermore, one might presume after reading such ethnography that the Futanke's opposition to the ban by the Senegalese government was somehow related to constructions of gender and ethnic identity through initiation and the "making" of a person through coming of age. If this was the case, one would imagine that the Futanke's opposition was a symptom of their holding on to so-called traditions that incorporate rites that are markers of ethnic identity and personhood. However, I show in this chapter that none of these presumptions are accurate.

This chapter explores how gender is made through female and male circumcision. West African ethnography on initiation shows that in many places, excision is part of reaching the status of a woman. Among the Mandinka in the Gambia (Ahmadu 2005; Ahmadu and Shweder 2009; Hernlund 2000, 2003) and southern Senegal as well as cohabitants like the Diola (Dellenborg 2004), becoming a responsible person is intrinsically tied to initiation ceremonies. Yet among the Fulani in Fouta Toro, things are different. The opposition to the law from Fouta Toro is not connected to the loss of "tribal rites of passage" and coming of age through circumcision, as might be expected among Mande subgroups (Ahmadu 2000, 2009; Bledsoe 1984), as female excision in Fouta does not involve such rites. Nonetheless, by contrasting how female excision and male circumcision are practiced according to local discourses, I show that gender is made through circumcision. As Griaule (1948) described among the Dogon, female excision and male circumcision are about feminizing or masculinizing the androgynous body (also see Ahmadu 2005, 2009). Excision and circumcision create the physical foundations for appropriate adulthood and render a person marriageable.

Furthermore, the imaginary boundaries between the state and the NGOs on the one hand and the traditionalists (those who want to hold on to the practice) on the other are by no means as clear as one might imagine. On the contrary, the division between those who uphold the practice as an ethnic and religious tradition and NGO workers is often blurred, and individuals move freely between the two conceptual camps. So-called tradition is a term that accords value to a practice because of the relationship it represents between those who have passed it on and those who have taken it up. "Tradition" does not mean that the practice has never changed, but that it is reinvented and accorded value by each generation who takes it up.

Initiation and Becoming a Person in West African Ethnography

The West African ethnography on female circumcision mostly focuses on the importance of the practice in relation to initiation and becoming a person and member of a group through it.

Fuambai Sia Ahmadu (2000, 2007, 2009), an American/Sierra Leonean anthropologist who underwent initiation among the Kono in her parents' home village in Sierra Leone but did research on FGC among the Mandinka in the Gambia, argues that circumcision for boys and excision for girls during initiation makes male and female gender (Ahmadu 2000, 2009). She explains that among the Kono, as for most Mande groups, children are seen to be part of nature, undefined and possessing both male and female elements (2009:14). In initiation rituals the male foreskin of the penis symbolizes femininity. Its removal represents the "masculinization" of the boy. In parallel, "the exposed clitoris represents the male sexual organ or penis and thus its removal symbolizes the feminization of the girl child and marks her adult status" (Ahmadu 2009:14).

Ahmadu (2000:289) argued that for the Kono, initiation affects adult female identity through the act of excision and realizes a novice's procreative value. Fertility is transferred to the *bain den moe*—the matrilineage—represented by the mother's brother and descendants (Ahmadu 2000:287; Hardin 1993; Amadiume 1987, 1997). It embodies a "motherhood" or "one womb" ideology whereby "relations are marked by closeness and familiarity" (Ahmadu 2000: 287). Although a woman resides in her husband's *fa den moe* (patrilineage), to which she contributes her labor, and her children will belong to her husband's lineage, she can count on her bain den moe as a check against her husband's fa den moe (2000:287). It is believed that only through excision, and the maternal uncle's ancestors' blessing, can a newly created female with reproductive powers successfully procreate (Ahmadu 2000:289).

Also focusing on a Mande subgroup in the Gambia, the Mandinka, who traditionally practice excision during initiation, Hernlund (2000) looks at "re-ritualization" of the initiation ceremonies without female circumcision. These "alternative rituals," run by an NGO, aim to eliminate FGC without losing the ceremony that people embrace as culture and tradition (and which provides a potent avenue for women's empowerment) (Hernlund 2000:235). Admitting that not everyone agrees that these expensive rituals are a good idea or that they can replace the original ceremonies, Hernlund looks at increasing incidents of girls who are cut outside the initiation ceremonies on a compound with no further ritual (2000:242). Hernlund establishes that for some families the expense of the lavish celebrations is perceived as problematic; others say that schoolgirls have no time for lengthy seclusions after circumcision. In a few cases (a fourteen-year-old and a seventeen-year-old), the girls concerned were considered too old to participate. Furthermore, some families who adhered to a more orthodox form of Islam insisted on "cutting without ritual" because they considered the traditional "circumcision" rituals un-Islamic (Hernlund 2000:243).

Although Hernlund is interested in "cutting without ritual" and discusses aspects of the practice that are not directly related to initiation, her research shows clearly that among the Mandinka in the Gambia, initiation and coming of age are strongly associated with excision. Ahmadu (2005) also shows that among the Mandinka in the Gambia, a noninitiated or unexcised woman would not be allowed to enter the seclusion area where the rites and ceremonies take place. Excision and initiation are inextricably connected to the making of a person among the Mandinka.

Dellenborg (2004) looks at excision in the context of initiation and personhood among the neighboring Diola in Casamance. She argues that the Diola adopted female circumcision from the Mandinka for several reasons (Dellenborg 2004:82), including the adoption of peanut cultivation, promoted by colonialism at the beginning of the twentieth century, which brought the two ethnic groups closer together. Young Diola men who wanted to gain independence from their elders went to the Gambia to sell their labor on the groundnut fields and stayed in Mandinka families. Dellenborg (2004:83), like Mark (1978:11), argues that "Islam offered a more rapid means of attaining adulthood." It bestowed on them the financial independence and authority to gain adult status and start a family without performing the traditional Diola initiation rite, *bukut*, which was held every twenty-five or thirty years. Islamic practice adopted from the Mandinka involved circumcision of men and excision of women. For Diola women, the declining importance of indigenous religion, according to which they were ascribed a ritually central role as guardians of agriculture and human fertility (Dellenborg 2004: 84; Linares 1992; Journet 1983, 1985), meant that new strategies for gaining ritual and religious authority had to be found. Besides becoming persons through Islamic practice, excision was incorporated into a new form of female secret society that allowed for unmarried and childless women to gain ritual power, respect, and authority in their communities. Dellenborg (2004) argues that whereas the prerequisite for being initiated into the secret society used to be childbirth, with Islam, the prerequisite became excision.

In Dellenborg's (2004) research, excision is also associated with coming of age and becoming a member of a group of women who are not just initiates but also Muslims.

Johnson (2000), who researched female circumcision among the Mandinka in Guinea-Bissau, and later migrants in Portugal (2020), argues that female circumcision practices must be understood in relation to the ritual of girls' initiation and the construction and transformation of religious identity and personhood. Initially assuming that female circumcision was linked to social adulthood through initiation, Johnson found that among the Mandinka of Guinea-Bissau, most male and female children are "circumcised" well before puberty and the practice did not bear any direct relationship to marriage (2000:218). She was told that whereas in the past initiation occurred shortly before marriage, nowadays girls are often excised long before marriage. As for adulthood, the Mandinka did not associate initiation with becoming an adult. Instead, the birth of the first child and the woman's move to her husband's compound designated the end of childhood. Circumcision and excision, on the other hand, were first and foremost linked to religious identity—being a Muslim (Johnson 2000:219).

The West African literature on FGC focuses on the Mande subgroups and cohabitants who tend to associate excision with initiation, either as a requirement for becoming an initiate or as part of the ceremony itself. Beyond excision in the context of initiation, Ahmadu (2005) focuses on the symbolic significance of the clitoris in ancient Mande myths, and the need to remove the "female penis." Johnson (2000) looks at religious personhood alongside initiation among the Mandinka in Guinea-Bissau. Although Amadou Hampate Ba describes circumcision and initiation rites in his tales of Fulani initiation (*Contes Initiatiques Peuls*; Ba 1993), which are presumably of the Peul of Macina (Mali) like himself, limited literature has been published on excision practices among the Fulɓe in West Africa (O'Neill 2018).

If excision is not important in the context of initiation in Fouta Toro, what is its relevance, how is it practiced, and how does the performance of female excision differ from male circumcision? Let us first of all look at the terminology of words for circumcision in Pulaar.

Terminology

In Fouta Toro, the noun for female excision is *kaddingol*, and the verb is *haddinde* or *sunninde* (derived from the word for religious recommendation, *sunna*). Although male circumcision and female excision are both considered religious recommendations, the term sunninde is almost exclusively used for female excision and rarely for circumcision. In some areas of Fouta Toro an unexcised woman is called *jiiwo*, but this is not a universally used term; it is common to say *mo haddinaaka*,[1] the one who was not excised, or *mo haddaaki*, the one who is not excised.

There are two words for male circumcision: *duhaade*, which means to knot up (a pair of trousers, for example) and *ɓoornaade*. In addition, ɓoornaade means "to dress up" in everyday language. Ɓoornaade resembles the word *ɓoorde*, which means to take off (for example, to strip bark off a branch). The word therefore has various connotations. An uncircumcised boy is called *solima* in Pulaar in Fouta Toro. Interestingly the same expression is used for unexcised women in the south of Senegal as among the Diola or the Mandinka (Dellenborg 2004; Ahmadu 2005). However, in addition to merely referring to an unexcised woman, the term also means impure in Mandinka and Diola. In Pulaar, *laaɓaani* means impure (negation of the verb *laaɓde*— to be clean/pure in the tense for accomplished actions), whereas *solima* is not used for impurity in everyday language. A newly circumcised boy is called *njulli* until his circumcision wound has healed. Adolescents also call circumcision *haddaade*, which resembles *haddinde*, the term for excision. However, this term is considered vulgar in the vernacular.

Terms for female excision thus refer to religious practice. Male circumcision, however, has connotations of getting ready for the outside world— "dressing up" or "knotting up one's trousers." Whereas female circumcision takes place in the realms of the private—besides those involved, no one really knows when or how it is practiced—the performance of male circumcision is more public and has the connotation of getting the boy ready for life.

In the following we shall explore how excision is practiced in Fouta Toro.

Excision in Fouta Toro: Conversations with Three Excisers

During my fieldwork in Fouta, I interviewed eighteen women who had performed excision either as traditional excisers or at health care centers. Some I knew quite well; with others I had just one in-depth interview; others I only asked a few questions. The procedure of the cutting and the techniques these experts used to stop the bleeding after excision differed. Some women said that, at times, a few girls are cut together; however, none of them said that there were any other ritual activities involved or that they had ever performed the practice during an initiation ceremony. Although the procedure of excision is said to be passed down from generation to generation, none of the excisers said that they had ever heard of any of their ancestors performing the practice as part of a female initiation ceremony. As far as they knew, it had always been practiced either at the exciser's house or the house of the family who was paying for the work, but there were no activities or celebrations to make public that a girl had been excised.

Most excisers said that the age at which the girls are cut depends on their clients. Some parents want their daughters to be excised within the first two weeks after birth. Others prefer to wait until the girls are four years old.

Besides excision, most traditional excisers tended to do work related to childbirth or gynecological operations. Some were also midwives and called when young women needed to be opened on the wedding night. Others also pierce earlobes and cure cuts and sprains with incantations. The cost of the cutting varies between CFA1,000 and CFA5,000 (~ USD 1–8),[2] depending on how much the exciser feels she can charge. If the family is well off, it is acceptable for her to charge more.

I describe in greater detail my conversations with three of these excisers. The first one, Awa Diallo, lived in my fieldwork village in Diawoury where no NGO-led sensitization against the practice had taken place. The second exciser, Kumba Kawry, also defended the family lore with pride. However, she is registered as an "ex-exciser," a member of an association of former excisers who sensitize against the practice at governmental and

nongovernmental-led events to promote reproductive health. The third exciser, Halimatou Gueye, is a midwife at the health care center of Weendouley, where she unofficially excised girls in hygienic conditions in what she
considers to be a less traditional manner. All three excisers either are part of
or have close ties to the health system; none considered the practice to be associated with initiation or coming of age.

Awa Diallo, Exciser of Diawoury

I met Awa Diallo on a cool late afternoon in January 2008. She was known to
be a good exciser, so I was told by many women in Diawoury. People come
from far to have their daughters cut by her. My friends had encouraged me
to go and see her before, but I had waited until my grasp of Pulaar was good
enough to be able to communicate without a translator. At this stage, I was
already well known to the *Diawourynaabe* and had spent the mornings joking with the women by the well fetching water and the late afternoons down
by the river with the unmarried girls (*mboomri*) and boys or working on the
fields. People knew that I had not come to change their way of life and to persuade them to abandon their customs (*woppude adaa*). According to many,
this is white people's only motivation for staying in these lands, with their
harsh climatic conditions and lack of commodities that bring comfort.

My teacher and host Samba Sarr insisted on introducing me to the exciser Awa Diallo. He spoke of her in an affectionate, respectful way as one of
his "mothers"—she belonged to his own mother's age group and had helped
to bring him up. The Diallo and the Sarr families had entertained strong ties
of friendship and solidarity in Diawoury for generations. Samba emphasized
that their families are tied together by more than just the friendship of the
two women. On this late January afternoon before dusk, when the households
liven up before nightfall, Samba and I go over to Awa Diallo's house. She is
an elderly lady dressed in a slightly torn boubou with a headscarf, like most
women of her generation on a normal working day on the fields or in the
household. We greet her respectfully for a few minutes as is customary, and
on shaking her hand, I can feel the curiously strong, rough, and leathery
skin that I have noticed so many times when shaking the hands of older
women—just as my hands must seem like the hands of a girl to her. Awa Diallo takes Samba by his hand and tells us that he is her son and she has seen
him grow up. Even though I have come with her "son" and my intentions are

good, the situation makes me a little uneasy. It is unusual for a girl, as I would appear to her, to come and ask questions accompanied by a man. Excision is against the law and by admitting to practicing, she admits to having committed a crime, which in theory could see her put in prison for up to five years.

Awa tells us that her family has practiced excision for five generations and that they do it from Nouakchott in Mauritania to Cascas and all over Fouta. She learned excising at the age of fifteen by watching her mother. Every time a girl was brought to their home to be cut, she and her siblings were called to watch and learn so that one day they would be able to do it themselves. "I was the oldest daughter, so I learnt," she says, "and started excising independently when I married." Some of her sisters who learned with her now practice in Mauritania. Others don't. Excising is not for everyone, she says. Awa is quiet about whether her own daughters practice. Times have changed. Excisers need to be more careful and some prefer to keep their practice quiet. As to the importance of the practice, she says that it is religious. The marabouts say that it is a *sunna*, a Prophetic recommendation. She says that when she cuts, she only cuts a little; otherwise the girl loses a lot of blood. Only the clitoris is cut; the labia stay the way they are. To soothe the pain and stop the bleeding she casts some incantations. These verses are part of the family lore (*gandal*) that has been passed down from generation to generation with pride. Awa Diallo tells us that to stop the bleeding they used to take the feces of a goat, boil them, and put them on the wound after the cutting. If the girls were old enough, they would ask them to sit down in the boiled goats' feces (*borgo*). Besides excision, Awa says she also opens up women on the wedding night if they are too tight to be penetrated by their husbands. Being tight, she explains, is something a woman is born with and is not caused by excision. Samba, who has worked for an NGO sensitizing against the practice, is confused: according to doctors and midwives, closure of the vagina takes place only when the labia are cut as well as the clitoris and the blood coagulates and heals as scar tissue. He asks her if she has ever opened a woman who had not been excised. Awa replies that in Diawoury, all girls are excised so she has never come across it here. However, once she was called to Toulnde, a village about 8 kilometers away, to open up a newly married girl whose husband could not penetrate her. She also excised her.

Having in mind the ethnographic accounts of excision and the spirit world (Boddy 1989; Gosselin 2000), I ask her whether an unexcised woman is thought to be more vulnerable to attack by jinne. She starts laughing and says, "Not at all, they have nothing to do with it! But when the clitoris gets big it can get in the way." She now has a passionate sparkle in her eyes as if something is about to burst out that she has tried to keep quiet:

> The clitoris can grow big, like a little boy's penis. Sometimes it grows bigger than the labia so it has to be cut away! I didn't want to tell you this but now you have started me off and I'm telling you everything! It grows huge like a boy's penis. You understand? And sometimes a white liquid collects inside the clitoris. So it needs to be cut to let it out. An excised woman has a big clitoris that splits into two big pieces of skin, like the ears of a rabbit! One rabbit ear hangs down on the right, the other on the left. [We start laughing.]

Dusk is approaching and calls for prayer are blaring from the mosque. Samba gets up for prayer. I say goodbye to Awa and leave with Samba. Awa Diallo was one of the few excisers I met in a place where the practice had not been questioned by most people. At the time, no NGO program or sensitization activities had called on people to stop practicing. Most women and men from Diawoury had taken the validity of the practice for granted. It was their *doxa* (Bourdieu 1977): unchallenged and unquestioned habits that are embraced as normal. Although Awa Diallo, like most excisers, might have been aware that her occupation was outlawed by the Senegalese government, ending the practice seemed even more ludicrous and wrong than continuing. However, it was said that she eventually stopped practicing before she died. She passed away in 2015.

The next exciser I introduce here comes from a rather different context, which is also typical for Fouta. In contrast to Awa Diallo, she has seriously considered abandoning the practice and is a member of the "ex-exciser association." However, despite discourses around and political movements against excision, Kumba eventually decided to stay with her family occupation.

Kumba Kawry and the Ex-Exciser Association

Thilogne was pointed out to me as a good place to meet ex-excisers—women who had realized that the practice was not good and had joined the abandonment movement. Ngoura Sy, the president of the ex-exciser association, whom I went to see in Ndouloumadji, told me that I should meet Hawa

Diawa. So on a cool morning in February, Seydou and I ride to Thilogne on a motorbike to meet Hawa Diawa and other ex-excisers. Her phone is not working. Not sure where she lives, we follow people's directions, noisily riding through the sandy lanes of Thilogne until we eventually find her compound. Dirty from the ride, we enquire whether Hawa Diawa is there. As we couldn't let her know that we were coming, she is not expecting us and is not at home. Her family are smiths who are making jewelry in the front yard. As the women in the compound cannot tell us where she might be and when she might return, we decide to look for another ex-exciser in the village after I have changed into Senegalese clothes. The smiths in Hawa Diawa's compound do not know much about ex-excisers, but they send us to an exciser who lives around the corner.

When we arrive, cheerfully greeting the family and the children, they welcome us into their home with curiosity as to what a white Pulaar-speaking woman, well-dressed in a boubou, and a Pulaar man have come for. The veranda is very lively. A very old man is sitting in the corner playing with a toddler; children are playing and laughing. After lengthy greetings Seydou tells them that we have come to speak to the member of the ex-exciser association. Kumba, the exciser, immediately starts explaining that a relative of hers had come to see her and her mother and suggested that they give up excising and join the ex-exciser's association. Instead of excising, the association would organize other income-generating activities. A few other excisers in Thilogne became members and Kumba introduced the president to some of her relatives so that they could join as well. But one day there was a meeting in Sinthian with French people about the abandonment of excision and Kumba found that the board members were sharing the money among themselves instead of doing as they had promised—sharing it with Kumba's relatives and the other members. Since then, she had decided not to go to any of these meetings.

> If I participate in something I want to be told the truth and not find out later that I've been ripped off or taken advantage of. Either you act with transparency or you have to go separate ways. That's how things are in life. If we are thieves together and one day I find out that you are trying to steal from me . . . I'm not going to accept that!

After listening to Kumba's disappointment with the ex-exciser association at length, we tell her that we have come to talk to her about excision and why the Futanke hold on to the practice with such pride. Kumba is curious as to what we want to discuss and explains everything in great detail. We ask her if this association has created any problems between the excisers of Thilogne, but Kumba tells us that there aren't any problems between excisers. Everyone practices in their homes on their own account, but before this association appeared, there was never a collective movement of any kind among excisers. "We all became members of the association because we trusted the president. She asked us to give up the practice so we joined her movement."

We ask, "So you have all stopped since Khadija came and asked you to leave the practice?" Kumba replies that she does not know. She has stopped going to the meetings, and as everyone practices in their home, it is hard to know who has abandoned and who has not.

> And if the religious leaders found out that this association even existed and that some excisers have stopped practicing there would be a big noise! Some would get very angry! Some people don't think it's normal to leave behind something that you have inherited from your parents and that has always been practiced in the past.

Kumba learned the practice from her grandmother, who herself was also taught by her own grandparents. She says that their family is one of the few in Thilogne who have practiced excision "traditionally," whereas many picked it up from others. The family tradition is not restricted to excision. They also assist women in labor and cure headaches and bruises and other illnesses. If someone in the neighborhood has an accident, their aid is called on first because, she says, they are known as healers and as very skilled at easing people's pains and bruises. Kumba learned how to excise from a very young age. Whenever a girl was taken home to be excised, she and her sisters were called to help hold the girl down. She therefore observed the procedure from a very early age. However, not everyone has the courage to take on the practice and excise girls. Her sisters, who are sitting with us during this conversation, did not become excisers. To emphasize how the family lore (*gandal*) is associated with pride and the identity of the matrilineal line, Kumba says that even her grandmother had once gone to Saint Louis to train in a different job for a few years. She was so good that she was offered a job there. However, it was more important for her to come home and practice the family lore. In addition to that, the exciser speaks of the tie of solidarity between their family and the Cherifian family of religious leaders.

The Ly do the naming ceremony[3] for all the children in our family. When someone dies, they are the ones who wash the body and say the last prayer. In return our family has always excised their daughters since the times of my grandmother. There is a very strong tie between our families.

As to the procedure of the cutting, Kumba's sister tells us that there used to be a very efficient technique to stop the bleeding. Sheep dung was taken and boiled and left to cool down and then the girl was asked to sit down in it after the excision. That would help to heal the wound well. However, these days only shea butter is used. Before the operation, the blade is boiled in hot water to disinfect it. Then incantations (cefi) are cast onto the blade. Then a third of the clitoris is cut. Only a tiny little bit is cut (she indicates on her little finger).[4] I ask if the girl bleeds a lot after the cutting. Kumba replies that after the incantations have been recited, the girl has been cut and the shea butter applied, it's all over. That is where the spiritual knowledge helps.

You recite the incantation and go over it with your hand and it's all over. The girl can go home and there will be no further complications. And no man will be able to penetrate the girl until she marries.[5]

The Midwife Halimatou Gueye

The last exciser I introduce here is a midwife at the health care center of Weendouley. A lot of Weendouleynaaɓe had participated in Tostan's education program, and many had stopped excising. However, Weendouley is also the site of renowned religious leaders who pass their knowledge on to taliɓe and who have opposed Weendouley participating in any kind of declaration of the abandonment of excision. I got to know Halimatou Gueye through my friend Bintou Sow, whom I had met the first day I arrived in Weendouley on my way to Diawoury. Bintou was adamantly against excision and had been raising awareness about the practice with Tostan for ten years. This year she was not working because her mother was very elderly and sick and needed to be cared for. However, whenever I stayed in Weendouley, Bintou and I spent many afternoons and evenings together during the rainy season and the cold season of 2007. She was in her late thirties, had three daughters, the youngest of them eight years old and the oldest in her early teens. None of them had been excised due to the many problems Bintou had experienced from her own excision. Bintou was divorced; her husband had left her many years before, though she did not seem particularly bitter. She was extremely independent and self-sufficient, interested in health care and education, and a great advocate of democracy and equality between people. Bintou liked to spend the afternoons at the health care center with her friends, the nurses and midwives. One day, Bintou and I arranged to meet at the health care center to talk to her friend, the midwife Halimatou Gueye.

Halimatou tells us that she has been in the service for twenty years. She trained as a midwife in Ndioum. She says that many people have stopped excision since governmental and non-overnmental awareness-raising program have been introduced. I ask how it is possible for so many people to abandon the practice if it has always been so important.

> "Excision was practiced so that girls guarded their virginity until marriage. However, now, since sensitization, women are told that childbirth is sometimes more difficult because of excision and so a lot of mums have decided to stop practicing."
> I ask, "Being a midwife yourself, have you found that this is true? That excised women have more problems in labor that others?"
> "No," Halimatou replies. "To be honest it's rare. If women come to their prenatal consultations it's rare to see any serious problems. Except for women with hypertension. They sometimes experience shock during childbirth."
> Bintou adds, "Don't excised women have problems during labor, for example, with tissue that tears?"
> Halimatou replies, "The majority of women are cut before labor so that it's rare to see tissue tearing these days."
> I ask, "Do you cut the women at the back, where it does not cause any harm?"
> Halimatou says, "If the woman's vagina is straight, yes. If not then on the side."
> I tell them that in Europe many women go through episiotomy as well, although they are not excised. Then I ask Halimatou if women come to have their daughters excised. She says that she used to do it but now she has stopped. A midwife taught her how to do it, she

says. But they used to cut just above the clitoris to conform to the fashion. Just a tiny little bit, not like the old excisers who cut everything.

"If women come to have their daughters excised we now say no. It's against the law. If someone catches you doing it. Ah! You've spoilt your life! And particularly as a mother of a household. It's not worth it!"

As midwives at health care centers are employees of the state, it is riskier for them to practice excision is explicitly outlawed and they can be sentenced to prison for up to five years. Whether Halimatou really does practice, as Bintou and some Weendouleynaaɓe say, or whether she has stopped, as she says, having excision performed at the health care center has been an alternative for many mothers deciding where to have their daughters cut. Because the procedure is said to be more hygienic and causes few complications, many people plead for medicalization, which the government has adamantly refused.

I ask if there are other excisers in the village and Halimatou says yes, but they are afraid, because "they used to practice with blades, whereas we cut with scissors and alcohol and sterile material. But these excisers did it with blades, which can lead to infection."

"And with cefi [incantations]," I add.

"Maybe, I don't know. Perhaps they learned it from their parents and their grandmothers [*laughs*]. But I don't know anything about that."

Halimatou says that there have been a lot of changes over the last twenty years. Before, you'd find a lot of women who did not come for prenatal consultation until the day they gave birth.

"They didn't take the antitetanus serum . . . but now, with sensitization, women come more regularly for consultation and if they have pains when they are due, they come and find the midwife. Women used to prefer giving birth at home but now a lot of them come to the health care center. And after birth we give women treatment and weigh the baby. Later on they come back for vaccinations. If the baby is undernourished we give the women advice on what to do.

A lot of women have stopped excision. I have seen women have three to four babies here who have not been excised."

Bintou adds that her daughters have not been excised, even the oldest one, who is thirteen.

I am still not convinced that it is possible for women to stop without being discriminated against by their neighbors and other members of the family. I have seen that in Diawoury it is not easy for people to stop even if they are against it. However, if there has already been ongoing discussion in a village about whether it may or may not be good to practice, and some are very outspoken against it, like Bintou in Weendouley, then it seems to be easier for women to stop. I remember what Awa Diallo told me in Diawoury about women growing rabbit ears—an image that many women in Diawoury think of with abhorrence when they even toy with the idea of not cutting a girl. I say to Halimatou,

> "I have heard women say in Diawoury that if a girl is not cut, her clitoris grows big and splits into two like rabbit ears."
> "Well, that is true," Halimatou replies.
> "It is true?" I say with astonishment.
> "Because the clitoris, you grow and it grows. You grow and it grows. Like a tree that you have seeded. If you cut it when it is small is it going to grow? Ah! It's going to die!"

We laugh and joke. I tell them that I have never seen a woman with rabbit ears. Then Halimatou continues.

> "I once spent three months in France in a hospital. But I tell you with the toubabs [white people] there you could think that it's the noses meeting each other."
> Bintou laughs and Halimatou says, showing her disgust, "It's true. You know that the white people don't practice excision. Hmmm!"
> She turns up her nose at the memory.
> "They smell?!" I ask.
> "Mmm," she affirms. "There is a very big difference."

We all laugh and Halimatou tells us that she has to get back to her duties. I thank her for her time.

The three cases provide insights about how the practice is performed and for what reasons.

Family Lore, Tradition, and the State

Although two of the women claim to come from a family that has practiced for generations, there is no reference to excision ever having been part of an initiation ceremony. Instead, they learned at home, from a young age, by watching their mothers and grandmothers, and they performed independently as soon as they married. The two traditional excisers learned how to excise along with other things: delivering children, opening women on the wedding night, and curing people of other aches, pains, and bruises when they've had accidents. They therefore also perform the role of midwives and healers for women's problems or minor injuries.

It would be interesting to record in greater detail how excision is passed on from grandmothers or mothers to daughters in clans that pride themselves on excising as a family tradition. The data I collected indicated that excision was practiced by women from a variety of caste backgrounds. Some of them were Tooroodo, like Awa Diallo and Ngoura Sy (see Chapter 4), the president of the ex-exciser association who took great pride in excision being an occupational lore (Dilley 2004) and family tradition according to Islamic practice. Other traditional excisers belonged to the caste of blacksmiths (Wayluɓe) or leather workers (Sakkeeɓe) and entertained strong ties of patronage with Tooroodo families, like Kumba Kawri (above). But I also met excisers who had taken up the profession to make money or because it was related to what they were already doing—as in the case of the midwife Halimatou Gueye.

All three cases show that the distinction often drawn between those adhering to the practice and those who adhere to governmental institutions implementing its ban is blurred. All three excisers are closely tied to institutions in different ways. Awa Diallo's "son" sensitizes against excision at an NGO. Kumba Kawry is officially a member of an ex-exciser association but continues practicing the family lore with pride. And Halimatou Gueye, midwife at a statutory health care center, has excised many girls and believes in it, despite governmental recommendations and legal sanctions. I want to emphasize here that there is no clear-cut distinction between those who adhere to traditional ways of practicing and those who are followers of the state. As

Hobsbawm and Ranger (1983) show, traditions are reinvented and celebrated over the passage of time. What people chose to call important traditions and which ones are redundant can change very quickly. When people refer to tradition in Fouta, they do not mean that these practices or beliefs have never changed. I argue that these accounts indicate that what is referred to as tradition often relates to habits and practices one generation has taken on from the previous generation. As we can see, the maintenance of a practice or a strong bond between people over generations increases the value of the relationship or the practice. Tradition is cherished because it points toward a form of stability that is highly valued. Although the exact procedure or relationship with the object or clan may change, certain elements of it are passed on to or taken up by the next generation, and the continuation is attributed with value. This is perhaps the root of the logic of "some people think that giving up a practice that was cherished by your parents or grandparents is not a good thing." Breaking a tradition means breaking the continuity of a habit that people cherish.

As far as the procedure of the cutting is concerned, the discussions with the first two excisers shows that knowledge acquired during apprenticeship is not just about the physical cutting but also is a spiritual form of knowledge (*gandal*) that has been learned from mothers or grandmothers. Part of the skill involved in the cutting and what is believed to render it safe comes from the fact that it is a family tradition. What has been evaluated as effective and safe by one generation is believed to be effective and safe for the next.

The interviews also show that the nongovernmental movement and the opposition to the law are both tied up with political and economic interests and motivations. In all three cases we can see that people joined the abandonment movement or NGO sensitization out of economic interests, without losing their personal convictions or beliefs about the benefits of excision. Taking on a position that some consider political does not necessarily mean dropping beliefs that are thought of as opposed to that political position. Someone may have joined the NGOs and the antiexcision movement out of economic motivation—because of financial recompense—but may not be completely convinced of the harmfulness of the practice. Others may say that they are against the law and the abandonment of excision because the tradition has always been there since "the beginning of the universe" (*kaddungal gila dawaa-dawi ina waɗe*) or because "we have inherited it from the ancestors" (*min tawri ko taaniraaɓe amen*). However, those who are personally affected by its harmful consequences may change their minds, although they would never publicly say so. If the practice no longer provides stability and associated social reward, an alternative ideology is found to justify change and replacement of what existed before. Some marabouts who officially speak out against the abandonment of excision based on claims of it being a religious recommendation are known to have avoided excising their own daughters and granddaughters for health-related or other reasons.

The Androgynous Body and Making Gender

All three women have beliefs about how a woman's genitals may mutate if not cut. Awa Diallo tells us that the clitoris grows big and splits into two big pieces of skin, reminiscent of rabbit ears. What she is describing is tainted by the gaze of a woman who is used to seeing a flat, empty vulva on looking at a grown woman's clitoris and labia. The midwife, Halimatou Gueye, who has delivered the babies of excised and unexcised women, agrees with Awa Diallo's description that unexcised women have rabbit ears. Their perceptions of uncut female genitalia illustrate the need to feminize the androgynous body by cutting away the ambiguous masculine parts, as seen in Griaule's (1948) description of the Dogon myth of origin. It implies that gender is made through excision.

Like most midwives I interviewed, Halimatou Gueye feels that despite governmental recommendations to stop practicing, unexcised women are "uncleaner" (*inpropre* in French, *laaβaani* in Pulaar) than excised women and that they can be clearly distinguished by their smell. Classen (1992: 134) argues that odor is used to ascribe characteristics of difference and is a marker of social identity. She looks at how "pleasant scent" and "foul smell" are attributed with meaning and social significance in different societies. She argues that something or someone "stinks" when it disagrees with our notions of propriety. In the same way that we may feel antipathy toward something because its odor offends us, we equally ascribe an offensive odor to something because we feel antipathy toward it (1992: 135).

Classen shows that distinctions are made between the smell of the sacred, pure, and divine on the one hand and the stench of promiscuous women, prostitutes, and witches on the other. Evil spirits are often chased away with incense and the odor of the sacred. Furthermore, through the act of smelling, one fills oneself with the presence of the divine, as in Hindu practices, for example (Classen 1992: 156). Maidens, wives, and mothers tend to be identified with pleasant, nonthreatening odors. The odors of seductresses are more ambivalent: sweet, heavy, exotic with overwhelming powers of fascination. Classen argues that Cleopatra and Marie Antoinette are classic examples, while perfume-vending models and film stars are modern ones (1992: 143). Prostitutes and "sluts" are often characterized as having an unpleasant smell and with a "failure to regulate their bodies in accordance with the cultural norms" (1992: 143). To exemplify how promiscuity can be associated with a foul smell, Classen cites Courbin's eighteenth-century example of a French reformer who said that the prostitutes disappeared along with the foul odor of the drains of Florence when the streets were cleaned and covered with flowers (Courbin 1986: 194). The association between corrupt women and corrupt odors is manifest (Classen 1992: 143).

We shall explore purity and personhood in more detail in the following chapters. For now, I want to focus on the perceptions of uncut female genitalia as "dirty" and ambiguously male. Kumba Kawry does not speak of purity, cleanliness, or mutating clitorises. However, she suggests that a woman is closed through excision and cannot be penetrated by a man before marriage. Thus, the practice renders a woman socially appropriate—she allegorically stays a virgin until marriage (*mboomri* is the term for both an unmarried woman and a virgin). It is assumed that an unmarried woman is a virgin in Pulaar language and society. The smell imputed to an unexcised woman perhaps points to the fact that she is socially ambiguous—androgynous because the male elements have not been removed. To what extent does male circumcision in Fouta Toro fit with Griaule's Dogon (1948) imagery of making the androgynous body "masculine" and what is the role of initiation here? We shall explore this in the final part of this chapter.

Male Initiation and Circumcision: Disappearing Practices

I have shown that female excision is not, and according to my interlocutors never has been, associated with initiation and coming of age in Fouta Toro. On the contrary, it is surprisingly lacking in ritual: every exciser performs the practice in a slightly different way.

Paradoxically, male circumcision used to be, and sometimes still is, performed during initiation. However, according to interlocutors' views and descriptions of their own initiation experiences, the practice seems to have changed since as far back as people can recall. In the following, I present views and memories of what circumcision and initiation were like and how it is performed now in order to compare it to female circumcision.

Myths and Memories of Male Initiation

I was frequently told that "in previous times," which no one I met actually remembered, all the boys of the same age group would be taken to "the forest"[6] together to be circumcised, as among the Diola and the Bassari in the south of Senegal today. The forest is called *dulndu* or *foonde* in Pulaar and denotes an area densely populated with trees in the Waalo along the banks of the river. It was dangerous because of wild animals such as lions and hyenas. However, since the beginning of the desertification in 1973, woodland has almost completely disappeared.

In the forest, young men who had been sheltered at home were faced with challenges that should teach them that life is hard and how to overcome the difficulties involved in looking after one's family. Initiates were taught that it is important to be brave and carry out one's duties with honor and not give up, even if the conditions seem dire. Some of the lessons they learned were how to endure pain without tears and hunger without complaint. This corresponds to what Turner says about the purpose of initiation among the Ndembu—for boys an emphasis is put on obedience to elders, endurance of hardships, and sexual instruction (Turner 1967: 7).

Many people have told me that in these times, circumcision would take place during late adolescence or when men were in their early twenties and considered ready to marry. Uncircumcised young men were not considered ready to marry or have sexual relations with women because their penis was not yet clean and virile and they were seen as not yet having been initiated into adulthood. Even after circumcision, a man was not considered an adult until he had sex and married. Newly circumcised young men or boys (njulli) are still teased with the phrase *Ittude ñaande paaka*,[7] which means "take off the leftovers of the knife" by sleeping with a woman. I have heard various interpretations of what this phrase signifies. My interlocutor Fall told me that, on the one hand, it reminds the boys that they are not yet men because they have not completed the initiation process until they marry. On the other hand, this phrase is an encouragement and consoles the njulli that the pain and discomfort they are experiencing due to their circumcision will soon pass when they have sex with a woman and will feel pleasure and gratification instead. Symbolically, circumcision and initiation are therefore not completed until the boy has sexual relations and marries.[8] It is also said that in the old days, a man should not wait for more than a year after circumcision before taking a wife and taking off the leftovers of the knife by sleeping with a woman.

Circumcision thus renders a man virile and takes away the impurities and the parts of the penis that are associated with childhood. In the same way, it would be considered inappropriate for a woman to have sex before she is excised and she is believed to be closed by the practice. The thought of a man having sex before circumcision arouses reactions of disgust—to the extent that some people I met in isolated areas believed that it was impossible for men and women to have sex if they are not circumcised or excised. Like excision, circumcision makes a man physically masculine and prepares him for adulthood—a stage that is not completely attained until he has sex and marries. Circumcision and excision therefore signify an entry into a liminal stage which is completed with marriage. They render the body appropriate for eventually becoming a socially recognized adult.

This account, however, is an abstract and idealized version of what circumcision used to be like and how it was tied to initiation and becoming an adult. Fall, who was in his mid-thirties, remembers how circumcision used to take place in his natal village, Waltunde Colli, when he was a boy. At the time, initiation took place just before puberty, between the ages of ten and twelve.

Memories of Circumcision in the 1980s

As in the myth of how circumcision used to take place a long time ago, Fall emphasizes that circumcision used to be a very important event in a boy's life because it meant becoming a responsible member of the community. When men refer to someone when they were young and naive they often say, "A long time ago, when he was young, not even circumcised," to emphasize that the person had not yet developed a moral consciousness, had no responsibilities, and was in the process of learning how to become an adult and valued member of the community. The companions with whom one was circumcised will always be close as they went through a significant stage in their lives together.

Fall says that in the 1980s, circumcision took place in the following way. All the boys and their parents, male and female, were assembled in someone's compound. Anyone could attend this part of the ceremony; there were no taboos or secrecies. The boys waiting to be circumcised (*solima*) were already wearing the traditional white or black dresses. The gowns were wide so that air could enter freely for the circumcision to heal. The cutting took place in the *taarorde*, the toilet area which is enclosed by a mud-brick wall or hut, depending on the compound. The boy entered the taarorde, encouraged and cheered by the members of the family and spectators who were waiting outside. As soon as he entered the toilet area, he was out of sight of the family and alone with the circumciser (*kaddinowo*). He sat down on the mortar (*howru*) that is normally used by the women to grind millet and other grains and is circumcised. After the cutting, a bandage with the powder of a herb called *gawde*[9] was wrapped around the circumcision wound, to help heal the cut. Outside the taarorde, people were cheering and encouraging the boy to endure the operation with courage. If the boys did not cry, they were considered courageous; if they did cry, they were consoled when they come out. Songs of encouragement were sung to all the newly circumcised njulli and to those who had to wait for their circumcision (*solima*).

After the cutting a celebration took place somewhere in the village to honor the boys. They received little presents to comfort them, and often an animal was slaughtered for the festivities. Over the next couple of days, the boys were fed food called *mbaⱬⱬungu* that was supposed to give strength. It consisted of millet and corn. From now on the newly circumcised boys (*njulli*) were always accompanied by an older boy, called *selɓe*, who had already undergone circumcision. He guided the boys in whatever they did, showed them how to walk with their wound and how to lie down to sleep, and when someone made a mistake or was naughty, he was the one who punished them. When the wound began to heal, the boys began to roam the village to prove themselves as men. They were often teased by the older boys who had already undergone circumcision as well as other villagers with the song:

njulli yoo booroo dotel, kalle maa caami e bolol, hanno maa yeƒtude
ndogaa, yimɓe fof yefti ndogii

which means

Oh circumcised boy with the naked bottom, your penis has fallen
on the path. Why don't you pick it up and run? All the others have
picked up theirs and run.

When teased with this song, the njulli often chased after the older boys to beat them or tease them back. The newly circumcised boys often teased each other with the following song:

Heedi cagal fowru ŋola
The one who is left behind will be eaten down to the bone by the
    hyena.

This song encouraged the boys to compete, run faster, aim with more focus, and perform better during the games played throughout the seclusion period in the village. There were also jokes between the circumcised and the uncircumcised. The uncircumcised were teased as being women. The njulli took pride in saying that the uncircumcised were not yet men.

One of the challenges for njulli was to prove themselves as men in front of the girls of the village. My interlocutor Fall told me that making women submit was part of becoming a man. They did this by obliging girls to kneel down in front of them. If the girls refused to do so, they beat them and told them that they were preventing the healing of their circumcision scars.

Part of the general mischief the njulli undertook in the village was the theft of chickens from villagers for slaughter. Although this would have normally caused anger and the owner of the chicken would have disciplined the thieves with the approval and encouragement of the boy's father, when the njulli did this it was tolerated, as they were known to be in a special phase of their life.

The boys did not go their separate ways until their circumcision wound was healed, about three to four weeks after the circumcision. The last thing they did together was go down to the river to wash for the first time since their circumcision, as they had not been able to wash while it was healing. They also washed their gowns and then went back into the village.

Fall's account of circumcision in the 1980s supports my interpretations regarding the myths of how circumcision used to take place a long time ago. The initiation represents a liminal stage; the njulli were no longer like girls, and they teased those who had not yet gone through circumcision as being like women. Circumcision therefore makes gender; it removes the parts of the genitals that are feminine or androgynous. It also represents the beginning of social manhood: the njulli practiced making girls submit to their orders. Refusal slowed down the healing process, they said. Metaphorically, the healing of the circumcision scar and becoming a man who is recognized as a responsible member in the community go hand in hand. Circumcision is not just about physically making the boy's penis virile, pure, and ready for marriage, but it also prepares the boy for social manhood—accepting one's role as superior to women. Making girls obey their orders is part of this process.

The fact that the njulli were teased by the older boys and adults and that their mischief was tolerated and laughed at also shows that they were in a liminal sphere until the initiation phase was over and they married and took on the responsibilities of grown adults. Turner, along with Van Gennep, argues that rites of passage are transitional moments in which individuals change status within the community. Neophytes are structurally "invisible" according to Turner (1967: 98). They belong to neither one group nor the other as they have not completed the final steps of the initiation rite. In that sense they are both androgynous and sexless at the same time, as long as they are in this transitional stage of ritual seclusion (1967:98). The njulli of Fouta Toro, as well as excised unmarried girls, have entered liminality. They are no longer androgynous children but have attained the first stage toward marriage and becoming adults—they have been made appropriately "male" and "female."

Fall said that when he was a child, he witnessed large circumcision ceremonies where sometimes sixty boys from various villages would be circumcised together. Such large ceremonies with boys coming together no longer exist in Fouta Toro. If communal circumcision ceremonies do take place, it is often boys of the same age group from a family or a neighborhood of a village.

Today most boys are circumcised between the ages of four and nine. It is rare to see an uncircumcised boy reach the age of puberty: this was considered to be too late by most of my interlocutors. Although I have seen boys wearing the traditional gowns and hoods the initiates wear after circumcision in different parts of Fouta, circumcision ceremonies are becoming rarer and a lot of boys tend to be circumcised individually at the health care center or by a Sakke (member of the hinnde of leather workers) in the village. Sometimes the reasons given for this include the risk of infection or fear of transmission of disease, such as HIV or tetanus.

Gendered Bodies and Changing Traditions

In contrast to Mende groups in Senegambia and West Africa, FGC is not important in the context of initiation and coming of age in Fouta Toro. It is about making female gender by removing the external genitalia reminiscent of a boy's penis. Thus the ambiguously androgynous body is rendered female. The excised woman is "pure," a "virgin," and socially appropriate. The process of becoming a woman, however, is not completed until she marries. For boys, on the other hand, there are initiation ceremonies, although circumcision is also frequently undertaken without them. Circumcision removes what is feminine and impure. It makes the penis virile and ready for sexual intercourse and marriage. A boy metaphorically enters a liminal phase through circumcision that is not completed until he has sex and marries. Until then he has not attained adulthood. Female excision and male circumcision thus both create the physical foundations for gendered personhood.

Why does male circumcision involve more ritual and why does it happen much later than female circumcision? We have seen that in Fouta Toro, most girls are excised during infancy without much celebration, at the exciser's house, at the health care center, or at home. We have also seen that even though male circumcision ceremonies exist, they are constantly changing. I have argued that traditions are never unchanging, but what is called "important tradition" signifies a practice or relationship between people that is cherished and valued. Most people I met in Fouta Toro did not feel much regret about male circumcision ceremonies disappearing. For them, the main thing was that the boys were circumcised—initiation was not necessary. On the contrary, it was considered expensive by many. Perhaps Futanke society has changed in ways that mean the emphasis on learning to become a responsible adult within the community, who is able to fend off wild animals and distinguish himself through bravery and endurance of hardships in the bush, is no longer necessary. The traditions associated with becoming a man are redundant in modern Senegalese society—where it is more important to provide for one's family by earning money.

We have seen that none of the elements associated with the procedure of excision, nor the celebrations around the practice such as initiation or coming of age, nor fear of loss of tradition associated with any of the aforementioned is the cause of the opposition to the law in Fouta Toro. In the next chapter I will look at how personhood is constituted through gender socialization and how excision creates the moral foundations for female personhood.

CHAPTER 3

Curbing Desire

Gender Socialization and the Physical Foundations for Moral Personhood

March 2007. I'm sitting on a mattress on the veranda of my teacher's house studying Pulaar. Every so often I raise my eyes and gaze across the family compound. It is almost midday, and the sun is beating down onto the hot soil. The children have moved into the shade and continue their play there. The only ones still occasionally walking across the compound are Fatoumata, who is preparing lunch, and her teenage daughter, who occasionally fetches things for her that are scattered across the compound. On these late mornings, when it was getting hard to concentrate, I had many long conversations with my teacher. We discuss how society should be, whether education should be guided by religious practice or by other values, about finding a balance between the freedom to do as one pleases and duties toward family and larger society. We spent a lot of time talking about Islam, pleasure, and eventually also excision. In the words below, my teacher explains to me why the Prophet Mohammed recommended excision to help women control their sexual desire better.

> No, it's not in the Qur'an, but the Prophet said that excision should be practiced. The Prophet was a kind man. Very kind. He only wanted the best for his wives and women in general, that's why he created these rules. Do you know how women were treated before? They were like domestic slaves. They were worth nothing. It didn't matter if you killed them or violated them, they were worth nothing!

But the Prophet loved women and said that a man is only allowed to
marry up to four if he can treat them equally. Since then, a Muslim
is not allowed to harm or treat them badly. He can't just do what he
feels like with women but has to abide by the recommendations of
religion. But the Prophet also knew that women have a great sexual
desire. They want to have sex and get aroused very quickly. That's
why they were not respected, because they were like animals. They
get aroused so quickly that the Prophet recommended diminishing
the clitoris just a little bit so that desire is diminished and women
are more respectable.

Excision, like Islam, brought law and order to the world, as some Futanke
see it. Lawlessness, injustice, and social disarray, which mainly affected the
weak, were replaced by divine law, faith, and solidarity between Muslims.
Throughout my time in Fouta, I was frequently told stories of times in the
past when powerful men kidnapped other men's wives and killed those husbands who could not defend themselves. Once in their possession, they
adorned their beautiful acquisitions with treasures of gold. Women, as the
"weak sex," were vulnerable not only to the aggressive, self-righteous, uncon-
trolled desires of men, but also to their own desire. According to the ideology, Islam brought an end to these barbaric times and helped to establish
harmony and solidarity between Futanke that most people would not want
to replace with anything else in the world. Excision is not only a social norm
defended by men and women, but it also ensures a certain level of safety and
maintenance of what is seen as social order and law, as I will show in this
chapter.

The quote above refers to key themes in this chapter: control of desire,
conceptions of law and order, as well as the untamed mayhem and lack of
civilization that would perhaps exist if the Prophet had not put forward his
recommendations. Since Hosken's radical proposition that "female sexual
mutilations" are a result of male control over women and "a systematic surgical attack on the essence of our female sexual being"[1] (Hosken 1982),
which caused outrage among female African intellectuals (Amadiume
1987; Ahmadu 2000), anthropological analyses have addressed the ways in
which excision is linked to the control of desire in local discourse (Boddy
1989; Gruenbaum 1991).

Janice Boddy, who undertook her fieldwork in Sudan around the same
time as Hosken, discussed discourses on women as "weak, morally inferior

beings, oversexed and inherently inclined to wantonness, devoted to sensuality" (Boddy 1989:53) As with Rosen's (1978) and Dwyer's (1978) descriptions of gender differences in Morocco, Boddy's Hofriyati stipulate that women and men differ in their amounts of animal force (*nafs*), which includes lust, emotions, and desires as well as their ability to reason and control emotions and behave in socially appropriate ways (*'agl*) (Boddy 1989: 53). Due to women's lack of ability to exercise conscious restraint, circumcision is used to curb and socialize their sexual desires so that they do not bring irreparable shame to their family through misbehavior. Boddy suggested, however, that this is an essentially masculine point of view. I found that a lot of my male interlocutors took a similar stance on women's capacity to constrain their emotions. However, mothers were also very concerned with the risk of undesired pregnancy before marriage for their daughters and the consequential shame. Hence women were also strong advocates and perpetuators of the idea that excision helps to control desire.

I suggest that rather than thinking of excision in terms of male domination over women and a symptom of patriarchal society, we need to consider the complex sociality of obligations and mutual expectations in the gendered spaces of the household as well as conceptions of civilization (Simmel 1997; Strathern 1990; Elias 1997; Gruenbaum 2001) in order to make different perspectives on excision intelligible.

I argue that, for women, excision creates the physical foundations for moral personhood as it prepares a girl for the responsibilities she will have to take on as a mature woman and mother. Besides gender socialization, excision makes a woman Futanke in local discourses—it renders her socially and morally appropriate in ways that mark the Futanke's sense of ethnic superiority.

We will first of all look at the making of the physical foundations for female personhood and how women consider that moral personhood and control of desire are related to the practice of excision. We will then see how "desirable womanhood" develops in childhood and how female and male traits differ from those of other societies whose members are not perceived as well brought up and accomplished. First, I show how obligations of reciprocity are constituted and responsibility develops throughout childhood and adulthood. Second, I look at the gendered spaces of men and women and what mutual expectations they have of one another in their domains of responsibility. I discuss how women's sexual behavior and reproductive capacity can lead to loss of honor and hence to shame and other consequences. In the last section of this chapter, I come back to the control of desire as an aspect of civilization, suggesting moral superiority over other ethnic groups whom Futanke perceive as less able to control their physical needs than themselves.

The Control of Desire and the Physical Foundations for Moral Personhood

The control of sexuality has been discussed in a body of literature on honor and shame and the role of women's behavior in boundary marking (Pitt-Rivers 1965; Caplan 1987; Goddard 1987). Pitt-Rivers argued that honorable behavior for men and women differed. Whereas a man must defend his own and his family's honor, women must preserve their purity (see Goddard 1987:167). Men's relationship to honor is therefore active whereas women's is passive (Pitt-Rivers 1965:45). Pitt-Rivers's view implies men's control over resources and women's submissive compliance with their standards of honor and reputation. Davis (1977) challenged Pitt-Rivers's view by suggesting that women's role in the preservation of honor is not just passive. Davis argued that they have an active role in upholding the family honor by looking after their husbands and defending their interests (Davis 1977; Goddard 1987:198). Despite Davis's challenge it seems that much of the 1980s literature on control of sexuality and honor somewhat victimizes women in their role as preservers of their group's reputation, rather than leading to a deeper understanding of how power and forms of resistance (Abu-Lughod 1999, 2008; Mahmood 2005) are negotiated.

Some anthropologists have looked at how different groups maintain their identity through strict rules and recommendations in everyday practices. Okeley (1983), for example, looked at Gypsy Travelers' conceptions of purity and pollution, and how they protect themselves from non-Gypsies who are perceived as threatening their purity. Goddard (1987) was concerned with women and honor in Italy. She argued that their role as boundary markers and carriers of group identity requires their sexuality to be controlled. Due to their capacity to bear children, they are a potential menace to the group they belong to—giving birth to the wrong kinds of children because of sexual encounters with the wrong kinds of men threatens the "purity" of the group (Goddard 1987:190).

The interest in honor and shame and the role of women as "guardians of race" (Gupta 2002) or preservers of ethnic identity continued to be explored in the literature in the 1990s and 2000s. Yuval-Davis and Anthias (1989) were interested in the delineation of the boundaries of the state, the nation, and civil society', not as reified entities but as processes in which women play a key role as "biological reproducers of members of ethnic collectivities" and "transmitters of culture" (Yuval-Davis and Anthias 1989:7). The centrality of gender in identity politics, be it fundamentalist, racial, or nationalist, has been explored further by Kandiyoti (1991), Hawley (1994), Moghadam (1994), and Wilson and Frederiksen (1995). This body of literature is concerned with ideas around keeping ethnic boundaries intact and demarcating the juncture between internal cohesion and external difference. Constructions of the "other" supply protective anxieties, be it with regard to numbers—fear around one's own population declining—or being overrun by the other who is more sexually charged and more fertile. For many, anxieties around declining populations are related to the loss of culture and the extinction of race.

Few of my interlocutors saw themselves as victims of male control. On the contrary, even when men asked the women in their families to stop practicing, they often continued, instead of passively obeying their male relatives' wishes. I suggest that it is far more inspiring and productive to consider how local categories are naturalized as God-given and represent the basis for gender socialization (Yanagisako and Delaney 1995). Mahmood (2011) argues that the transnational feminist analytical and political agenda of gender equality may be misplaced when looking at women's agency within patriarchal social structures. Instead she suggests that "the meaning of agency must be explored within the grammar of concepts within which it resides" (2005:34). In the following I explore the contextual meaning of control of desire and how the necessity for excision is naturalized among women and men.

Controlling Desire

In Pulaar, desire for something or someone is expressed in different ways. The verb *yidde* means to want or to love. *Mbada yidmaa*—"I love you" or "I want you"—is, however, rarely said between couples in love; there are more subtle ways of expressing one's desire through gestures or by doing things for each other. For example, a woman might cook a meal or dress in a particular way for her husband, which arouses his desire for her. Men show their love or desire by giving a woman presents.

As far as physical desire or sexual excitement is concerned, men and women express their feelings differently, according to my interlocutors between the ages of twenty and their early forties from rural Fouta. A man may express his desire to sleep with a woman as *mbaɗa yidi yettaade ma*, which figuratively means "I want you, I desire you," but literally is "I want to arrive at you/with you." Some, however, would consider this too direct. A woman would never voice her desire to sleep with a man so explicitly. It would be vulgar to do so and there are more subtle ways of showing one's desire through gestures or looks. I was told that if a woman does verbally express sexual desire for a man it could be with the words *Mi rokkiima hoore am*, "I give myself to you," or *wad ko welmaa e am*, "Do what you like with me," or *Kala ko woni e am hannde oo ko aan jeyi*, "All that I am belongs to you today." Other words for sexual desire regardless of gender do not exist in Pulaar in Fouta Toro. As we can see, men actively want/desire, whereas women submit to men and give themselves away, in words or speech at least.

For my interlocutors in Fouta, control of the body is essential to social etiquette. This is most explicit in humor, where lack of (physical) control (*jogaade hoore mum*) is often subject to jokes and laughter—for example, in common jokes about lack of control during mealtimes (*fonngi* or *saali*). When people get together for a meal and someone notices in the course of the meal that a member of the family is not present around the bowl or on the compound and asks "Where is so and so?" everyone laughs and says that the speaker was so hungry that they did not notice that the person was not there at the beginning of the meal and are only remembering them now that their stomach is beginning to fill up. Forgetting the other at mealtimes is a sign of weakness because the hunger was greater than the care for the other and it represents lack of honor on a small scale, which, in everyday life, translates into jokes about lack of control. In a similar way, farting is against social etiquette and is a popular theme in joking relationships (Smith 2006; Launay 2006; Galvan 2006). "Joking cousins" (*dendiraaɓe*) take pleasure in accusing each other of being bean eaters. It is asserted that one's own clan never eats beans because "bean eaters smell and you cannot enter their rooms." Farting is a sign of weakness. In fact, black-eye beans (*ñebbe*) are a major element of everyone's diet and, due to the relative scarcity of food, no one can refuse to eat beans.

The importance of self-control (*jogaade hoore mum*) is reflected in other spheres of everyday life as well. For example, I was told that it was a sign of weakness to ask for food and one should wait until it is offered or served. Even a husband who incessantly asks his wife when lunch will be ready displays a lack of control. His behavior elicits laughter and humiliating comments. In a similar way, a man who is in love with a woman is sometimes teased by his age-mates: "Go and wash, go and practice ablutions, you can't control your-self" (*Yah lootoyo a roŋkii jogaade hoore ma*). What they are stressing is the need to be pure for prayer after being sexually aroused to the extent of "wet-ting oneself" (see also Chapter 4). These jokes point to a social code of honor and humiliation that treasures the ability to control desires and physical needs in general. In fact, endurance and self-discipline (*muñal*), intelligence and forethought (*hakkille*), shame or modesty (*gacce*), and bravery or courage (*tin-naade/cagataagal*) are all part of the Pulaaku (Riesman 1974; Stenning 1959) code of honor for which the Fulani are famous.

Foucault (1975) argues that discipline in eighteenth- and nineteenth-century Europe produced docile bodies. On the one hand, discipline in-creases the forces of the body by turning the body's power into "'aptitude', a 'capacity' which it seeks to increase; on the other hand, it reverses the course of energy, the power that might result from it, and turns it into a relation of strict subjugation" (Foucault 1975:138). With regard to Fouta Toro, being in control of one's body, being disciplined, and being able to constrain one's physical needs are seen as an asset in which people in Fouta take pride. A person who can control himself is powerful, superior, aware of a social ideal, and conforming to it. Although, as Foucault suggests, disci-pline of the body implies strict subjugation to social order, it is experienced as empowering. For Foucault (1975), power is not "possessed" by the domi-nant classes, nor is it a privilege acquired or preserved by them: "but the overall effect of its strategic positions—an effect that is manifested and sometimes extended by the position of those who are dominated [. . .] this power is not exercised simply as an obligation or a prohibition on those who 'do not have it'; it invests them, is transmitted by them and through them; it exerts pressure on them, just as they themselves, in their struggle against it, resist the grip it has on them" (1975:26–27). With reference to Foucault (1975), I argue that the ability to control desire should not be attributed to a particular social group or gender in Futanke society but should be seen as a characteristic of civilization, refined social conduct, and moral person-hood among all strata of society. Control of desire is a *doxa*, the experience by which "the natural and social world appears as self-evident" (Bourdieu 1977:164).

The Control of Desire and Sexuality

The greatest fear with regard to not cutting one's daughters that has been expressed to me is that an unexcised girl might not be able to control her sexual desire when she reaches a certain age. This might tempt her to sleep with a man before marriage. In Pulaar it was said that *o waawa fadde gorko makko*, "she cannot wait for her husband," or *o waawa jogaade hoore makko*, "she cannot control herself." In French, people tended to use the expression *elle ne peut pas controller ses pulsions sexuelles*, "she cannot control her sex drive." Considering that virginity on marriage is extremely important to Futanke, and a family's honor and social standing are contingent on their daughters' virginity, this is seen as a serious threat.

In Sinthiou Sebbe, a village where the majority of women had decided to stop practicing excision, I interviewed a middle-aged woman called Juulde, who was opposed to a collective abandonment of the practice. Even though the option of not practicing had become the subject of open discussion between families, Juulde, like many other women, considered excision important for the following reasons:

> If a girl is not excised, her clitoris will continue growing, like the girl's body is growing as well and that will weaken the rest of her apparatus. [. . .] When an excised girl's husband is not there, she will not look for another man to sleep with. If the clitoris is not cut, the girl will not be able to rest still. She will not be able to sit and wait for her husband. We are not for the abandonment of excision. It is a good thing.

Since the desertification of the 1970s, it has become increasingly difficult for people to live from subsistence farming and herding. Men search for paid labor in urban areas and abroad, where they hope to be paid higher salaries. Many women I met had husbands working in Mauritania, Ivory Coast, Central Africa, and Gabon, as well as European countries and the United States. Juulde emphasized the importance of two things with regard to excision. First, a girl cannot wait for her husband while he is away working. Second, Juulde brings up the notion of the "weakening of the girl's apparatus." I frequently came across this belief in comments suggesting that an excised girl is physically stronger—her life force goes into her physical and moral strength, turning the body's power into "aptitude" (Foucault 1975) as a socially appropriate woman who performs her duties in the household well, rather than her life force going into the development of her sex organs and sexual desire, which could potentially become dangerous. It could also be argued that Juulde is using "the weakening of the apparatus" in a metaphoric sense to describe an unexcised girl's incapacity to control herself, which signifies physical, mental, and moral weakness. The image of an unexcised girl not being able to "sit still" was also frequently used. It conveys the idea that she is waiting restlessly for her husband to satisfy her sexual desire and lacks the patience (*muñal*) an excised girl possesses. Similar images of a girl being tempted to commit adultery when her husband is away were expressed to me by Hawa, a close female interlocutor of mine in Diawoury: "Excision is practiced when girls are babies. It is practiced so that when the girl has grown up, if her husband needs to emigrate she will be able to wait for him. She will be able to go without sleeping with a man for a long time." Another woman explained the importance of the practice to me in a village where many other women had abandoned it:

> *Gedda* We have practiced excision since the generations of our grandmothers. If you hear people say that it is a practice that needs to be done, it is because if a woman's husband travels to France or to the US she cannot stay without a man for more than two months. An excised woman can wait for her husband for years.
> *Sarah* Aren't there excised women who look for men as well?
> *Gedda* Yes, there are, but without excision it would be worse.
> (Gedda Sy, in Semme)

In both comments, excision is seen to help women to wait for their husbands and to control their sexual desire. These women's views are those of mothers who want their daughters to be socially successful in a society where the domestic sphere is associated with women as reproducers while men are charged with the responsibility of producing income to support their families. According to local ideology, the spheres of production and reproduction are strongly gendered.[2] But even beyond social recognition through marriage to a man who is "successful," it makes mothers proud and happy to see that their daughters are able to contain their desires and devote their lives to their husbands, in-laws, and children.

To what extent can these women's views be seen as a result of male oppression over women, as Hosken (1982) suggested? Strathern (1988:26) stipulates that feminism's theoretical concerns focus on the extent to which women suffer from systematic social injustice because of their sex. As the practice of female circumcision has been under sharp scrutiny from feminist scholars who suggest that it is a result of inequality in gender relations, I briefly assess how my ethnographic data corresponds to some feminist academic notions of inequality and gender relations.

Gender Differences and Feminist Analyses

Kandiyoti (1998) discusses to what extent perceptions of personal interest and concern for family welfare help sustain "traditional inequalities" as put forward by Sen (1990). Sen suggests that the absence of protest and lack of questioning of inequality are not evidence of their absence. Instead, he argues, acute inequalities often survive precisely by making allies of the deprived; the underdog, accepting the legitimacy of unequal order, becomes its implicit accomplice (Sen 1990:126).

Kandiyoti discusses Agarwal's (1994) disagreement with Sen's vision of inequality as tied to "false consciousness." Agarwal (1994) favors a position that presents subordinates as conscious actors generally capable of penetrating the ideological fabric woven by the privileged (Kandiyoti 1998:139). Agarwal (1994) argues that it is the material impossibility of fulfilling needs that stands in the way of alleviating disadvantage. She suggests that, instead of sharpening women's sense of self-interest, an improvement in the ability to pursue that interest by strengthening their bargaining power should be sought (Agarwal 1994:54).

Kandiyoti (2002) further looks at Apffel-Marglin and Simon's (1994) stance on inequality. They go so far as to suggest that Sen's argument about lack of awareness of personal interest and great concern with family welfare (Sen 1990:126) exemplifies the imposition of the women-in-development discourse, which Apffel-Marglin and Simon (1994) call the "direct heir of Victorian colonial feminism." What is at stake is not degrees of consciousness about self-interest but a radically different sense of selfhood expressed through a fundamentally different set of values and priorities (Kandiyoti

1998:140). Apffel-Marglin and Simon's (1994) stance echoes African feminist critiques of what they called "White Western Feminism," the project of middle-class educated women, whose mission it was to expose sexism in public life and to alter the male bias in scholarly work and popular culture (di Leonardo 1991:2). What African feminists reacted to most strongly were the racist and ethnocentric assumptions of feminist academic writing on motherhood, marriage, and sexual practices (Amadiume 1987). Yanagisako and Delaney suggest that "assimilating 'them' to 'us' can do violence to what people cherish that is distinct about themselves. [. . .] The superficial assessments of similarities in the roles and sentiments of women in different societies can lead to the naïve conclusion—rampant in U.S. white feminist scholarship in the 1970s—that all women can readily comprehend each other's suffering, sorrows and joys. In short, they can lead to patronizing representations of other women as 'ourselves unclothed' (Rosaldo 1980)" (Yanagisako and Delaney 1995:16). With reference to my data on why excision and control of desire were perceived to be necessary, most women did not see themselves as seriously disadvantaged because their desire had been "controlled." On the contrary, the ability to control desire through excision was perceived as an asset, something that enabled them to behave in a way that they were proud of and perceived as honorable. From a feminist perspective that focuses on the manner in which certain structures are perpetuated to the advantage of men (Strathern 1988: 26), it is possible to argue that gender inequalities in Fouta Toro exist because of the material impossibility of women acting in their personal interest due to lack of bargaining power (Kandiyoti 1988, 1998). For local women, however, such notions of inequality did not make sense. Rather, they regarded gender roles as complementary and that each sex had a heavy burden to carry due to the responsibilities they were expected to take on.

This resonates with feminist scholarship on agency that addresses how women perceive their own position and make decisions within social structures where they are expected to be submissive to men, either due to local traditions or due to religious injunctions (Abu-Lughod 2013; Mahmood 2005; Wardlow 2006). Mahmood (2005) looked at how pious Muslim women in Cairo consider their options and make decisions based on the recommendations of the four schools of Islamic law. Rather than judging the performance of certain actions or activities in terms of gender equality, women in the mosque movement decided on the most appropriate ethical conduct by choosing from the given options in the Islamic scriptures.[3] Following Foucault and Asad (1986, 2003), Mahmood is interested in the discursive formations and pedagogical practices that allow women to make decisions.

Rather than equating Futanke women's and men's wishes to control sexual desire with Western notions of gender equality and satisfaction of needs (Sen 1990; Agarwal 1994; Kandiyoti 1998; Apffel-Marglin and Simon 1994), I prefer approaches that explore how gender relations are naturalized and how agency is justified "within the grammar of concepts within which it resides" (Mahmood 2005). Yanagisako and Delaney argue that "cultural domains are culturally specific, but they usually come with claims of universality, which are part and parcel of their seeming to be given-in-nature and /or god-given. The apparent logic and naturalness of these domains is a consequence of the way they are made real through the institutional arrangements and discourses people encounter in everyday life (1995:12)." Yanagisako and Delaney (1995) suggest that unlike explicit ideologies, which can be traced to people with particular social position, cultural domains seem to emerge from each person's own experiences. The separateness of domains is encountered directly by people whose lives are organized along institutional fault lines that are themselves the products of hegemonic cultural distinctions. As a consequence, religion seems to be about God rather than about gender; the family seems to be about reproduction and childbearing rather than about gender and religion (Yanagisako and Delaney 1995:12).

In Fouta Toro, notions of desire, sexuality, and satisfaction are expressed through idioms of kinship and the honor of the family. We shall explore in further detail how kinship is not merely added to an abstract notion of bounded individuality but kin relations are perceived as an intrinsic part of the self (Carsten 2004:107). Doing things for other members within one's group (status group, clan, or ethnicity) according to social expectations and preset patterns of agency is intrinsically linked to local notions of personhood and ensures a sense of self-value and pride. I argue that social identity (ethnicity, caste, clan group) cannot be conceptually separated from individual desires and the will to control one's physical needs.

Creating the Physical Foundations for Moral Personhood

When women explained the importance of excision to me, they used metaphors to emphasize the need to cut the girl when she is young "to diminish the force and size" of the clitoris (*sedere*): "Before a field is seeded, it needs to be worked on and prepared to make the harvest a good one." This metaphor has various connotations. It could be argued that she is speaking of the importance of excision for women's fertility and producing good children.[4] More important, however, is the idea that a girl cut young can be physically prepared for her responsibilities in the household and community. Like a field that, if tilled, weeded and looked after, will produce good crops, a girl who is cut when she is young will not develop the threatening comportment an unexcised girl is imagined to develop. With regard to excision preventing a woman from behaving inappropriately, Halimatou Gueye, the midwife and exciser of Weendouley, used the following metaphor: "It's like a tree, you know, that you have seeded. If you cut it when it is small, is it going to grow? It is going to die." This metaphor suggests that a girl who is cut when she is young will not develop the desires of one who is not cut. In addition to the frightening image that one's daughters might turn into sexually insatiable beings who risk damaging the family honor for their personal gratification, pregnancy before marriage causes sadness and social loss. Furthermore, women expressed other fears and concerns to me related to aesthetics, childbirth, and purity.

Gendered sociality is based on a conception of personhood according to which reciprocity between the sexes is an a priori presumption (Strathern 1988). As among Strathern's Eastern Highlanders, the person in Fouta is not self-evidently "an individual" who, as in "Western" formulations, derives integrity from his or her position as prior to society (Strathern 1988:93). Instead, persons define themselves through what they do for others. To elucidate how this takes place, I discuss how boys and girls are socialized into the gendered spaces and relations of reciprocity. What people understand as reciprocity is associated with a particular comportment and duties toward the elders in the community. To locals, the obedience necessary to fulfill one's duties toward others requires the ability to control one's personal desires and interests for the common good of the family and community.

Gender Socialization

In Fouta, a person is likely to be identified by who they are related to and how well they fulfill their duties toward their family. Most of my female interlocutors did not know how their husbands and sons or fathers actually earned their money and, unless they were influential in local politics or a famous religious cleric, men got little recognition for what they actually "did" in life. To most people, what was far more important was how well a man supported his family, how generous he was toward the community, and who his children married. A person's wish to strive for the realization of personal pursuits and passions was considered selfish if they did not serve the common good of the family.[5]

A person, whether a child or young adult, who refuses to serve others they have obligations toward based on age or rank is considered badly educated. There is a customary rule in Fouta that the younger ones always have to give way to and serve the older ones. This applies to all ages. I was told that even if a sixty-five-year-old asks a sixty-year-old for a favor which requires them to walk to the other side of the village on an errand, they cannot refuse without appearing extremely impolite. Even if they are physically not capable of doing it themselves, it is their responsibility to delegate to someone else and make sure the task gets done. If the task is not done suitably, it reflects badly on their honor and reputation. The person is at risk of being considered unreliable, disobedient, or impolite.

Children are taught from a young age how to serve elders and perform certain tasks in the household. Boys and girls below the age of five are often asked to run errands for the elders[6] without gender distinction. Besides greeting correctly, one of the first things a child learns from the time they can walk is how to bring things from one person to another. Although this is initially only a game, as soon as children understand "give," "take," and "bring to," they are asked to give and bring things to adults such as pots of water or empty bowls. If they refuse, they are considered either impolite or as not yet having reached a certain stage of development. The jobs young children are asked to do are never very difficult, but the challenge lies in doing them properly. When, for example, children lose coins in the sand on the way to the shop or bring back the wrong things, they are often disciplined, sometimes through beating. If they have performed the task correctly, their achievement is merely acknowledged but not necessarily rewarded; it is considered their duty to do these things. Toddlers and young children who do not understand or perform the "give, take, bring to" game properly are often compared to older children who do understand. A child who follows these orders is considered "cleverer" than one who does not.

This understanding also relates to schoolwork and obedience at home. In the family with whom I spent a large amount of time in Weendouley, there were a few girls between the ages of five and ten. One of the girls, Penda, who was about five and did not yet go to school, loved playing around at home and doing things for the elders. She would try to sweep the ground and help the women in the kitchen, and she keenly obeyed when someone gave her a job to do. When she was called to go on an errand, she did not get distracted by play and it was well-known that she transmitted messages correctly. For example, when members of the family spent the mornings in other areas of the village, she would be asked to call them home for lunch, and she always gave the message to the right person. Mariama, another girl in the same household, who was about seven and very good at school, was considered a little slow because she did not manage to do some of the basic household chores properly and often gave messages incorrectly or to the wrong person. Women in the household would say about these two children, "Penda [the little one] is clever, she obeys and understands when you give her jobs, whereas Mariama does not. She is not so clever."

I noticed the importance of such obedience in well-brought-up children all over Fouta and not just on the Ile Amorphile, but, interestingly, not among Wolof families in Dakar. Whereas in Fouta every child has to greet and serve a guest and obey the elders' instructions as far as they are capable, children in Wolof families in Dakar often do not greet and they often refuse to help or serve strangers even if asked to. To a Futanke, this behavior is a sign of being badly brought up and extremely rude.

One day a French girl about four years old came to spend the morning with me and my friend in Weendouley. She had grown up in France but her mother was from Fouta. I spoke to her in French, which she was more familiar with than Pulaar. My male friend gave her a coin to get us some matches from the shop to heat up some water. The girl refused. He asked her again to go, as it is unusual for an adult to go to the shop if there is a younger person capable of doing so. I told him that she had not grown up in this society and that she would not understand these orders. When she heard me say that, she took the coin and went to the shop, which was just around the corner. We waited and waited. Half an hour later she came back with cigarettes instead. My friend said to her, "I told you to bring matches and you brought cigarettes? Why is that? That does not make sense." Instead of returning the cigarettes for matches as he ordered her to do, she refused and said that it was not her fault, she asked for matches but the shopkeeper gave her ciga-rettes. From my friend's point of view the child was extremely impolite because she argued back instead of obeying and refused to do as she was told. From my point of view, it could not be assumed that such a small child who had not grown up learning to follow orders from the elders and to whom everything was foreign could understand what she was expected to do. My friend told me later on that he witnessed a conversation between the mother and the girl, in which they discussed why she had been "naughty" on vari-ous occasions. For my friend it was remarkable that there was a dialogue between them instead of the elder just telling the child what to do, as is com-mon in Fouta.

Teaching children to serve and obey elders from a young age makes them aware of their responsibilities. This arrangement is experienced as "solidar-ity" (*jokkere endam*)[7] by many: in the same way you have obligations toward others, you can rely on help from others who have obligations toward you in times of difficulty. Whereas someone who has grown up in northern Europe, like myself, would consider it their own responsibility to carry heavy luggage, a Futanke would not hesitate to whistle the boys in the neighborhood together to carry the luggage to wherever it needs to go, even if a fifteen-minute walk is involved. Instead of seeing this as a burden, the children enjoy tackling challenging tasks because of the recognition they receive. To make the im-portance of solidarity and obeying the elders explicit, I was told a story of a boy who caught a big fish in the river and was on his way home full of pride to show his parents. On the way, an elder saw the boy with the fish and asked the boy to hand it over to him. The boy could not refuse, as he knew that the old man was of his grandfather's age group—he was one of his "fathers." After handing over the fish, the boy ran home crying. When his father found out why the boy was upset, he became angry and scolded him. It was the boy's duty to hand things over to the elders if they claimed them. Instead of cry-ing, he should have felt proud that he had been able to give something to the elder.

Instead of pursuing personal interests, recognition and respect are re-ceived by acting in the interest of the community and by creating and suc-cessfully maintaining networks of solidarity between people. Loyalty and respect are achieved through fulfilling responsibilities toward elders and, in addition, children become socially aware and are socialized into the gendered spaces of the household and their duties as a boy or a girl. They learn, from a very young age, what their duties toward their male and female elders are and how to meet expectations.

Becoming a Woman: Girls' Duties in the Household

Girls learn to perform and take over certain responsibilities in the household until they are considered marriageable. As soon as girls reach a certain level of maturity, little time is spent playing, but I noticed that they take pleasure in participating more and more in the activities of the household. Initially some of the tasks girls try to perform, such as fetching water or searching for firewood, seemed dangerous to me. However, girls pride themselves on trying as they are then taken more seriously—it shows that they are becoming adults and will soon be marriageable. In the family I stayed with in Diawoury, women and their daughters had to perform extremely hard physical work in the household, according to my perception, because the family was large and there was no running water, electricity, or gas for cooking. One of the girls, Khadi Sarr, was ten years old, lean and strong, and took on several duties to help her mother, who was pregnant with her ninth child. One day Khadi asked me to help her lift a heavy bucket of water up onto her head. I told her off for trying to lift such a heavy weight; her body was still growing, I reasoned and she could damage her back. Khadi would not listen and half a year later she had become one of the main water carriers. Rather than trying to avoid certain tasks, a clever and ambitious girl quickly learns and understands what needs to be done. In this way she builds up respect in the community and comes to be seen as a good catch, which increases her chances of finding a good husband.

A girl is not considered marriageable until she demonstrates that she can run the household independently and perform all the duties a wife has to perform. This includes sweeping the compound in the morning, setting the fire alight to heat water for breakfast, fetching water, preparing lunch. She must demonstrate that she can look after small children responsibly and treat guests (*hobbe*) with hospitality and respect. At times I witnessed discussions among women who were wondering whether a girl was marriageable or not and commenting on how she performed household chores independently. My friend Dickel, who was fifteen years old, desperately wanted to get married. Her parents and other women, however, considered that she was not yet mature enough to run a household by herself in a respectable fashion. Although she performed all the household tasks well and was reliable, she was very boisterous and rebellious, which is not desirable in a newly married woman.

When a girl marries, she is fully in charge of her husband's household and has to obey her mother-in-law. She has years of hard work ahead of her until her own children are old enough to help with the chores. Her views will finally be heard and her wishes executed by others when her sons bring daughters-in-law into the family, who then take over the chores and serve her. When I first did fieldwork in Fouta in 2007, Fatoumata and Ndeye Sy had a lot of small children and most of the housework and cooking was done by them. They also had their mother-in-law's orders to obey. When I returned in 2019, each of them lived in a separate house that their husbands, who were brothers, had constructed for them. Their mother-in-law, whom I cherished very much during my first stay in 2007, had passed away. This meant that they were fully in charge as their husbands both worked hundreds of kilometers away in different parts of Senegal. When Ndeye Sy showed me her new house with lots of rooms that she called "my rooms," she said to me with an overjoyed expression on her face, "Sarah, now I do nothing. Absolutely nothing! The children do everything for me now. I have no more work to do."

Becoming a Man, Becoming a Breadwinner: "It Is Better To Go On Until Death Than to Sit Down in Shame"

For very young boys and girls the chores are the same. However, in the same way that girls around the age of eight participate more actively in housework, boys are charged with responsibilities outside the compound, running errands that are considered too risky or unsuitable for girls, such as fetching something from another village that requires them to walk for hours or running errands at night. In my host family in Diawoury there was a boy called Mamadou who was fourteen years old and went to secondary school in Toulde about eight kilometers away. He had a very old broken bike for a while, which he spent a great deal of time repairing, and he often ended up walking to school instead. The journey was long and tiring and he often did not eat anything all day. In addition, he was routinely asked to pick things up from places eight to twelve kilometers away, which also required him to go for a long time without food. If he did not get the jobs done because of tiredness or schoolwork, he would get into serious trouble as the elders relied on him to perform jobs that required responsibility, like carrying money or delivering important documents. He reasoned that although the girls had to help with the household, at least they got their meals regularly and did not have to walk long distances during the hottest hours of the day.

I also witnessed that if a roof needed to be repaired or scorpions killed, the boys would be called. Many boys were asked to accompany herds and search for livestock that escaped or got lost. Subalɓe boys also practice their fishing skills. Following livestock and fishing involve the risk of encountering potentially dangerous wildlife such as snakes, crocodiles, and hippos.[8] Boys' tasks therefore often require bravery.[9]

In terms of formal education, boys would also be encouraged to go to Qur'anic or state schools, whereas many parents would arrange for girls to leave school to stay at home once they reached puberty. This was because their help was required in the household and because state school was seen as potentially corrupting of girls' morals and virtues. A girl learns what she needs to know in life on the compound instead of at school, whereas a boy may benefit from learning things that will help him to get a better job than farming. Some uneducated men regret that their chances of employment are compromised by a lack of literacy that would qualify them for well-paid jobs in urban areas.

A young man is not considered a responsible adult until he marries and has a family to support. Furthermore, to be considered an honorable, important, and respected man (*jontaaɗo*) he needs to earn a good salary and be able to show his success by supporting as many members of the family and the community[10] as possible. To become someone whose opinion carries weight in the village community, he needs to either be a scholar of the Qur'an or earn a good salary and impress locals with his generosity and kindness. It is acceptable for him to stay away for months or even years to earn money; however, he cannot come back into the heart of the family if he has no money to bring home.

To take an interlocutor of mine as an example, Hamidou Ndiaye had been working for a local NGO for years. He started off as a simple teacher in the literacy program of an NGO, but, as he was a very ambitious man and a hard worker, he managed to work his way up and became one of the regional managers of the NGO's program in Kaolack, the center of Senegal about 1,000 kilometers (by road) from his home village of Waaltunde Colli. With promotions and increases in salary over the last couple of years, he has gained more and more consideration and respectability at home. His wife and fiancée both lived in his mother's compound and looked after the household and his children. Because of the distance, he could rarely go back, although he missed them dearly. In addition to the distance, the more respect he gained the less acceptable it was for him to go back if he did not have enough money to make his return an honorable one. At the end of the Ramadan celebrations in 2007, Hamidou could not go back to Waaltunde Colli despite the fact that he was incredibly lonely, homesick, and tired and had time off because it was a religious holiday. He had not managed to save enough money to distribute among the family and other relatives he had obligations toward. A return with empty hands would have been dishonorable. "*Yahde haa maaya buri joodaade haa hoya*," he said: It is better to go on until death than to sit down in shame.

Hamidou's case was not exceptional. Most men who worked for local NGOs or the council and were beginning to be highly respected could not return home just for one night while they were away working if they had nothing to take back to the family. Even if they were in the area, it was preferable to spend the night in the neighboring village than to come home with empty hands.

Relationships between men and women therefore are imagined in terms of the man being the breadwinner and providing for the family and the woman being in charge of the household. Women know that it is hard for their men not to be able to come home when they are away working. Yet for a man to come home with empty hands is not honorable. A man who cannot support his family is not a good husband and is undesirable. Although, according to this ideology, women merely wait for their husbands to return with food, money, and gifts, women actually spend a lot of time acting as producers by working on their farms, selling cooked food, ice, bissap juice, water, beans, corn, or milk at the market, and making a living to feed their children beyond their husband's support and without their income being acknowledged as a household contribution. According to the local ideology, divorced and widowed women should not remain unmarried for long to ensure that their children are well-fed and financially taken care of. In fact, women without husbands have a lot more freedom to move around, work, and trade than married women. Some find good jobs and become well-respected members of the community, as I explain later on.

Choice of Marriage Partner and the Family

A girl is not considered mature enough to choose her husband at what is seen as the age of marriage, between ten and twenty years. Although girls might be infatuated with the idea of being married to someone in particular, marriages between relations or allied groups (e.g., caste, friendship, parents' age group) are considered safer because these marriages are thought to be long-lasting. Choosing a partner in marriage is not a personal issue but concerns the future and respectability of the lineage. Even if husband and wife do not love each other passionately and may not satisfy each other intellectually, sexually, or personally, the bond that has been created through marriage, by bringing two families together, ensures that the marriage will be successful, rather than relying on passing emotions, which only last for a number of years and are not a solid basis for a household. An arranged marriage between kin groups is thought by many to secure the respectability and honor of the family and the bride. Furthermore, if the daughter-in-law is a relative chosen by the family, it is more likely that she will fit into the household well and that mother and daughter-in-law will get on, as there is already a strong bond of affection due to kinship between the two.

This ethos of being married to the right person is encapsulated in the proverb *Dewgal bonngal ɓuri innde bonnde*: a bad marriage is better than a bad reputation. Especially for the older generations, companionship or passion between husband and wife are not considered relevant. What matters is that their children are well brought up. Many women and men do divorce, which brings sadness to the family, and the women have to return to their parents' compound and secure financial means for themselves.

It is a young man's responsibility to make sure that his mother has enough support in the household from daughters-in-law and grandchildren. As soon as the sisters marry and leave, young men become conscious of the fact that their sisters' housework needs to be replaced by that of their own wives, who will live with their mother in the compound. This explains why it is hard for young men to refuse their mother's chosen daughter-in-law in marriage.

As a young man, Thierno Diallo loved indulging in Pulaar language, grammar, and poetry. He personally aspired to marry a woman whom he loved and who would stimulate him intellectually. However, his mother had chosen for him his maternal cousin in the neighboring village as a gesture of gratitude toward her father. Thierno refused, and continued following his intellectual passions and interests in Dakar with other Pulaar scholars while his mother was waiting for him to return to take her niece in marriage. After a year, Ramata, Thierno's mother, grew very upset—believing that her son had abandoned her. Eventually Thierno's older brothers, who had also given in to their mother's choice in wives, told him to come to his senses. They said that it was his duty to follow his mother's wishes and accept her chosen daughter-in-law. Begrudgingly, Thierno gave in, left his personal pursuits behind, and began to earn a living to support the family.

Dishonor and Shame

Notions of loss of honor and shame for a family are mostly provoked by incidents where it becomes known that a girl engaged in sexual relations before marriage or a married woman had sexual relations out of wedlock. For unmarried girls this may become known either through pregnancy before marriage or because a girl is found not to be a virgin on the wedding night. Both cases are devastating for the girl's family as this brings shame on them and the girl's reputation is ruined. In most cases pregnancy before marriage means that a girl cannot marry her parents' chosen groom, a respectable young man with whom a union would secure social standing and tie the families closer together. At such a respectable wedding, the praise singers (griots) would have sung in her honor and praised her lineage and reputation. The praise singers would have reminded the wedding guests of the groom's and the bride's distinguished ancestors and their unforgettable deeds. This would have made both the bride's and the groom's families proud and happy.

If a girl falls pregnant before marriage, the degree of dishonor very much depends on who the father of the child is. It is less grave if the father is of the same status group. In that case, marriage can be arranged once the child is born. For a noble girl it is extremely shameful if the father is of a lower status group. The worst-case scenario is if he belongs to the status group of slaves (Galluŋkooɓe/Maccuɓe). Not only is marriage between a noble woman (Dimo) and a man of skill (Ñeeño) unthinkable, but the child would be considered of inferior "pedigree" growing up in a noble household. Parents whose daughters are impregnated by a Galluŋke find this outrageous.

To make the indignation this might cause explicit, I was given an example in a Subalɓe village where the population consists of 80 percent Subalɓe and 20 percent Galluŋkooɓe. There are no other noble inhabitants. In this village lived a young and extremely attractive Galluŋke man who was sporty, charming, and very popular with the girls. One of the unmarried girls fell pregnant with his child, which infuriated the elders. They summoned a meeting to come to an agreement on how Galluŋkooɓe men who impregnate Subalɓe girls should pay for their crime. It was decided that a fine of CFA100,000 should be paid to the girl's family in compensation. Many young people in the village ridiculed this regulation because if a slave girl fell pregnant by a nobleman, which frequently happened, it was unthinkable that a compensation payment would even be offered.

I often heard people say that only thirty years ago it was rare to see girls raising illegitimate children in their parents' village. A girl who fell pregnant before marriage had to leave without further ado and never come back. She would flee to a distant relative or acquaintance far away, where no other villagers had acquaintances who could report back on the girl's life. She was forced to bring her child up there and perhaps marry a local man in this area. Families found this very sad as it meant losing a daughter or sister who was not able to marry her parent's chosen groom.

Nowadays a girl does not have to break off all contact with the family and vanish forever, but having a child before marriage still has consequences. When I returned to Weendouley in January 2010, I found that one of the girls in the family with whom I had spent much of my time was not there. I asked where she was because I missed her—she used to cheer everyone up and make me laugh while she was doing the housework. I was told that she had moved somewhere else. One day we were sitting in front of a boutique and she walked past with a baby tied on her back. Rather than greeting us loudly and warmheartedly as she would have done a year before, she seemed embarrassed, looked at the ground while shaking our hands, and walked on without exchanging much news. I said to my friends that I did not know she had had a baby and that I was happy for her. They replied that she was not married, which was why she had left her father's compound and lived with a relative. Although girls are not shunned for pregnancy before marriage as they used to be, they still bring shame on themselves and often have to leave their homes. In 2019, we were thrilled to see each other again. She was married to a cousin who is a local marabout and lived in the same neighborhood as her parents' compound. She showed me her house and introduced me to her husband. However, she didn't talk about the child she had in 2010 and I did not dare to ask.

Another woman I knew was married to a cousin who had spent the last twelve years in South Africa without returning. In 2015 she was raped by an older man. She got pregnant and was pained by the shame and the complete lack of support from the man who had fathered the child. She left her home and went to Ziguinchor, where no one knew her. She gave birth to a child who sadly died a few months later. She eventually returned to her family home, and the marriage with her husband continues. Although those closest to her know, no one speaks about this pregnancy any longer. Despite the fact that her husband has not returned in such a long time, divorce is unthinkable as it would upset the harmony of the larger family.

Rather than having to go through this humiliation, some seek other solutions. One is a clandestine abortion with a herb cocktail prepared by knowledgeable women. However, no one speaks of this publicly; these women are consulted secretly at night because if the abortion is discovered, the consequences are socially even more devastating than pregnancy before marriage. Abortion is condemned by religion and by society. There are also known cases of infanticide. I was told of a case that happened in the 1980s, when a dead newborn baby was found in the bush outside a village. The villagers were outraged and tried to find out whose child it was and who left it there. The mother was an unmarried girl who claimed that the baby was already dead when she left it. The case was referred to the police. According to the penal code, abortion is prohibited and those providing abortions or aborting their own pregnancies are liable to receive a five- to ten-year prison sentence. According to Western journalists, a large number of incarcerated women in Senegal were convicted for abortions or for infanticide.[11]

The consequences of a girl not being a virgin upon marriage are not so devastating. Nevertheless, if it becomes known to everyone in the village through gossip, it does bring shame on the girl and her family. To prevent this from happening, techniques have been developed by girls, their accomplices, and sometimes prospective husbands to pretend that the girl is a virgin. Most families proudly display the bloodstained sheet of the bride the morning after the wedding night, and the bride receives visitors in her bedroom for the rest of the day, displaying CFA10,000 banknotes the groom has attached to the bride's hair to show that he is pleased that he found her a virgin. If the groom knows that his bride is not a virgin but he wants to preserve the family honor, the couple may arrange for the sheets to be stained with the blood of a secretly slaughtered chicken. I have also heard of girls, eager that their grooms believe them to be virgins, placing a bag with animal blood or red liquid inside their vagina that bursts on penetration.

Even if some grooms do not object to their brides not being virgins, most grooms feel deceived if they only discover this on the wedding night. I have heard on various occasions that most marriages where this happens break up within a year, regardless of what the family thinks, because of loss of trust by the groom. It is said that he cannot be certain of her not lying to him again and of her not taking more lovers when he is away. A woman's self-restraint and control of sexual desire when her husband is away are crucial to her reputation and his.

Men feel loss of honor when they fail to be taken seriously by the local community due to their own misbehavior or the misbehavior of close kin. As I have explained, the more a person helps others and fulfills his or her obligations, the more recognition he or she receives from the community and the more likely he or she is to be considered a respectable, influential person. If a man's behavior is shameful, he loses recognition and is less likely to be consulted when decisions are made by elders or important family members. For some men, being denied a say in communal decisions because of their past misbehavior or display of weakness is so shameful that it is preferable to move elsewhere.

It is also said that a man's sexual behavior can reflect badly on his reputation and can result in him being considered a threat. For instance, I was told about a man called Ablaye who was known to have extramarital relations frequently. On one occasion the solar panels of the water pump outside his village were stolen and the villagers decided to patrol the village at night in order to catch the thieves. Everyone was instructed to stay in their homes unless urgent business required them to leave. Respectable men of the community could still move around if they explained where they were going and for what purpose. However, when patrolling villagers caught Ablaye walking through the village at night, they did not hesitate to beat him up because he had broken the curfew. Even though Ablaye was not a thief, the village security did not refrain from punishing him for breaking the agreement because his moral personhood was already compromised. Lack of honor can therefore lead to lack of respect and denial of rights.

Some people, especially close kin, consider it a grave matter if a man has a child before marriage or out of wedlock. However, I knew a few men who had children before marriage and this did not seem to reflect badly on their reputations—they were still considered honorable men. It seemed to be far more shameful if a man's wife conceived a child outside wedlock. It was unthinkable for the real father to recognize the child as his own—the mother's husband had to recognize the child as his own, even if he was not physically present during the period when the child was conceived and born. Such cases bring dishonor and sadness to the husband, the wife, and the child, who is not told who its real father is. I was told of a case where a young man resembled his biological father a great deal and was often mistaken for that man's son, instead of his mother's husband's. This was extremely embarrassing for him as well as his parents.

These examples may serve as justifications for the importance of control of desire and excision. The social consequences of a man having a child out of wedlock do not affect his professional life and long-term respectability to the same extent as women conceiving illegitimate children. Illegitimate children are somewhat less respected and have less status than those born in wedlock. While I was in Diawoury, two women named their daughters after me in my honor. One of the children was from a respectable Tooroodo family; the other was illegitimate. I was encouraged to go and see the legitimate little Sarah more than the illegitimate one. People would avoid mentioning the latter's existence. It seemed that her having been named after me did not count toward my honor to the same degree as the legitimate Sarah.

We can see that a man's honor can be more easily compromised through women's sexual misconduct than the other way round. A woman's upright behavior is what keeps Futanke society in order. The woman is the pillar of society, some marabouts told me. As long as her behavior is exemplary, the honor of the family remains intact. If she does not behave well, however, the consequences of her behavior affect her husband's as well as her children's and parents' reputations.

Ethnic Stereotypes and "Othering" Sexual Behavior

In interviews and conversations about control of desire with people all over Fouta Toro, I found that Futanke women's sexual containment and moral virtues were juxtaposed against the sexual behavior of women of other ethnic groups, who were known not to excise their daughters. In Senegal, Wolof women served as such an example, as well as women in other countries, such as Ivory Coast, Central Africa, and Angola. This view becomes explicit in my interlocutor Hame Sy's views on the control of sexual desire and the Wolof:

> *Sarah* The Wolof for example don't excise and guard their virginity until marriage. Guarding one's virginity until marriage doesn't necessarily depend on excision.
>
> *Hame* Yes, but the Wolof are not considered to be good women. They cannot control their sexual desire and they do not follow the rules of the religion. Have you seen the way they dance? Uhhhh!
>
> *Sarah* Yes.
>
> *Hame* The majority of the Peul in Fouta would say that the Wolof are not good people, they don't have honor. Dancing like that in public is not honorable. . . . A Peul would not trust a Wolof because they are not good people. All they do is follow the money. I would never trust a Wolof, they are criminals.

After I challenge the idea that excision controls desire because the Wolof, who do not excise, hold similar expectations as far as their respectability and sexual containment is concerned, Hame Sy reveals his beliefs on what he thinks are Futanke conceptions of this particular ethnic group. He thinks that Wolof women are sexually promiscuous based on the way they dance and that most Futanke would ascribe to the Wolof in general such characteristics as corruption, disloyalty, and dishonesty. The Wolof's dancing—by which he meant *mbalax*, as I gathered from subsequent conversations with him—clashes with the moral and social code of behavior in Fouta Toro, presumably because the dance involves a lot of hip rotation and sexual innuendo.

At the beginning of the chapter, I presented some Futanke women's ideas on the importance of control of desire that showed that unexcised women were thought to be physically incapable of staying faithful to their husbands. In the following we shall see how men explain the importance of excision:

> *Diop* The Prophet said that circumcision is an Islamic tradition. It is a sunna. Excision is the honor of a woman. I do not agree to abandonment as I have seen the importance of excision. There are more women than men on earth, to every boy born there are three girls [I questioned this fact and was told that in Fouta the women-men ratio is believed to be 3:1].[12] As far as

Islam is concerned, every man can have up to four wives. If
every man sufficed with only one woman—there would still be
another three women strolling through the streets. They are in
need of satisfaction as well. At the moment men emigrate too
much, they go away for six or seven years without coming
back. A man cannot sexually satisfy a woman. Even you know
it [*to me, laughing*]. A woman who is not excised cannot
control her sexuality. Even when she is asleep she thinks of sex.
Islam does not want adultery.

Sarah How do you know that unexcised women cannot control
their sexuality?

Diop I went to Ivory Coast and saw some unexcised ethnic groups.
Women prostitute themselves over there. Do you think
prostitution is a good thing?

(Marabout Diop in Wallé)

This marabout bases the need for excision on personal experience of living
in an un-Islamic African society. For him, Islam and excision ensure law and
order, which differentiates Fouta Toro from other places where this "order"
does not exist and women are more sexually enticing and promiscuous. Excision helps women control their sexual desires better, which is essential for
Islamic life—otherwise there would be chaos and social disarray, as the marabout makes clear by describing women strolling through the streets in search
of men to satisfy their desires. Although this might be the norm in other
societies, it is abhorrent to him when he considers Fouta Toro. This image of
what happens in big cities or among other ethnic groups haunts many Futanke minds. Similar views were expressed by a man I interviewed in Semme,
a village where many women had decided to stop practicing excision.

Oumar The practice of excision exists for the fidelity of the woman.
Those who want to abandon the practice are corrupt.

Sarah Does excision really increase the fidelity of the woman?

Oumar It diminishes a woman's sexual pleasure during sex so that
when her husband is traveling she can patiently wait for her
husband. If she is not excised, she cannot wait the way she
should.

Sarah Are women in countries where excision is not practiced less
faithful?

Oumar I lived in Angola for a few years and while I was working there I realized that women in other African countries search for men and for sex more than here in Fouta. In central Africa as well, I had conversations with women who cannot wait for more than six months for their husbands. During discussions with these women, I realized that they were amazed that women in Fouta have to go for six years without seeing their husbands. They could not understand how a woman could stay without sex for that long. This is why we are for excision. Excised women can wait for their husbands the way they should.

Again, experiences while traveling made Oumar believe that women in societies where excision is not practiced are different. He had also formed a negative image of what Futanke society would be like if women were not excised. In both examples we get a sense not just of men's fears that their wives will be unfaithful when they emigrate but also their perception of Futanke moral superiority and "civilization" in contrast to other ethnic groups.

In these discourses around the benefits of excision, Futanke women are put on a pedestal in terms of their moral superiority and capacity for controlling themselves in contrast to Wolof women, for example, whose dances are perceived as more sexually enticing and erotic. Excision thus renders a woman Futanke—a Fulɓe woman of Fouta Toro with the virtues and values embraced by its people. Many women refer to excision as a Pulaar custom and say that "If you see a Pulaar woman you can be sure that she is excised." And, "All Pulaar women are excised." Whether this belief is factually accurate or not is a different matter. What I want to underscore here is the idea that excision is perceived as an essential element of belonging and gender identity.

We therefore have an affirmation of what is seen as Futanke moral superiority built through a negative image of unexcised women from other ethnicities who lack civilization, morality, and proper Islamic practice.[13] The practice of excision defines a woman as virtuous and morally superior in contrast to those who do not follow the recommendations of the Prophet, who are seen as deficient in morals and reduced to the uncivilized barbaric state of human beings before civilization began with Islam.

The lawless, barbaric image of society ruled by brutish, self-interested individuals somewhat resembles Hobbes's image in *Leviathan* of what society is like without a "commonwealth." In the state of nature, man is driven by competition, envy, and glory. Like the stories I referred to at the beginning of the chapter about glorious men who stole other men's wives because they desired them, in Hobbes's image of society without the commonwealth, we would be in a condition of war "of everyone against everyone; in which everyone is governed by his own Reason" (Hobbes 2002:189). It follows that in such a condition, "every man has a Right to everything; even to one anothers body. And therefore, as long as this naturall Right of every man to every thing endureth, there can be no security to any man" (Hobbes 2002:190). However, the second natural law says that, to secure the advantage of peace and defense of himself, man is required "to lay down his right to all things; and be contented with so much liberty against other men as he would allow other men against himselfe. For as long as every man holdeth this Right, of doing any thing he liketh; so long are all men in the condition of Warre" (Hobbes 2002:190). Like the commonwealth for Hobbes, Islam brought peace, law, order, and civilization to Futanke society. In Chapter 5 we shall look at this juxtaposition of civilization through Islam and the foreign invasion represented by images of NGOs and the state that conjure up fears concerning a loss of culture.

The image of Futanke men and women constantly having to control themselves with regard to temptations that bring pleasure or to egotistical pursuits postulates a vision of human beings in constant search of personal gratification. Many Futanke are convinced that, without excision, their desired form of civilization would not be possible. Instead of social cohesion, morality, and culture, there would be fornication and dissidence. Marabout Souleyman Diop in Daande Lao, in May 2007, articulated the link between civilization and excision in the following way:

> A woman can be a source of all evil in society. She is at the center of society. Before Islam authorized marriage between men and women, if you saw a woman you liked you could take her if you were stronger than the man who was in charge of her. That does not exist anymore. Islam abolished these ancient customary practices. It is authorized that she should be excised because it is her honor. If a person loses their honor they[14] will gain a bad reputation. She will have no value whatsoever. A woman who remains unexcised is devalued in a way. An unmarried woman would be more prone to give herself to men. Sinner.

I initially found marabout Diop's first statement that women can be the source of all evil in society shocking as I assumed he meant that women are inherently evil. However, I came to understand that many men believe women to have the power to make men do things for them, even if they are not in the man's interest. There is a saying that there are three things in life a man should beware of: women, children, and money. All three things make a man lose his senses and do things that are irrational or harmful to others. Furthermore, it is said that most problems between men arise because of women. The proverb *Debbo yid, kono woto hoolo*, meaning "Love a woman but never trust her," is linked to the belief that most great men in Africa were brought down by seductive but malicious women. The source of all evil in society is therefore the passion and senselessness a woman can invoke in a man. However, Islam is believed to have enabled a solution to this problem because it brought an end to the chaos and anarchy of the past in which men were driven by their desire for women.

Most locals I spoke to held that men's desire was controlled through the sexual control of women. However, whereas women seemed to comply with this more for practical reasons, to save their daughters from ruining their future as respectable wives and mothers through the consequences of sex before marriage—men who were concerned with women's control of desire were riddled with fear of what their wives might get up to when they were away. I also found that rather than seeing women as in need of control and men being able to get away without having their sex drive controlled, men were far more concerned with the idea that sexual temptation outside marriage was linked to the devil. A man's lack of being able to control his sexual desire was linked to Satan seducing him to go to hell. The following example is illustrative:

Sarah Why is too much pleasure not good?

Ly Well, anything that gives human beings too much pleasure is dangerous. Because Satan always tries to persuade us to do things that are evil, that give us pleasure to take us off track so that we don't follow the religion. So we have to beware of any pleasures in life because Satan is trying to seduce us so that we go to hell.

[. . .]

Ly According to religion we should avoid all kinds of perversions and women in Senegal experience too much pleasure anyway. So much pleasure needs to be reduced.

Sarah What do you mean?

Ly Well, just the way of life in some parts of Senegal—in Dakar the way women behave, what they do, the way they dress, they just get carried away with pleasure. And that way of life is penetrating Fouta as well. Many people have ideas and conceptions that did not exist before, that they should not have because of the religion. The influence coming from Dakar is bad.

Sarah Hm. I see what you mean.

Ly There are many perversions in Dakar that are brought about by a different way of life. It's better to reduce women's pleasure to protect us from perversion.

This was one of the first conversations I had with Ly and he became a good friend. After many subsequent conversations it came out that he had had a very promiscuous past with sex workers in Nouakchott when he was a young man, which he felt bad about because of his religious faith. A decade later, when he was ready to have a family and choose a wife, it was important to him that she was a good woman who would not fall for the temptations of the devil. He believed this to be facilitated by excision. Men do not fall out of the parameters of control of desire but rather than being concerned with shame and social consequences—which do not affect men to the same degree as women—I found that they were worried about their own loss of control affecting their afterlife and evil coming over the society they live in and cherish.

As in most patriarchal societies, men's moral and social well-being is contingent on the extent to which women invoke desire in men. If men cannot control their desire within the boundaries of what is seen as legitimate, it is the fault of "evil" women or the incarnation of the devil in female form. Women, on the other hand, are concerned with their daughters' control of desire for their own safety and to prevent the consequences of pregnancy before marriage in a society where this is associated with shame and social disarray.

Desire and Civilization

In this chapter I have explored the ways in which excision is linked to the control of women's sexual desire in local discourses. I have argued that although structural inequality between men and women exists, it is not useful to think about relations between men and women in such terms if one seeks to understand the need for desire to be controlled. Yanagisako and Delaney's (1995) approach helps our understanding of how particular cultural concepts are naturalized as God-given or "given in nature" in a society. Considering how things are naturalized as cultural helps in observing how local people relate what they call desire to other concepts that have positive or negative connotations.

In Fouta Toro, desire, as in a singular individual's personal quest for sexual satisfaction, is not considered positive—on the contrary, any kind of behavior seeking personal gratification is considered barbaric and uncivilized. Moral personhood is intrinsically linked to the ability to control one's desires and go through the hardships of life with the ability to constrain one's personal needs and wants for the good of family and kin.

I have shown how girls and boys are taught from a young age the necessity of serving and obeying elders rather than pursuing their personal interests and passions—which in turn provides them with the certainty that they can rely on others' help if in need. Being able to rely on the support of relations—whether that relationship is through kinship ties or solidarity between age sets—represents a form of social security that requires strict subjugation to the rules. Those who refuse to participate in this social arrangement are considered not to be moral persons and are said to be "not like us" or "not Futanke" or "not Pulaar." A person who does not adhere to this moral code of behavior is therefore outside the boundaries of what the Haalpulaar of Fouta Toro identify with. Other ethnic groups, who are not concerned with the control of their needs to the same degree or in the same way, are perceived as less moral and civilized than the Futanke. A society without excision conjures up fears of perversion and temptation, illustrated with references to women not behaving in an appropriate manner, dressing and dancing differently, and getting "carried away with pleasure."

We have seen how women can bring shame on themselves and their families through their sexual behavior. The consequences of sex before marriage are not just devastating for the girls, who will no longer be trusted and respected by their kin, and unable to pursue the marriages their family want. Although men can lose social recognition through their sexual behavior, a woman's lack of control of her sexual desire does not just concern herself but risks bringing shame and sadness on her husband, parents, in-laws, and children because the place of a child resulting from sex out of wedlock is compromised in Futanke society. Most mothers therefore do not want to run the risk of this happening and so prefer to help their daughters by excising them.

Desire is therefore not seen as an enjoyable pursuit of personal pleasures but a threat to social harmony.

For some, Futanke values and culture are already penetrated by outside influences associated with sexual libertarianism and fornication. Stopping excision represents a threat to moral propriety and the possible disintegration of Futanke culture due to foreign ideas that are permeating Fouta Toro. I will come back to the role of marabouts in the abandonment movement in the final chapters of the book, but I want to emphasize here the relationship between the image of safety and social harmony that excision seems to represent, in contrast to the fornication, lack of civilization, and sadness that, for many, accompany the idea of stopping the practice.

CHAPTER 4

Pleasure, Desirability, and Purity

> If uncleanness is matter out of place, we must approach
> it through order. Uncleanness or dirt are that which
> must not be included if a pattern is to be maintained.
> (Douglas 1966:50)

This chapter is about pleasure and the boundaries of appropriate sociality. It is about what draws people close and pushes them away without words or action, what people find attractive and desirable or repulsive—the thin layers of familiarity and difference between people with which our senses nourish us. For many of us it is hard to give in to desires if we perceive the object of our desire as impure or unclean. In this chapter I am concerned with what the Futanke perceive as desirable and attractive and how their ideas of the unexcised body trigger feelings of repulsion.

In the previous chapter I argued that excision creates the physical foundations for female moral personhood. A girl cut at a young age is believed not to develop the uncontrollable sexual appetites that an unexcised woman will. I have also shown that failure to control desire is associated with a lack of decorum for Futanke, and a mark of their own moral superiority over other ethnic groups who are "known" to be more promiscuous, less sexually contained, and less civilized. On this basis, one might assume that sexuality in general is seen as something evil, and giving in to desire a sign of the human weakness of flesh. Yet, the enjoyment of sex within the legitimate realms of marriage is encouraged in Fouta Toro and is fostered using sexual stimulants and aphrodisiacs. These practices are not seen as having come into Fouta from the outside but are embraced as customary (*aada*) and existing since the beginning of the universe (*gila dawaa dawi*). Older women are experts who tease and instruct the young ones on marriage.

I observed that many women in Fouta Toro take pride in the art of charming their husband into having sex with them through aphrodisiacs and stimulants. They do not perceive themselves as mutilated, as the Senegalese law defined excised women when outlawing female genital mutilation. On the contrary, many women expressed abhorrence at the image of unexcised women whose genitals they considered to be mutating into repulsive impure growths that get in the way, not just in childbirth but also during sex.

The first part of the chapter focuses on how pleasure and desire are fostered. We then look at the ways in which boundaries of appropriate sexuality are demarcated and how sexuality is located within the realms of what is socially desirable. I show that there are practices undertaken to render oneself pure again after sexual intercourse, without which social interaction is inappropriate. Although we have explored women's role as markers of the boundaries between "them" and "us," we have not discussed the conception of religious purity on which appropriate everyday sociality depends and which concerns women and men.

Marriage and the Enjoyment of Sex

Enjoyment of sex within the realm of marriage is encouraged and fostered. Outside marriage, women have to keep sexual experiences secret. The best way to convey how sexuality is celebrated and made public on marriage and kept quiet outside of wedlock is to draw on my experiences as an unmarried woman on my arrival and how this changed when I married.

As I have shown in previous chapters, a girl who has kept her virginity until marriage is highly respected in Futanke society. It is taboo for her to speak of any sexual experiences in public. Openly admitting to having lost one's virginity before marriage is shameful, and unmarried women are talked of as if they were virgins, even if it is unlikely that they are. As in Mali, even when a girl is found not to be a virgin on marriage, the family is often in denial and pretends that marriage expectations were met (Diallo 2004:177). Instead of openly admitting to no longer being a virgin, the bride and her parents are congratulated in public through songs and compliments. However, this is possible only if the bride has not had any children before wedlock (Diallo 2004:177).

When I arrived in Diawoury, it was assumed that I was a virgin (*mboomri*), and I was treated like the other unmarried girls in the household. It was extremely shocking to people if I was seen outside the compound of my host family after dusk. When I did go out and was seen with men, the women in my family would show disapproval of my behavior on my return. They did not fear just that I might lose my virginity but also that my behavior might jeopardize their reputation in the village, as they and others considered them to be my guardians. It apparently did not occur to them to ask me whether I really was a virgin, but their behavior showed concern about my personal safety, since being publicly exposed as not being a virgin and being unmarried would have reflected badly on my reputation as a responsible, respectable person. Whenever I did speak to anyone who inquired about my marital status, of past boyfriends or sleeping arrangements, sexuality and intimacy in Europe, I was told that such talk would bring dishonor on me and potentially on my guardians. Linguistically, unmarried women and virgins are the same: mboomri. Unmarried women are treated like virgins, and girls have to conform to a comportment insinuating virginity; failure to respect this code of behavior dishonors the girl and her guardians.

Beyond the presumption that unmarried women/virgins need protection, they are treated as if they know nothing about sexual pleasure. This is because women and men who engage in sexual relations before marriage have to do so secretly without the things that are considered to make sex good and satisfying—the aphrodisiac, the chains of beads women wear around their stomach to excite their husbands (*binbin*), and the erotic underskirts (*njodom*) that people associate strongly with marital sex and pleasure.

During my fieldwork, older women spoke to me as if I knew nothing about life, pleasure, and duty as I was not yet married. They often jokingly insinuated what was waiting for me when I married. This was particularly the case if I remarked on the lovely smell of incense in their bedrooms or teased them about their binbins. Besides being a sexual stimulant due to their clacking sound, wearing these beads shows that a woman is sexually interested because the sound is seductive to men. When women's husbands were not around it was not appropriate for them to wear binbins or to burn aphrodisiac incense (*cuuray*) in their bedrooms. Habi Sarr, a close relation of my teacher who lived on another compound in Diawoury, was a middle-aged lady who had about eight children and was known to joke and tease young women and men in a sexual way. As her compound was closely linked to my family's and she was "our" grandmother's daughter, I spent a lot of time with her, her husband, and her children. She often teased me when I remarked on her lovely-smelling gowns (*boubou* or *wutte*), saying that the day I married I was going to encounter a huge surprise. With sounds and gestures she crudely imitated what my husband would do with the binbins when I wore them on my wedding night. Initially confused about what I perceived as the contradictions within this conservative society, which did not allow me to go out at night and assumed that I was a virgin with a reputation to lose, I was not sure how to react to such vulgar depictions of sexual acts and explicit advice. I laughed and was left perplexed.

Habi's teasing of unmarried young people for knowing nothing about life or sexuality indicates the difference that people in Fouta Toro perceive between the childlike ignorance of sexual pleasure on the part of an unmarried woman and married adult life where women (*ceemeedo*) and men are encouraged to enjoy sex. Whereas premarital sex is shrouded in silence and regarded as shameful and dangerous, marriage represents a transition to adult life, the taking on of responsibility, the running of the household, and indulgence in corporal pleasures.

After I married, women, particularly of older generations, began to tease me, asking if I had learned their customary room preparations with aphrodisiac incense (cuuray) and the *petits pagnes* (njodom), which are loin cloths with holes in them believed to arouse men. Some women sent me presents of incense; others showed me how to sprinkle the incense, made of African spices, over hot ashes and explained how else I could make the sheets and clothes smell nice. When I was seen walking down the village paths with bowls of hot coals for cuuray or with other utensils, women cheered and told me that I was doing well, learning their customs, and surely my husband would be very satisfied.[1] If women found out in the mornings that I had not burnt any incense the previous night, or had forgotten to wear the binbins, they looked worried. It did not make sense to them why I was so slack in preparing what they perceived would make sex good. They were concerned that if I did not perform these customs correctly, my husband might not be satisfied and that I risked losing him. Besides making me aware of my duties, the emphasis in many conversations with women was on learning how to use these sexual stimulants.

I do not want to imply that my experiences were similar to a Futanke girl's. Moreover, I was spared most of the duties of a newly married woman (*jombaajo*). However, these examples serve to illustrate the importance of sexual pleasure, and its enjoyment, to Futanke women and men. I suggest that despite the existing measures of control that are taken to ensure chastity in women, the enjoyment of sex (*ngende*) and expression of desire through the use of these utensils in the legitimate realms of marriage are not taboo in Fouta Toro. A wife's and a husband's failure to satisfy one another sexually can be a reason for divorce.

Diallo (2004) also discusses the seeming contradiction between excising women in Mali to take their pleasure away and simultaneously enhancing pleasure of married couples through sexual stimulants. She argues that in Mali, marriage imposes sexual duties on a woman. Some say that, "In general, wives' sexuality is based on values and practices that aim primarily at satisfying their spouses' needs" (Diallo 2004:182). Western conceptions of marital rape are laughed at because it is a woman's duty to give herself to the man. However, Diallo adds that marriage provides women with a right to sexual fulfillment (2004:182). Women request and enjoy sexual intercourse in perfect harmony with religious and customary requirements.

I encountered mixed views about sex being an obligation or a right during marriage. Some women evidently enjoyed making themselves desirable and motivating their husbands to have sex with them. Men react strongly to the smell of incense. I heard men say that the smell of cuuray "calls the husbands home and into the bedroom." According to local discourse, the smell of cuuray is irresistible to men. I witnessed various occasions when a woman strongly smelled of cuuray, was dressed beautifully, walked slowly, and spoke gently, and men would say, "she wants to kill him tonight," referring to the way in which she invoked desire. Although I showed in the previous chapter that women do not express their desire in words, making themselves desirable for their own man and seducing him is considered the art of Futanke women by many. Other women I met enjoyed sex less and performed the bedroom preparations only occasionally, reluctantly, or as a response to social pressure rather than personal enjoyment.[2]

Diallo (2004) writes about the role of the *magnonmakan* on a girl's marriage in Mali. The magnonmakan is an elderly woman who advises the virgin bride on how to give pleasure to a man, or helps an already sexually active bride to improve her sexual performance. Besides advising on the preparation of the bedroom, she prepares special drinks made of roots and plants that are known for their aphrodisiac effect (Diallo 2004:177). Although I have not heard of such experts being involved in marriage preparations in Fouta Toro, there certainly are experts on aphrodisiac tinctures who can be called on by men and women. Men consult these experts if they suffer from impotence, or to improve their sexual performance. Women seek their help if they are worried about infertility or to ask for products that lubricate the vagina if they suffer from dryness that makes sexual intercourse painful.

Besides the experts that are consulted in cases of emergency, the aphrodisiac effect of different types of food often comes up in everyday conversation. I witnessed on numerous occasions during mealtimes how men praised the strengthening effect of yam. They claimed that it helped them to keep an erection at night. Similarly, expressing a taste for ginger juice is associated with liking its aphrodisiac effect. Such conversation often produces jokes and laughter at meal times, despite unmarried people being present. I also observed on various occasions people laughing when white volunteers bought dried roots at the market in Ourosogui to put into drinking water to improve its taste. Men laughed, asking these women who they were waiting for at nighttime. To locals these roots are known to have a lubricating effect on the vagina.

So far I have discussed how people talk about and prepare for sexual activities in the realms of the legitimate. None of what I have presented above is taboo or makes people feel uncomfortable; it is part of everyday sociality and banter. However, people also joke about what happens in the realms of the forbidden at nighttime when no one can see. In contrast to the ways in which sexual pleasure is enhanced without much concealment during marriage, the ways in which unmarried lovers meet each other are secret but also known to people. Although it is not possible to admit having lovers, people gossip about what happens at night and who has been seen wandering down the village paths in the moonlight.

Secret Encounters in the Dark

Sexual relations also take place in the sphere of the forbidden (*haram*), the secret (*suturo*), and, if made public, the shameful (*gacce*).

When the moon waxes, everything becomes visible in the dark and villages without electricity in rural Fouta are lively and animated.[3] Children roam through the village playing. They can be heard running along the village paths singing, cheering, and laughing everywhere. Adults take pleasure in sitting outside in the moonlight drinking tea, listening to the radio, and visiting each other. Evenings at full moon are a time when people relax, all the housework has been done, the heat of the day has disappeared, and people socialize. In 2019, more houses had electricity, and the TV attracted a lot of young people from neighboring houses to visit to watch popular soap operas. But not everyone watches TV. I was lying outside under the stars with Fatoumata and Fama Ly, like we used to, chatting in the absence of our husbands. Despite the fact that some households now have electricity and light, the village tracks are not lit up, and the light is turned on only when needed,[4] for instance, in the early evening when schoolchildren are doing homework or when dinner is served. But adults still like to sit outside in the evening breeze with the lights off.

During my fieldwork in 2007, girls of a certain age were not allowed to leave the compound at night; their friends had to come and see them and they played in the far corners of the compound, visible to their parents' eyes. This was because no one could be sure what they might get up to in the dark and no one wanted to risk them falling pregnant before marriage. When the moon wanes, the village quiets down and children and young people are discouraged from going out. It is said, however, that this is the time when lovers go and see each other because no one will be able to recognize them in the dark. These lovers could be unmarried men and women or married men and women and it would be very shameful for any of them to be caught. People sometimes jokingly accuse each other of having been seen walking down the village paths at night. The connotation is that they are going to see the secret lovers whom they cannot see throughout the day. To some extent these jokes may point to a sphere of secret activity that exists. For others it may just be a fantasy of things they dare not do because they are forbidden.

There are widespread legends in Senegal that Pulaar wives receive lovers in their bedrooms when their husbands are away. It is said that this is why Fulɓe men (herders) always carry knives—in case they find a man in their wife's bed when they return home late at night. The men then fight and the stronger kills the weaker, without losing his honor. According to these myths, the wife would never be blamed for having committed adultery, and men secretly take pride in their wives being desirable to other men.[5] However, they see it as a matter of masculine honor and strength to kill the other. None of the Subalɓe men I knew during my fieldwork carried knives, and it would be extremely shameful for adulterers to be caught out in that way, which would lead to dishonor and eventually divorce. The Subalɓe and Tooroɓɓe I knew think that these practices only exist among nomadic Fulɓe herders who carry knives.

Despite the strict morality that exists about legitimate and illegitimate sex and all the measures that are taken to control desire through excision and observing women, myths of the secret practices of Fulɓe women, and jokes about having been spotted walking through the village at night, point toward a fear of lovers seeking each other's company in the dark. Although romantic encounters and enjoyment of sexual pleasure can only be openly talked about and made public if a couple are married, jokes about forbidden encounters in the moonlight point to the fact that sex in the realms of the secret and the illegitimate is also present in people's minds. Some may fear what would happen if women were not controlled. Others fantasize about what they would like to do but dare not. Some may seek their lovers in the dark. In any case, these encounters are forbidden. Personal stories only shared with closest friends or shrouded in silence are the material of which legends and jokes are made.

Purity and Sociality

In this section I am concerned with other ways in which boundaries of appropriate sexuality are demarcated. We shall look at the ways in which sexual activity takes place in the realms of the clean and the pure. I show that there are practices undertaken to render oneself pure again after sexual intercourse, without which social interaction is inappropriate. We will also examine how perceptions of what is impure and what is clean in everyday sociality are related to excision and circumcision.

Impurity and uncleanliness are called laɓaani in Pulaar, which is the negation of the word laɓɗe—to be clean or pure in a spiritual as well as a material sense. Laɓaani is used for uncleanliness in terms of religious impurity (see below), as well as for dirt, such as a child that has a dirty mouth or a dirty mat or a dirty bowl of food. The other Pulaar term for unclean and impure is soɓe, which can also have spiritual connotations. In French, laɓaani and soɓe are both translated as impure and pas propre.

Why is it that people in Fouta Toro turn up their noses at the idea of an unexcised girl? I heard activists against the practice say that their mothers sometimes were not as warm and loving toward their unexcised granddaughters as they were with the excised ones. This was to do with purity. I, too, witnessed Demba Sow, Habi Sarr's husband, asking his granddaughter not to sit on his prayer mat because she had not yet been excised. Unexcised girls are sometimes emotionally rejected not just because of the women they will become but for reasons to do with a form of purity and cleanliness that is necessary for appropriate social interaction.

This form of purity is linked to Islamic ablutions. These ritual washings are a meditative preparation for prayer. Anything sinful that has been seen, heard, felt, or thought since the last prayer is washed away so that the believer can address himself to God in a way that is perceived as pure. Purifying washings are called *sallige* in Pulaar. For devout Muslims, male or female, the day begins with the first prayer, *Salaatu*, at 5:00 a.m., before dawn. Thereafter, *Tisubaar* is performed at 2:00 p.m., *Takkusaan* at 5:00 p.m., *Futuro* at dusk, and *Geeye* about an hour after Futuro. These prayers are said to be compulsory. Many devout Muslims in Fouta Toro also perform a prayer called *Wolluha* at 11:00 a.m., which is not compulsory. Before each of these prayers, a small ablution (*sallige*) needs to be performed. This consists of washing one's hands and arms, the mouth, the nose, the eyes, the top of the head, the ears, and the feet with water. If a person has had sexual intercourse, the whole body needs to be washed according to a particular procedure called *lootngal janaaba*, beginning with the genitals, then the loins and thighs, hands and arms, mouth, nose, eyes, top of the head three times, and the ears. Then, the body is divided into two. The right-hand side of the body is washed first following the procedure described for sallige, finishing off with the feet. Then the left-hand side of the body is washed. These washings need to be performed with pure water, meaning water without soap or any other contents or additives. If a person has not performed these ablutions after sexual intercourse, they are not clean enough to address themselves to God. Even when a person was merely aroused, as soon as liquid is excreted from the genitals, lootngal janaaba needs to be performed, according to religion. Men and women are both subject to the same procedure after sexual intercourse or arousal; however, in addition, women also need to practice lootngal janaaba after their periods and to end the period of sexual abstinence forty days after having given birth. Men have to practice these long ablutions on Fridays before going to pray at the mosque as well, even if they have not had sexual intercourse throughout the week.

Most Futanke men and women therefore constantly assess their own purity and practice purifying ablutions before addressing themselves to God.

At prayer time, people often pass around the water jug (*satalla*) and do sal-lige in front of each other before they pray together. The small ablutions are therefore performed very publicly and people notice if someone does not do ablutions. Being impure (laaɓaani) is considered inappropriate. If there is no water available, it is preferable to refrain from sexual activities until there is water, as not being able to pray at prayer time because of impurity is very em-barrassing. It is not appropriate to interact with people before having ren-dered oneself pure. I therefore suggest that religious purification through ablutions does not just serve a spiritual purpose but has also become a code of social decency and cleanliness without which social interaction is inappropriate.

My male interlocutor Ba explained how excision and circumcision are linked to purity in the following way:

> The Prophet wanted all men to be circumcised, and the same
> applies to women in order for them to undertake prayer. Because for
> example, there is a white liquid under the foreskin before a man is
> circumcised and that is dirty and smells bad. It prevents a man
> from being able to undertake prayer in a way that is appropriate
> because all human beings have to be pure before addressing
> themselves to God. So it needs to be cut for the man to be pure
> because too much dirt would collect under his foreskin so that he is
> never clean when performing prayer. The same applies to women.
> Women too excrete this white liquid around the clitoris that makes
> them impure and prevents them from being able to undertake
> prayer, at least not with the same purity, so just a little bit of the
> clitoris needs to be cut off. Not all of it, just a third. That is what
> the Prophet recommended. It needs to be undertaken so that the
> woman can pray with the appropriate purity, just like the man
> needs to be circumcised because of this inappropriate impure white
> liquid. (Diawoury, March 2007)

Circumcision is about being able to address oneself to God with appropriate physical cleanliness, which is perceived to ensure spiritual sanctity. The be-lief that a circumcised man is cleaner than an uncircumcised man, and that the latter cannot address himself to God with the same purity, is trans-ferred to women. However, the circumcision of a man is not associated with the control of sexual desire, it is merely thought to reduce the amount of bodily fluids that need to be washed away through ablutions. According to local religious discourse, ablutions are merely a preparation for prayer, to be able to address oneself to God after a purifying procedure described in the Qur'an. Ablutions are not supposed to make someone a better or more spiritual person—they are said to render a person clean for prayer.

For women, however, the implications are different. Many people feel that for unexcised women, it is not just about the amount of bodily excretion washed away through ablutions but also about how much more "impure liquid" is produced. I was told on numerous occasions that it is practically impossible for a woman to cleanse herself of impurities if she is not excised. This is because her clitoris is constantly stimulated by her underwear or the cloth of her skirt (*pagne*), which means that she is sexually aroused and excretes this impure white liquid. In the same way that she cannot address herself to God with the purity of an excised woman—because she cannot help but think of sex more than is appropriate—she is considered dirtier in everyday life as well. This was why many marabouts to whom I spoke said that it was inappropriate for an unexcised woman to do housework and look after children. This liquid did not just inhibit praying with an appropriate standard of purity but also meant that she soiled others with whom she was interacting throughout the day.

Some people show disregard for unexcised women because they fear their uncontrollable lust; some feel repulsed by them because they are thought of as dirtier. Local discourses on cleanliness and dirt, whether rooted in concerns about sexual control, preservation of group identity, purity, or social decency, have become embodied in people's physical reactions to bodily practices that do not conform to this order (Foucault 1975; Douglas 1966). Bourdieu's concept of "bodily *hexis*" is helpful for thinking about how particular social and cultural values become embodied in local discourse as well as people's emotional reactions to practices that are not part of the local habitus: "Bodily *hexis* is political mythology realized, *em-bodied*, turned into a permanent disposition, a durable manner of standing, speaking, and thereby of *feeling* and *thinking*" (Bourdieu 1977:93–94). Bourdieu suggests that particular "cultural" principles are embodied beyond the grasp of consciousness and "hence cannot be touched by voluntary, deliberate transformation, cannot even be made explicit" (1977:94). Many of these principles are *doxa*, part of Bourdieu's concept of "the universe of the undiscussed and undisputed," which are only ever fully revealed when they do become subject to discussion and are confronted by competing discourses (1977:168) The questioning of what is taken for granted (doxa) is brought about by "culture contact," which brings the undiscussed into discussion and the unformulated into formulation and can potentially lead to crisis (1977:168). The crisis is "when the social world loses its character as a natural phenomenon" (1977:169) and the conventional character of social facts can be questioned. Bourdieu argues that crisis is a necessary condition for a questioning of doxa but is not in itself a sufficient condition for the production of critical discourse (1977:169).

Mary Douglas's analysis of purity and pollution makes the visceral reaction to what is perceived as "dirt" or "smell" more explicit. She argues that purity and dirt are intrinsically linked to the categories of the beholder. The world is divided into things that smoothly fit into these categories, and those ambiguous things that are categorized as either-or. Ambiguity is unpleasant (Douglas 1966: 46). Anomalous things are dangerous (1966: 49) and can cause anxiety. We could therefore argue that Douglas's "ambiguity" and "abnormality" are what represent crises to Bourdieu's doxa. The emotional reaction is shock and discomfort, disbelief, and sometimes anger.

Douglas argues that

> dirt is essentially disorder. There is no such thing as absolute dirt: it exists in the eye of the beholder. If we shun dirt, it is not because of craven fear, still less dread of holy terror. Nor do our ideas about disease account for the range of our behaviour in cleaning and avoiding dirt. Dirt offends order. Eliminating it is not a negative movement, but a positive effort to organise the environment. [. . .] In chasing dirt, papering, decorating, tidying, we are not governed by anxiety to escape disease, but are positively re-ordering our environment, making it conform to an idea. There is nothing fearful or unreasoning in our dirt avoidance: it is a creative movement, an attempt to relate form to function, to make unity of experience. (1966:2–3)

If we use Douglas's interpretation as a lens through which to think about Futanke notions of cleanliness that are believed to be achieved through ablutions and circumcision, what is it that is positively made and created? What kind of dirt are people in Fouta clearing from their society and what society is being positively created? We shall explore this further in the following section on images of unexcised women's androgynous bodies and what happens during childbirth.

Repugnance and Shame:
The Aesthetics of the Unexcised Body

We are revolted by something because it disagrees with our conceptions of what is normal or aesthetically pleasing. Disagreement with the unexcised body is to some extent linked to notions of social decency as I explained above, but it also constitutes a rejection of its physical appearance: the idea of an impure growth resembling a penis between a woman's legs. The image of the rabbit ears that we explored previously is evocative. The androgynous body of an unexcised woman is anomalous (Douglas 1966). It is different, ambiguous (Douglas 1966), something to be ashamed of. I suggest that these images of what an unexcised girl's clitoris will grow into encourage many mothers to excise their daughters. On the one hand, these images are repulsive to them personally; on the other hand, they do not want to expose their daughters to the shame of growing something impure and ugly between their legs. What is undesirable to mothers is also believed to be undesirable to men, as the following extract taken from an interview with, Juulde, a middle-aged woman in Sinthiou Sebbe on February 8, 2008, conveys:

> If a girl is not excised, her clitoris will continue growing, like the girl's body is growing. Her vagina will not be big enough to facilitate penetration by her husband. And when she gets ready to have a baby, when she is pregnant, her clitoris will split into two, which can cause the tissue to tear. When a man wants to sleep with a girl and he realizes while touching her that she is not excised, he will abandon her because he will be afraid that her clitoris will cut his penis. The clitoris can cut a man's sex [tergal][6] and hurt him if he is not careful and touches it with his own sex. So men are afraid to sleep with unexcised women. If a girl is not excised, there can be little grains that collect around her sex everywhere and all the way into the vagina.

The ambiguous, unexcised genitals clearly convey images of danger, impurity, and potential disease as well as the threat of being sexually rejected by a man for Juulde. We are already familiar with the idea that the clitoris splits into two when a girl is fully developed. In addition, Juulde believes that the clitoris may cut a man's penis. I have heard other people express similar ideas. Although evidently not all men fear their penis will be cut if they have intercourse with an unexcised woman, such myths are common in Futanke discourses.

Fears of disease and impurity suggest that people perceive the unexcised woman as being "other" because she is different, unknown, unpredictable, and ugly. She may cause harm, which is why she is rejected. More specific examples follow.

Rabbit Ears and Childbirth

It is the evening after our visit to Awa Diallo's house. Samba Sarr, his wife Fama Ly, Seydou, and I are lying under blankets on the veranda of their mud-brick house in the dark, before going to bed. It is a cold and clear January night. Samba and I recall what the exciser said about an unexcised woman growing rabbit ears and laugh about the image she has put into our heads. None of us has heard anything like that before. Fama Ly and Samba talk to each other; I temporarily drift away from their conversation until Samba and Seydou suddenly burst into laughter. Fama Ly has just said that an unexcised woman's clitoris gets in the way when she is in labor. The clitoris and the labia need to be tied around the back of her bottom with a piece of string so that they don't get in the way when women are giving birth. Samba says to his wife,

> "Do you really believe that, Fama Ly?"
> "Yes. That is what women say. That is what I have heard happens when a woman is not excised. The exciser said that the rabbit ears need to be tied back so that they are not in the way when a woman is in labor and I have never questioned it."

Samba has been telling his wife to stop having their daughters excised for years, but she will not agree. All the girls are excised, and in this social environment it would be strange if someone refused. Besides, Samba's mother is a strong defender of the practice because it makes a woman "cleaner." While Seydou and I continue laughing, Samba tells Fama Ly not to believe everything people say. Fama Ly is my friend. We have spent a lot of time together and joke a lot. I have met her brothers and sisters and her mother, who live in the neighboring village. I also had met her father, who died half a year before. The pictures of him that I took during our first visit are greatly cherished. Fama Ly has never been further away from home than to the main road in Weendouley, about 10 kilometers away. She did not go to school, does not speak any French, and has hardly watched television. When I first arrived in Diawoury she asked me if we cook with firewood or charcoal in Europe and was surprised to see that I was not used to carrying water or performing household chores. She had never seen a creature like me. But she helped me, and my need to communicate with her forced me to learn Pulaar quickly. I admire her for the hard work she does in the household and I often take her side against my teacher, who I know can be very severe. I say,

> I am not surprised that women insist on excising their daughters if this is what they think happens if they are not excised. I would excise my daughters as well if I believed that their clitoris would grow like rabbit ears one day that need to be tied back when my daughter is in labor. If this was what I heard from other women and did not know anything else I would not want to leave my daughter unexcised.

Fama Ly gets up, while Seydou is laughing and Samba continues telling her to stop believing such things. Fama Ly's expression of disgust is visible in the moonlight—caused both by being told off by her husband and the image of letting her daughters grow rabbit ears. She spits on the floor.
I ask Fama Ly in a joking manner,

> "Excision is good?!"
> "Yes, it's good. Do you think it's good?" She replies.
> "No, it's not good.[7] Why should it be good?" I say.
> Fama says, "Why shouldn't it be good?"

I don't answer. Fama Ly continues more seriously:

> "It's a custom we have practiced since the ancestors."

I reply:

> "It doesn't hurt?" Fama Ly and I have had this conversation many times before this one but I am bringing it up again for the sake of the discussion.

"Noo," Fama Ly says soothingly. "It's done when the girls are just
little children. It doesn't hurt. It doesn't do any harm at all."

I say,

"Do you think people will abandon one day?"
"I don't know what people will decide," she replies. "At the moment
everyone practices. If everyone decides to abandon it, then maybe
yes, if it is in God's will. If everyone sees a reason to stop, maybe,
but at the moment everyone practices and we have not seen any
reasons to give up the practice.'

It is getting late. We continue conversing about other things until we go inside the house to sleep.

* * *

Fama Ly's sense of repulsion is based on the thought of what an unexcised
woman's body might look like, how the genitals might mutate into ugly-
looking rabbit ears, and how embarrassing this situation might be during
childbirth. She rejects the image of her daughters being different and exposing themselves to ridicule. Excision has proven itself because it has been practiced for a long time, as she affirms by mentioning that it has existed "since
the ancestors." Stopping the practice, however, would mean leaving girls' genitals to grow into something that is unknown, not just morally ambiguous
and potentially dangerous, and possibly exposing unexcised girls to embarrassing situations where they might be stigmatized.

In the following conversation we return to the idea that unexcised women
are impure and how this might be potentially embarrassing.

Ngoura Sy, President of the Ex-Exciser Association

Being the president of the ex-exciser association, Ngoura receives visits
from researchers who want to interview her about the practice as well as
from NGOs who ask her to mobilize other ex-excisers for sensitization activities. When I arrived at her house in February 2008, she asked me to write
down who I was in a visitors' book, what I was researching, and with what

organizations I was affiliated. I noticed the names of familiar researchers in
her book. She also expected me to give her a sum of money in return for an
interview, which rarely happened in Fouta Toro. Despite her unusual profes-
sionalism, which many Futanke would perceive as calculating and rude, she
was friendly and helpful, although careful. Ngoura Sy was a Tooroodo woman
but said that she used to cut anyone regardless of their caste and background.
Like the other excisers, she had learned the skill from her mother at an early
age. In her teens, she trained as a midwife at a hospital and turned against
the practice of excision as a result of the problems she saw excised women
going through during childbirth. When her mother was getting old, Ngoura
asked her to stop practicing. But her mother replied, "I cannot stop as long
as you have not taken up the practice." Although Ngoura felt that there were
risks and she had already started her training as a midwife, she decided to
take up the practice so that her mother could retire. Years later she became
the founder of the ex-excisers association. Although Ngoura is a well-known
activist against the practice, she expressed similar views to the excisers cited
in Chapter 3, that excised women are unclean and the growth of the clitoris
resembles "rabbit ears." When I asked her why excision was practiced, she
replied in the following way:

> *Ngoura* Ah! The importance is that it is our culture . . .
> *Sarah* Is it the religion or . . .
> *Ngoura* It's the religion! It's for the religion and to be clean (pure).
>   A woman who is excised is cleaner than a woman who is not
>   excised.

It seemed hard to imagine how people can stop practicing if they perceive
nonpractice to be impure and against the requirements of religion. So I
ask her,

> "Do you really think that people can abandon the practice if they
> believe that their daughters are not clean?:

Ngoura replies,

> "Yes, normally you can smell that."
> "Hmm!" I say, unsure of how her response was related to my
> question.

She continues:
"A lady who is excised, she is clean. More than the unexcised."
"Ah, really? Is that what you have noticed?" I reply, knowing that as a midwife she has delivered the children of excised and unexcised women.
"That is what we have noticed," she replies with certitude.
"How?" I ask.
"That is what we have noticed, *dey*!"[8] says Ngoura.

Not sure what exactly she is referring to, I repeat my question: "In what way?"

"In all the ways!"

Sedina, my research assistant, who is present during the interview and a supporter of the practice, says,

"In all the ways."

Ngoura agrees with Sedina:

"The men as well have noticed that."
"The men as well have noticed?!" I ask, perplexed about hearing this from an activist against excision.
"Aha!"

To find out what exactly she means by cleanliness I ask for more detail:

"She does not excrete as much liquid?"
"Hmm. No, it's just cleaner," Ngoura says.

Sedina, referring to the religious recommendation that the man's foreskin should be cut for religious purity, says,

"There is the prepuce."
"Mhm." Ngoura affirms Sedina's statement.

I recall what Awa Diallo, the exciser of Diawoury, said about excision and ask,

"I have heard an exciser say that if you don't cut the clitoris it becomes big, as big as rabbit ears."

Ngoura replies:

"Mhm. It will grow big, *dey*."

And I repeat Fama Ly's statement:

"And there are women who think that during childbirth you have to take a piece of string and . . ."

Ngoura finishes my sentence for me: "And attach it."

"And attach it behind the bottom," I repeat, surprised that she says it before I finish.
"Mhmm, sometimes that happens," Ngoura says calmly.
"That is what happens?"
"Yes, sometimes that happens," she replies. "Not everyone. Persons are different. Sometimes it's big, eh? Sometimes it's not."
"Really?" I am astonished to hear this from a midwife and ex-exciser.
"It depends on the women. There are some very big women and their clitoris grows big as well. It depends on the size of the woman and on her body. Sometimes you get a large woman, when it comes to childbirth you are obliged to attach it."
"Hm?" I utter questioningly.
"Mhm," Ngoura affirms. "It is very embarrassing! Very embarrassing."

I listen. Ngoura repeats:

"It is embarrassing, *dey*."

Ngoura thus shares the views of other Futanke women and men who perceive the unexcised woman to be less clean than the excised. She also perceives the "rabbit ears" that need to be tied back during childbirth as embarrassing. Although her depiction of the unexcised woman is not as shocking and full of danger as Awa Diallo or Fama Ly seem to perceive it, she ascribes lack of purity to it, and potential embarrassment. It seems contradictory that as an activist against female circumcision and the president of the ex-excisers association, she maintains local discourses on hygiene and smell at the same time as embracing the national and international discourses on the harmfulness of the practice. I argue that this underscores the fact that local beliefs and discourses around bodily hygiene, poise, and social decency are embodied and become part of people's *habitus* (Bourdieu 1977). Even though Ngoura Ly has adopted the national postban biomedical discourse of medical professionals, her visceral reaction to unexcised women reflects embodied local conceptions of purity and pollution.

Douglas (1968) argues that the physical body is polarized conceptually against the social body. Its requirements are not only subordinated, they are contrasted with social requirements (Fraser and Greco 2005:80). Particularly in "complex social systems," ways of behaving are devised that suggest that human intercourse is disembodied compared with that of animal creation (Douglas 1968). Different degrees of disembodiment are used to express social hierarchy in the following way: "The [more] refinement, the less smacking of the lips when eating, the less mastication, the less the sound of breathing and walking, the more carefully modulated the laughter, the more controlled the signs of anger, the clearer the priestly aristocratic image" (Douglas 1968 in Fraser and Greco 2005:80).

This contrast of the physical comportment of the body to social sophistication and refinement relates to Classen's analyses of the role of smell in social differentiation. Classen argues that "It is common, for instance, for the dominant class in a society to characterise itself as pleasant-smelling, or in-odorate, and the subordinate class as foul-smelling" (1992:136). As an example, Classen describes the Dassanetch pastoralists of Ethiopia, who consider everything associated with cattle as good—even the smell—so that they do all they can to augment their identification with this prestigious odor: men smear manure on their bodies to advertise their herds' fertility, women smear butter on their shoulders, breasts, and hair, which serves to attract men and is the perfume—so to speak—of women (Almagor 1987: 109 in Classen 1992: 138). The smell of fish and lower-class fishermen, on the other hand, are repulsive to the pastoralists. The social and olfactory codes of Dessanetch society perceive pastoralists as smelling good and fishermen as smelling bad, as the odor of cattle is held to be superior to that of fish.

If we apply this reasoning of the Dassanetch to Futanke society, we can say that their moral superiority is not merely a feeling that their women can control their desires better than the Wolof, for instance, but is an embodied perception of unexcised women being "impurer," "dirtier," and inferior. Describing the unexcised female body as odorous and impure is not just attributing social and moral inferiority to it but also points toward the fact that it is socially undesirable.

Control and "Foreign Invasion"

With reference to the control of girls' virginity in the HIV/AIDS crisis in South Africa, Wickström (2010) follows Mary Douglas in arguing that rituals expressing anxiety about body orifices are connected to the protection of political and cultural unity. Ritual protection of the body becomes a symbol for social care. "The individual body is the most direct, the most proximate area where social truths and disputes take place, as well as the place for personal and social resistance, creativity and struggle" (Wickström 2010:545).

Fears around loss of control of the body and foreign invasion or loss of culture are indeed a common theme in anthropology. Emily Martin (1990), for instance, suggests that discourses on the body's immune defenses in the twentieth-century United States are often imagined in a similar way to a nation state at war, constantly fighting foreign intruders. The life of the body apparently depends on its ability to keep all its functions under control. According to this imagery, loss of control equates with being defeated by disease.

Veena Das's work on abducted women during the partition in India analyzes women's role as reproducers of citizens within a nation-state and shows how honor is associated with national identity, purity, and the need for sexual control (Das 2007). She argues that a political community is dependent on reproduction. Within this scheme, women's allegiance to the state is proved by their role as mothers who bear legitimate children. A corollary is that a woman's infidelity, even if brought about inadvertently by violent rape in times of war or conflict, is an offense not just against the family but also against the sovereign (Das 2007:36). Thus, in this context the political community is also hinged on women's chastity, lack of which is perceived as a threat to the group's integrity as a cultural and moral unity.[9]

In addition to what I have shown about the importance of the control of desire, I argue that the Futanke's abhorrence of images of the unexcised body as impure and socially indecent is an embodiment of fears around a loss of civilization and foreign invasion and concerns with the preservation of ethnic identity. Whereas in the previous chapter I discussed how the ability to control one's desires is linked to kinship ties and a sentiment of pride and honor that arises from successfully maintaining these ties, I want to underscore in this chapter that emotional rejection of the unexcised body is linked to social decline in an embodied way.

Conclusion

I have shown that excised women do not consider themselves and are not considered mutilated, sexually handicapped, or unable to experience pleasure. Sex in itself is not taboo, dirty, or shameful. On the contrary, some women enjoy making themselves desirable and performing pleasure-enhancing customs with aphrodisiacs. There are, however, inappropriate, dirty, and repulsive aspects of sexuality. For unmarried women, the open use of pleasure-enhancing utensils would be shameless. Extramarital sex is shrouded in silence, the stuff of which myths and gossip are made, but not openly practiced. It is inappropriate to interact with people if they have not rendered themselves pure through ablutions after sex. Uncircumcised men and unexcised women are perceived as unclean because of the accumulation of impurity around the parts of their genitals that have not been cut. I have argued that many Futanke men and women perceive uncut genitals not just as dirty but also as ambiguous due to their androgynous status—being neither what is perceived as male or female. Ambiguity is potentially embarrassing and dangerous (Douglas 1966, 1968). On the one hand, such images are associated with fear of the unknown and the unsafe; on the other hand, the fact that a smell and impurity are ascribed to the uncut woman points toward moral and social inferiority. An unexcised woman is not just potentially loose, unable to control her desire, and uncivilized but also dirty, dangerous, and repugnant for some people. With reference to Douglas (1966), I argue that excision creates social order by removing the inappropriate desire that threatens to arise in women if they are not cut. This sense of desire is associated with the demise of Futanke society and the values that people cherish, and is largely associated with pregnancy before marriage and illegitimate children.

The consequences of illegitimate sex (childbirth before marriage or illegitimate children) lead to social chaos. The sense of repulsion that people feel toward unexcised women and their imagined impurity is an embodied reaction to the fears associated with discourses around what society might turn into if women no longer managed to control their sexual desires.

CHAPTER 5

Whose Law, Whose Body, Whose Rule?

The Opposition to the Law and FGC
Sensitization in Fouta Toro

"Female circumcision is a Prophetic recommendation!"

"We have practiced it since the beginning of time, it's an Islamic tradition!"

"The purpose of the practice is to protect women!"

"We will never abandon!"

"Westerners are fighting Islam by combating practices that are recommended!"

"They are trying to efface our identity!"

"You are traitors!"

These were the angry admonitions voiced by Fulani religious leaders in the aftermath of the trials of Matam that condemned a traditional cutter and the grandmother who had arranged for the cutting of her grand-daughter to a six-month prison sentence. The trials took place in 2009 in the regional lawcourt of the district of Matam in northern Senegal, the region known as Fouta Toro, ten years after the Senegalese parliament decreed a national ban on female genital mutilation. An angry mob of hundreds of people blocked the regional law courts to show allegiance to their mar-abouts, who had demanded that the offenders be released. The trials took place under strong police surveillance; access to the law courts was denied to the public. My friends at the Tostan office in Ourosogui, about 10 kilometers from Matam, were surprised to hear about the trial over the local radio. When the verdict was made public, the outraged crowds started throwing stones at the police force, who countered the attack with tear gas.

What was going to happen next? Why did that particular case get reported and not one of the thousands of other excisions that happen every year? How were people going to react? My friends at Tostan Ourosogui were afraid. Not just afraid that their work would be spoiled (*bonntide* in Pulaar) and that people would no longer dare to speak out against excision, but also afraid of the marabouts' spiritual power. Working for Tostan was not easy because of the rumors that its aim was to destroy their religion, despite the fact that all Tostan employees in Fouta were Muslim. Some were threatened that they would not be buried in their home villages when they die. Others were religiously condemned. In the stories I was told by Tostan staff, they always managed to convince their naysayers in the end. Some of those who were spreading polemics against Tostan ended up dying suddenly, unexpectedly. The reasons for their death are subject to interpretation. But there were places where Tostan never dared to return because of the religious leaders' power.

In 2007, Fouta Toro was referred to as the most difficult region in terms of reaching the goal of complete abandonment of FGC by 2015 (now 2030). When asking development agents and governmental officials what was different about Fouta and why working there was so challenging, they often referred to the religious leaders' power without giving a lot of details. Commonly cited events took place in 2003, such as the Aere Lao event and the tire burning incident in Ourosogui, during which NGO workers, representatives of a funding agency, a minister, and other government officials were threatened not to publicly discuss excision in their village. They were forced to stay inside their hotel and tires were burned outside to mark the crowd's disagreement with the ban and national and international politics promoting the abandonment of FGC.

After the first events occurred, researchers of governmental, nongovernmental, and international organizations experienced more difficulties interviewing research subjects about reproductive health in Fouta Toro than in any other region of Senegal. Senegalese researchers I met who were contracted by international organizations to collect data on attitudes toward FGC were frequently asked to leave, were refused accommodation, and were told that neither the government nor anyone else was welcome to ask inappropriate questions about their private lives.

Yet, these events of opposition in Fouta Toro are, in many ways, intangible as they did not receive the same press coverage and somehow remained nonevents (Farge 2002) in the making of a national success story. In contrast to the Malicounda Bambara declaration of 1997 (Mackie, 2000), for example, which was heralded as "the beginning of the end of excision in Senegal" by the national and international press as well as the Senegalese government (Farge 2002; Handelman 1990; Meinert and Kapferer 2015), the events in Fouta Toro are mainly known to those who were around at the time and who heard about them on the radio in their language or in the mosque. Emma Tarlo (2003) notes that "certain characters, moments and events are splashed large across the canvas of public memory; others are watered down, diminished, reduced, faded out of the picture altogether" (Tarlo 2003:21). Similarly, the events of opposition in Fouta Toro have somehow been forgotten or ignored. They are silenced—to use Trouillot's term (Trouillot 1995)—as they are absent from the official discourses around the beginning of the end of excision in Senegal. Since the start of my research, I have not come across many official versions of the events of opposition that I discuss below; they only seem to exist in the memories of those who were involved or directly affected. They were, however, "critical events" in Veena Das's sense (Das 1996), because they propelled people's lives into unprecedented terrains and brought about new modes of action that changed the way in which people perceived the role of the state and women's bodies.

The first part of this chapter addresses the trial of Matam and the religious leaders' interpretation of governmental and nongovernmental efforts to stop the practice as an attack on their Islamic way of life orchestrated by "Westerners who will do anything to destroy Futanke culture and identity." I argue that their public outcry and pain about what they saw as an attack on their culture and religious faith is strongly related to the challenges that national and international policies represent to the politics and religious authority of the leaders of Futanke society. To many, the implementation of policies that seem contradictory to religious beliefs and cultural identity, and appear to be an imposition by the West, bring back memories of the colonial experience.

However, the opposition between those who dislike the law/state and the NGOs addressing this issue is not clear cut with the Futanke on one side and the "white people's NGO" and the state on the other. Gupta (2001), Ferguson (2006), Hansen and Stepputat (2001), and Foucault (Foucault 2007) have shown that the authority of the state is diffused and represented in many forms of power in different bodies of society and its institutions. Ferguson (2006), for example, suggests that governmentality in Africa seems to be suffused by transnational processes that reach from beyond the state all the way through imagined hierarchies down to the local level. It is not at all a top-down process whereby governmental officials act and take decisions according to a vertically arranged hierarchy. In a similar way, I show that in Fouta Toro governmental and nongovernmental intervention, the state and the law are not superior entities hanging above citizens; they are manifest in everyday transactions and interactions through different bureaucratic forms associating government employees and the rest of the population.

The Trials of Matam

Let us return to the trials of Matam. I followed this event closely when it happened in 2009. The U.S. Department of State's Human Rights Watch described the event as follows:

> On May 28, the Court of Matam sentenced a woman who had
> carried out FGM on a 16-month-old baby. The court also handed
> down the same sentence to the baby's grandmother, who had
> requested the FGM to be performed. The baby's parents received a
> suspended sentence of six months' imprisonment. After failing in
> their efforts to pressure government authorities to abandon the
> case, local religious groups influenced local persons to stone
> security force members.
>
> (US Department of State, 2010)

This incident is listed along with other events under categories such as "unlawful deprivation of life," "sexual violence," and "torture and other cruel, inhuman, degrading treatment or punishment." Despite the strong views of many Futanke, there are no longer any articles on the Internet interpreting state intervention as a form of cultural colonialism or the infringement of the right to practice one's religion. The latter, incidentally, is also a human right.

Jeune Afrique described the event as follows on the 28th of May 2009:

Senegal: a female circumciser sentenced to six months in prison.
A Senegalese court on Thursday sentenced a traditional exciser to six months in prison for mutilating a 16-month-old child in northern Senegal, a human rights organisation said.[1]

The grandmother of the girl, who had taken her to the exciser, was sentenced to the same penalty, according to a representative of the African Meeting for the Defence of Human Rights (Raddho). The court in Matam (680 km north-east of Dakar, near the Senegal River) sentenced the parents of the child less severely, as their six-month prison sentence was suspended. After the judgement was handed down, "talibés" (followers of marabouts) clashed violently with the police in Matam, according to the private radio station RFM. The demonstrators threw stones at the police, who used tear gas. Excision—the term most commonly used to refer to "female genital mutilation"—has been banned by law for ten years in Senegal. But this legal action was strongly contested by religious leaders in the Matam region, who defend the practice in the name of tradition. On 14 May, a crowd of demonstrators had already laid siege to the court to demand the release of the accused, according to the local press.

The girl's excision in the locality of Ourossogui (a few kilometres from Matam) had been reported to the gendarmerie by the Raddho. The exciser and the three members of the child's family were imprisoned.

"This is the first conviction for excision in the region. The Raddho wanted to give a strong warning sign, to signify that excision is banned," explained its regional representative, David Diagne. "We are going to continue raising awareness throughout the Matam region to point out that excision does a lot of harm, particularly from a health point of view, with all the risks of infection for girls.

This account of the event in a pan-African magazine appears disimpassioned. It is not clear to a reader who does not know the context why the religious leaders and their followers disagreed with the sentence and why violence broke out. Nor were there any other articles in the national press explaining or discussing the marabouts and their followers' reactions in more detail. The absence of local views on the subject echoes Trouillot's historical analysis in *Silencing the Past*, where he reveals how various events linked to the Haitian revolution between the 1790s and 1802 were silenced in historiography. Despite the fact that the French and the British lost more soldiers and generals in Saint Domingue than in the battle of Waterloo (Trouillot 1995:99) and that Saint Domingue was the most valuable colony of the Western world at the time of the revolution, perceived as vital to France's political future and economy (Trouillot 1995:99), the revolution itself is strikingly absent from historiography. At the time of the revolution, the French denied that it was happening, and it was unimaginable that slaves would be able to permanently succeed in an organized revolt against their owners—they were perceived to be mentally incapable of such acts. "The revolution that was unthinkable became a non-event" (Trouillot: 1995:98). Trouillot shows that years later, historical research has more of a tendency to look into who helped the slaves revolt, rather than examining the existing evidence that this revolt was an entirely self-driven act to gain freedom from ownership and self-determination. In relation to the insurrection following the arrest of the exciser in Matam, I suggest that the absence of perspectives from those who rioted against the law's enforcement authorities is important. The event is described as an irrational form of violence against the law and the law's enforcement. Reflecting on the role of religious leaders in revolts against the French colonial government, it is interesting that no link is made between their authority and the imposition of external law foreign to the Futanke and the Senegalese.

In 2009 I got hold of a press statement made by the ulamas, imams, and religious leaders of Fouta, the Ferlo, and the Bundu shortly after the arrest of the exciser (May 29, 2009). This statement is also nowhere to be found on the Internet or in the national storytelling of the beginning of the end of excision in Senegal:

Press Declaration

Since the cold war and the demise of the Sophiet Union ex USSR [*sic*], Westerners led by the United States of America have been fighting Islam with intelligent methods which consist of combating certain practices that are recommended by Islam, to efface Muslim culture, since a society without culture will disappear.

This conflict is taking place in various ambiguous forms [*sic*]. NGOs have been created and say that they are there to help citizens understand their rights and duties, but in reality they are there to make Islam disappear. **They will never succeed.**

Today, the Senegalese state (95% Muslim) allows itself to outlaw practices that are recommended by Islam, such as:

—Excision was practised by Arabs since the time of the Prophet **(peace and greeting be with him)** [*sic*] who came to us with Islam. Non-Muslim African societies do not practise it. Our illustrious

ancestors [*sic*] practised it without problems. Shame on those who
voted for this satanic law! Shame on those who voted for this
impractical [*sic*] law in Senegal![2]

Among the religious leaders who released this press declaration was the son
of Thierno Mountaga Tall, the marabout who had opposed the national ban
on FGM ten years before. The arrest of the exciser had nothing to do with
Tostan, and the staff I knew in Fouta agreed that prosecuting the grandparents and parents of the girl was harsh—especially as some members of
their own families continued practicing despite their professional efforts to
stop excision. Yet, it felt as though this press declaration was directly addressed to NGOs like Tostan in Fouta and they needed to respond; otherwise further violence and "poisoning" might turn against their own program
facilitators and other staff.

Rumors spread across Fouta Toro that Tostan had been involved in de-
nouncing the exciser to the police. In response to this, some marabouts ordered all Tostan education classes in Fouta Toro to be closed and said that
the NGO should leave Fouta Toro if it turned out this rumor was true. To
prevent further poisoning (bonntide), Tostan Fouta invited the marabouts
to a meeting in Ndioum in the district of Podor. Marabouts and Imams came
from all over Fouta to attend. The meeting was not open to the public, but
my former research assistant, who was employed by Tostan when this meeting took place, was able to attend and wrote everything down with the per-
mission of the organizers.

Below are three comments from marabouts at this meeting that capture
the sense of anger, distrust, and fears around loss of tradition and the conviction that the forced abandonment of excision is an intelligent Western
method to destroy religion and culture.

> Even if excision was not sunna, it is our tradition, our identity! That
> is why we will never abandon. Tostan, you are frightening! What
> hurts me most is that the children of Fouta are being used to
> eradicate their own culture. An ethnicity that loses its language and
> customs will disappear! Why have other countries like Mali,
> Mauritania, the Gambia and Guinea not become part of the United
> Nations Embargo?[3] Even the politicians are supporting them. It is
> shameful to want to efface one's identity. [*He starts crying.*]
>   (Thierno Hassirou, marabout, May 2009)

Westerners have tried everything to win Fouta: Thierno Mountaga Tall himself predicted the arrival of NGOs whose mission it is to destroy Islam. I regret that the Futanke is too easily corrupted. The state and those who support it are the same. What I hope is that you as Futanke can help us to fight against those who are combating religion.[4]

(Zackaria Thioune, imam, May 2009)

All the activities organized by the state and the NGO are pure trickery and a way to fight Islam. The law against excision was passed against the Futanke—but to let you and those who have sent you know: We will continue to excise our daughters until the end of the world. No one can stop us! I have been told that Senegal is a secular state. If that's true, why don't you let us practice our religion? [. . .] The problem is that we are blinded by the Westerners who are ready to do anything to destroy our culture and our identity. The most shocking and abnormal thing is that we have to undergo French influence and even the unleashing of homosexuals.

(Thierno Hamidou Aliou, imam of Ndioum, May 2009)

All three citations express an immense fear of loss of Futanke tradition, culture, religion, and identity. They represent an imminent threat to Futanke way of life and religious practice. Although the exciser was arrested by the police, the *ulamas* associate this event with nongovernmental and foreign intervention. The rights and duties promoted by NGOs like Tostan and Raddho are seen as intelligent methods to annihilate existing Islamic forms of order and justice. Where does this fear of loss of culture and identity come from? And why is it directed toward the West and international organizations? David Berliner shows that this sense of loss of culture is not a new occurrence but an incredibly common social phenomenon driving identity politics, economics, and a concern for cultural heritage: "It is in this current climate of losing-everything that the notions of culture, heritage and authenticity—a great obsession of the Moderns—form an inseparable trio. They have become moral justifications in themselves, surrounded by an aura of evidence and authority. Faced with the acceleration of globalization that produces erasure [. . .], the transmission to future generations, so precious because it is in crisis, is now an individual as well as a political value" (Berliner 2018:12–13).[5] Berliner (2018), Herzfeld (2016), and others have argued that anxieties

about loss of culture or loss of tradition are closely connected to trepida-
tions about how culture, tradition, or heritage should be protected, preserved,
and transmitted to future generations. The transmission of cultural aspects
of identity or tradition seem to become even more vital when they were
subject to destruction—as is the case for populations that lived particularly
traumatizing and violent experiences, such as colonization, extermination,
and genocide (Berliner 2018:15). Although the international NGOs basing
their policies on human rights see themselves as *post*colonial, bringing
positive social change, gender equality, and social justice, the marabouts'
reactions above show that they are very much seen as a continuation of the
colonial past, still threatening cultural and religious identity.

Human rights educational approaches are often seen as innovative, new
and completely detached from the colonial past. Those who have little knowledge of the historical context in which human rights emerged often dis-
miss those who reject the doctrine as ignorant or backward. Goodale
(2022:79) argues that the early history of human rights and colonialism
reveals ambiguities of economic exploitation, legacies of racial violence, and
revolutionary mobilization. Between the end of World War II and the ratifi-
cation of the Universal Declaration of Human Rights, the processes through
which human rights were conceived, debated, and eventually drafted took
place in a deeply colonial world. Vast territories, including most of Africa
and Southeast Asia, were under the control of a few European countries.
Furthermore, a number of founding members of the UN security council
exercised colonialist control through military intervention, financial control, or self-proclaimed hemispheric hegemony (the UK, France, the US,
and the Soviet Union). Goodale argues that these dominant actors "took
great pains to ensure that the 'Magna Carta for all mankind' could do nothing to threaten a global colonial order in which hundreds of millions of
people were not full members of the category 'all mankind', but were rather
captive subjects of a parallel economic and political system whose raison
d'être was exploitation" (2022:80). Early critics doubted whether a universal declaration of human rights could be adopted that excluded the voices
and perspectives of such a vast variety of peoples, nations, religions, and cultural traditions and whether the enormous cultural diversity among people
under colonial control would be taken into consideration during the delib-
erations. Eventually, anticolonial movements drove back the colonial system by harnessing the language of human rights in ways that grounded

their struggles in the right to self-determination and thus exposing the in-equalities and injustices inherent in the structural violence of colonialism itself. The representatives of newly independent nation-states confronted the international human rights system by using human rights language in transformational ways (Goodale 2022:89–90).

The above citations also show a lack of trust in the Senegalese government to protect its people from the trickery of international organizations and Western influence that are thought to destroy Islam and culture. Although the NGOs tend to refer to the national law in their sensitization activities and discourses against the practice, the marabouts do not see this law as result-ing from a national consensus but as an imposition by the United Nations and Westerners. They interpret the renouncing of excision and Senegalese officials' collaboration with NGOs as due to corruption and loss of moral-ity, which results in the demise of Futanke culture. This loss of holy law and order clearly disturbs and saddens many marabouts, leaders of what they perceive to be a glorious society built on the foundations of Islam.

In addition to reading the religious leaders' anxious and violent reaction to the law as a threat to their cultural identity, reflecting a continuation of the colonial experience, I suggest that their claims to authority over law and justice during the trials of Matam should be read in the light of the status of religious leaders as Tooroɓɓe and their historical role in Fouta Toro. They still hold the highest rank within Haalpulaar'en social hierarchy as political lead-ers within Futanke society alongside the official governors of the colonial and postcolonial state since the most recent Islamic revolution in the 1760s.

Willis (1978) explains how the *Turudiyya*[6] *ulama*[7] developed in Fouta Toro in the seventeenth and eighteenth centuries. He argues that a number of Haalpulaar'en warriors who strongly believed in Islam, Malik Sy being one of the most famous, created an Islamic community in the Bundu. Protection and asylum were offered to various sociolinguistic groups (Dianicunda, Tenda, some Dulet who had difficulties with the Wolof of Saloum, some Fulɓe groups, some Mande-speaking groups, and various Sarakhole peoples) (Raffenel 1856, cited in Willis 1978: 201). In this community (*Jama'a*), Pulaar was spoken and Sharia was practiced. Non-Muslims, who were ex-cluded from the *Jama'a*, were kept as slaves. European travelers at the time noted that Europeans as well as "all Sudani infidels" (Hecquart 1853 in Willis 1978) were not allowed to enter certain urban settlements and were excluded from the *Jama'a*. Willis points out that "One of the striking features of the Torodbe *Jama'as* was the clear distinction which evolved between dar al-Islam ('the land of Islam') and dar al-harb ('the land of war' or polytheism)" (Willis 1978: 205).

The Tooroɓɓe clerisy became the dominant occupational group among Pulaar speakers across what is Senegal today. Initially it was possible for people from any ethnic or caste background to join the Tooroɓɓe if they were devout Muslims and agreed to settle (some people who lived in "caves and trees" or were nomadic had to give up their way of life to join the community, according to Willis [1978]). Other free men and landholders (such as the Fulɓe, Jaawamɓe, and Subalɓe status groups[8]) were integrated into the newly forming hierarchy. They kept their land but had to pay revenues to the imam (*ushr, zakat,* and *Jizya*) in return for internal and external security (Willis 1978: 206). The imam was everywhere recognized as the principal political and religious figure: "It was to the *imam* that believers looked for maintenance of Islamic traditions, the enforcement of the Sharia, and the wisdom necessary for a sound economic and social policy" (1978: 206).

It is commonly believed that Islam brought law and order to Futanke society and offered people protection. For many, following Islamic recommendations is still important for this reason—the holy law and order it has brought to Futanke society. Although this sense of sanctuary has not remained unchallenged since the Islamic revolution (Robinson 1985; Wane 1969), statutory and NGO intervention seems to defy this order that has offered protection from invasion and offered spiritual salvation as well as socioeconomic order for three to four centuries. It is important to note that the Tostan Fouta staff were all practicing Muslims and had grown up respecting their local religious traditions and marabouts. Yet NGOs aiming to raise awareness about FGC were labeled anti-Islamic because excision is endorsed as a sunna—a Prophetic recommendation. Although the colonial and postcolonial state has imposed its power alongside this socioreligious system, not only the law against excision, but also foreign intervention through NGOs have directly challenged their authority. The Islamic leaders, all traditional Toroodo elites, see secular interventions and recommendations against this religious practice as undermining their authority. Within Futanke society, religion belongs to the domain of the Tooroɓɓe clerisy of which the colonial and postcolonial governments mostly stayed clear.

These reactions to the law, international NGOs, and social change seem incredibly striking and reveal a genuine threat perception to cultural identity. Yet, there is a multiplicity of voices that have not been heard and that are silenced in the marabouts' pleas. The opposition between those who are against the law, the state, and international human rights recommendations is not clear-cut with the Futanke on one side and the "white people's NGO" and the state on the other. The following explores the complexity of decision making that activists are confronted with when facing vehement opposition to the abandonment of FGC.

The NGOs and the Opposition: Understanding the Conflict in Fouta Toro

In the following, I introduce Khalidou Sy's version of the events. Khalidou was the Tostan national coordinator when I met him in January 2007 at the beginning of my fieldwork, and he had managed the implementation and running of Tostan's education program in Fouta Toro from 1992.

I interviewed Khalidou in a small hotel where we were staying along with a delegation of officials who were going to the public declaration of Koumbidia. I began by asking Khalidou how the program was introduced in Fouta Toro. He replied that when the program was implemented in 1992, Tostan entertained good relations with communities in Fouta. However, at the time, the program covered only basic education: teaching literacy, problem resolution, hygiene, health, management of resources, finance, and doing a feasibility study. There were no modules on human rights, democracy, or reproductive health. In 1997, Tostan added a module[9] on reproductive health, aiming to sensitize women about their rights. Khalidou explained that this was when the image of Tostan changed, and after a successful beginning, the first problems occurred:

> Then, the communities started seeing a different NGO in Tostan: a reactionary NGO that does not just try to put women before men but also touches on a very sensitive subject: excision. So when that started off, the Senegalese government voted . . . the parliament passed a law against excision, the most influential marabout of Fouta wrote an oath to say that he was for excision.

The national call for abandonment was paralleled by movements that questioned whether it is legitimate to stop practicing on religious grounds. Those who argued that excision was a Prophetic recommendation called the state's policies into question. The high point of this movement was the appeal by renowned religious leader Thierno Mountaga Tall to the parliamentarians not to pass a law criminalizing the practice because prohibiting Muslims from practicing a religious recommendation is sinful and an injustice that retards "human rights" (Tall 1999). Khalidou explains the effects of these opposing views on local people:

> Suddenly two different things happened: the government said we will now abandon in Senegal and someone who practices is sentenced to between two months and five to six years in prison. Whereas on the other hand he [the religious leader] says: listen, continue with excision, your religion recommends excision. So that created problems! Everywhere it was suddenly said that it's UNICEF, it's Tostan, it's ASBEF [another Senegalese NGO working on Sexual and Reproductive Health] it's . . . they cited various NGOs and funders that were there working for community development and they asked for these NGOs to be chased out of Fouta. This was how the difficulties started!

Khalidou noted how people found themselves in a conflicting position between what the government orders and the religious leader recommends. Faced with having to take sides, many blame the NGOs and, apparently, want them to be chased out of Fouta. In these new circumstances, Tostan had to rethink what they were going to do. To provide a stronger sense of how NGO workers in charge of the implementation of the program perceived of the opposition, what it consisted of, and why they decided to continue raising awareness against FGC, I want to look briefly at the founder and former director's account of how the NGO Tostan experienced the problems in Fouta.

I did a long interview with Molly Melching about Tostan's interventions in Fouta in Paris in November 2008. She confirmed that when Tostan first started working in Fouta, FGC was not part of the teachings. However, Molly emphasized that many religious leaders perceived Tostan's teachings as beneficial for their communities. So despite the opposition to the Tostan program that began after women's health (including FGC) and human rights were introduced, Tostan decided to stay because they were also supported, sought after for help, and encouraged by others.

[Molly explained] how we got into Fouta introducing the subject of FGC. I went to see the religious leader [Thierno Ahmadou Ba] and he said, "because you've been here in our community since 1992 and you've never before discussed FGC . . . now, if the women are talking about it, if they're having those problems—then I will support you." [. . .] because I told him, "if you say to me to not do this now, I will stop!" And he told me, "Since you've included me in the process, and since you tell me it's detrimental to women's health and they're afraid of talking about it, I say, yes, go ahead and you will be victorious because it is a noble cause." So it was very beautiful. [. . .] that was how we decided to leave the sessions on FGC in the women's health module because previously, even the supervisors were really afraid of discussing this! They were very, very afraid of discussing FGC and even told me not to say anything about it.

In view of the anger caused by the added module to the education program, Molly Melching was confronted with the decision of whether to continue it. Given the threats of religious condemnation if the awareness-raising activities continued, she was potentially risking her staff's safety. Although the program was backed by the government and the international community (e.g., UNICEF), it visibly caused disarray among local authorities. However, Thierno Ahmadou Ba encouraged her to continue raising awareness on FGC because it was beneficial to women.

The Aere Lao Event

In 2004, before my involvement with Tostan, I met a schoolteacher in Kedougou (south-eastern Senegal) who was originally from Fouta. He immediately associated the NGO Tostan with the marabout's religious condemnation of their staff in Aere Lao and religious leaders' defense of excision as a religious practice. It was difficult for me to find out exactly what had happened in Aere Lao and why people were so shocked. The general sense I got, without being told any of the details, was that Tostan had gone too far and should not have discussed issues against the religious leaders' will in Aere Lao. It was implied that the NGO and the parliamentarians who were present at this meeting were put right by the religious leaders and had been successfully chased out of Fouta. The religious leader who condemned Tostan had put this foreign NGO, and the parliamentarians who had been bought by the "white people," in their place and let them know that they were not welcome. People who remembered Aere Lao as a positive event alluded to the religious leader's success in doing what was in the interest of the Futanke as devout Muslims. Although absent from the national storytelling, Aere Lao was therefore critical in many people's memory in terms of defending Futanke cultural and religious identity against the state and international NGOs.

I was strongly advised against doing interviews in Aere Lao because of hostility toward people bringing up the subject of female genital cutting. Things had calmed down when I was in the field, seven years after these events, and I frequently passed through Aere Lao and occasionally spent the night there. Nevertheless, I always felt uneasy despite the polite hospitability. I knew that many associated white people with social degradation, sexual libertarianism, and the demise of Futanke culture.

Besides uncertainty about what exactly had happened, I noticed that many people were afraid of the spiritual forces and the religious power of the marabouts.[10] The shock that the event had caused was not just due to conflicting opinions about excision, Haalpulaar'en cultural heritage, and ethnic identity; there was also a great element of fear of those who opposed the law and sensitization against what they called a religious practice.

The marabouts of Fouta are thought to be extremely powerful and adept in spiritual knowledge practices. Many people believe that the reason for this is that Fouta Toro was the first area to be Islamized in Senegal. Others think that many marabouts in Fouta are skilled in what are called Islamic sciences (Dilley 2005). Others think that a lot of the spiritual power is based on the knowledge practices of the Haalpulaar'en of Fouta in general. As Dilley explains, these are based on occupational lore. Fear of what happened during the events in Fouta and of the marabouts' power seems to be strongly associated with these Islamic knowledge practices.

In view of the ambiguity about what exactly happened and why the events were so frightening, we can now explore Khalidou Sy's and Molly Melching's accounts of the incidents. As I have mentioned, their versions are the only stories I managed to elicit about these events—partly perhaps because many Futanke who had heard of what had happened did not witness these events themselves, and partly because they did not want to talk about it in order to avoid inflicting evil on themselves.

Khalidou's Account of Aere Lao

"In Aere Lao they [participants of the women's health module and people who wanted to abandon excision] organized an event to discuss FGC and child marriage, but on the day the discussion was to take place, the minister of health was there . . . everyone was there [the officials], but on that day no one dared to speak of excision! No one! The authorities . . . no one dared to speak of excision even though it was supposed to be a public debate on excision. But on the day, all those who were for the abandonment and who wanted to talk about it suddenly changed their minds because people came to them and told them: Listen as far as the abandonment of excision is concerned, it would be a catastrophe and there will be deaths!"

"Ah!" I interject.

Khalidou continues: "So instantly people [the participants at the meeting] changed their language and spoke of the promotion of children's rights, of women's rights, of health and child marriage . . . all that. So many returned [home]. It was difficult to keep the meeting going but luckily some stayed. But no one dared to talk about excision."

"What were they afraid of?" I ask.

"It was because in the communities, the marabouts stood up and said, these are maraboutic villages, the marabouts stood up to say, 'Listen, they [the NGOs and the ministers] have come here to fight against religion, they have come here to create difficulties.' This is why we told ourselves that we [Tostan] would continue with the work providing information on the consequences. But while the program continued, people were speaking of it everywhere. There were teams of marabouts who went to inform other marabouts about the practice of excision."

Khalidou emphasizes that "these are maraboutic villages." He is referring to two things: first, the leaders of these villages are marabouts who belong to the Tooroɓɓe status group. The Tooroɓɓe have been the most powerful status group since the Islamic revolution under the Turudiyya (Dilley 2005; Johnson 1974; Robinson 1985; Willis 1978). They are those who are learned in the Qur'an and, with few exceptions, tend to be the village chiefs in Haalpulaar'en areas. Second, maraboutic villages are places where renowned religious leaders and marabouts reside. Many are believed to have demonstrated their spiritual power and skill on plenty of occasions by healing the sick or helping people with their personal problems. A lot of these famous leaders have *Taliɓe* (students of the Qur'an) who come from far away to learn the Qur'an. It is common for Taliɓe who have already memorized the Qur'an, the first step toward becoming a marabout, to move to other places to learn the Sharia or other religious sciences from another religious leader.

Khalidou also speaks of "teams of marabouts" who "inform each other about the practice of excision." I often heard from NGO staff and people working for the promotion of the law in Fouta Toro that some marabouts regularly communicated with each other about what kinds of sensitization activities had gone on in their villages and who the main actors were. Some NGO literacy projects were welcomed. PIP (Programme Intégrale de Podor), for example, was a Senegalese education program that exclusively focused on teaching Pulaar literacy and numeracy. The PIP program was widely accepted and experienced no problems because the teachings did not include any controversial recommendations such as human rights, health, and nutrition, which are associated with the "White man" (*tuubaako*). Whether they appreciated it or not, most people I talked to felt that such teachings on health and human rights were foreign to Futanke culture.

A lot of the marabouts who became involved in this movement against Tostan, ASBEF, Raddho, and the law had strong views on excision and came to a consensus with the renowned religious leaders that the practice should be encouraged and defended as an Islamic tradition. Many marabouts, who have to take position on the practice, orient themselves according to what the most influential marabouts recommend. In interviews with marabouts all over Fouta, I found that they almost always referred to what other marabouts had said and decided. According to my interlocutors working for the NGO, it was therefore crucial for Tostan Fouta to communicate with the marabouts in the villages where the program was running to prevent what they called "poisoning" (*intoxication* in French). Such poisoning was perceived to arise when people felt that the subjects being discussed were against the Futanke way of life or were anti-Islamic. As many of the modules

touched on contested issues, such as human rights based on equality, and leadership through democratic elections instead of birthright, poisoning regularly needed to be prevented.
I ask:

> "Isn't it strange that they opposed in this way? The reasons for practicing excision are the same in all the regions of Senegal but in this case there was an opposition."
>
> "Yes," Khalidou replies, "there was a very strong opposition! Because here, as I said, the people are very tough and they speak of religion. And they are unforgiving as far as religious issues are concerned. They are very tough; you see, here the people are convinced that the religion requires it, and that others want to change and turn them away for other purposes. That's where the difficulty lies!"

In other regions of Senegal, among Mende groups and the Diola in Southern Senegal, for example, excision is not immediately associated with the supposed Prophetic recommendation but with initiation (Ahmadu 2000; Dellenborg 2004; Hernlund 2000). However, in Fouta Toro, the belief that excision is a religious recommendation seems to strengthen the marabouts' justification to defend excision against the law and international organizations. Recommendations based on the Qur'an and the Sharia are seen as having more legitimacy than recommendations of non-Islamic origin. Any legal, social, or political issue is discussed with regard to the Islamic point of view on the matter. But in addition to Islamic jurisprudence, something else led to opposition to the law: the authority of Tooroɓɓe marabouts and their recommendations based on their occupational lore: the Qur'an and Sharia (Dilley 2004). Their public outcry against the law on excision thus represents a clash in authority between religious and secular leaders and contradictory ideas of justice.

Khalidou goes on to explain why Tostan decided to stay despite opposition to the program by local authorities:

> That's the difficulty! But we tried to work out a strategy and see how to explain and then, when the program started, again . . . certain religious leaders said, "No, we don't want this." But the women wanted the program! So we said, "Okay. Women, we're going to

work with you. The men, if you don't like the program you can stay
at home and keep your girls by your side if you don't want them to
come, ask them not to come to our classes, but all those who want
to come, this country is a country that is governed so all those who
want to, everyone has the right to learn what they want!"

Khalidou justifies Tostan's resolution to continue with their work by saying
"this is a country that is governed" and "everyone has the right to learn what
they want." He strongly believes in democracy and human rights and in the
state as a democratically elected entity governed by values based on human
rights and equality. The Comaroffs coined the term *fetishism of the law* not
merely as an enchanted faith in constitutions, but also the "culture of legal-
ity" that "seems to be infusing the capillaries of everyday life, becoming part
and parcel of the metaphysics of disorder that haunts all postcolonies" (Comaroff and Comaroff 2006:25). Khalidou's enchantment with human rights,
freedom of speech, education, health care, and freedom of choice clashes with
traditional and moral authorities (Tooro6be), who do not agree with this national law jeopardizing women's honor and religious recommendations.

However, this disagreement is about more than political differences between secular and religious authorities, the sacred against the profane, and
differing conceptions of what "justice" is based on. In Molly's version of the
events in Aere Lao it becomes clear that a battle between these two types of
authority took place in the spiritual realms as well.

Molly Melching added the following about the Aere Lao event:

Many religious leaders came to Aere Lao the day before the intervillage meeting was to take place. They called the women organizers
and myself to meet with them. This is where they told us that they
were not against having people come to the event, but rather that we
should not ever—not even once—mention the word "excision." We
explained that this was not a public declaration to abandon FGC,
but rather an intervillage meeting to discuss. We had assured both
Abdou Fall, the Minister of Health and Mamadou Wane from
UNICEF that we would not dare to frame this as a declaration as it
would have been dangerous at that point in time, given all the
problems. [On the day of the meeting] all the religious leaders went
up there and told us that we could not pronounce the word FGC
and they became very angry and afterwards they held a meeting

and one man got up and said that my soul and the other woman, Aissatou Tall [the woman who was the main organizer of the women from Aere Lao], that our souls would be damned for even having held that meeting and then that man from what I understand, had a diabetic crisis and his two legs were amputated because of his sickness. But everybody felt like, well okay, then maybe. . . .

Molly hesitates before continuing her story. Aware of how this incident might have been read, I finish her sentence for her:

"Mystical reasons," I say, referring to spiritual knowledge practices and powers many people believe in.
"Yes, mystical reasons," Molly replies. "He should not have gone that far and maybe there is something related to him being against ending FGC."

In our conversation we borrow a term that many Senegalese use when they speak about human interference through spiritual means. In French, such practices are commonly referred to as *des choses mystiques* or *mysticisme* in Senegal. The term *mysticism* is controversial in academic English, yet it is a local term that is commonly used particularly in Sufi religious practice (Brenner 2001; Smith 2009). Let us just step back and think about how anthropologists in diverse settings across the African continent have described so-called mystical forces and spiritual forms of affliction as witchcraft (Ashforth 2005; Evans-Pritchard 1976), occult forces (Geschiere 2008), and spiritual knowledge practices. Ashforth (2004:162) notes that most English terms for witchcraft are not satisfactory for understanding spiritual practices and local definitions for them. The same is the case for the French Senegalese blanket term *mysticisme*, so I briefly describe how such spiritual afflictions are understood and distinguished in Fouta Toro.

In Pulaar, spiritual knowledge practices are referred to as *gandal*—literally "knowledge." Gandal may refer to *maraboutage*, the manipulation of the powers of letters, words, and numbers using the names of God by marabouts or *seernaabe*—scholars of Islam. *Gandal bileejo/mbileewu* refers to the knowledge and power of what Dilley (2004: 140) calls "witch-hunters" and healers. *Ñengi* is the trade of precious possessions like one's own organs or the death of family members for desired material objects like money. Dilley (2004) extensively discusses the distinction between what is called the "white knowledge" (*gandal danewal*) practices of Islamic clerics and the "black knowledge" (*gandal balewal*) practices of the men of skill but acknowledges that, despite the dominant ideology that the marabouts' white knowledge is good spiritual practice in contrast to all spiritual knowledge practices sought after by locals, it can also be used to inflict evil. My interlocutors sought out both Islamic marabouts using white knowledge and local wise men (*ganndo* or *bileejo*) using indigenous herbs, potions, and spiritual practices. According to them, the latter was called black knowledge because it was the spiritual practice of the Black man, not of the white man or Arab nor of Islamic origin. Both black and white knowledge could be used for good and for evil.

Let's come back to the events boycotting NGO sensitization against FGC and Molly's account of what happened in Aere Lao. I prompt Molly to talk about the mystical interpretation of these events because I have heard many people say that Tostan is protected by spiritual forces.[11] The fact that the religious leader lost both his legs two weeks after an important event attended by ministers, NGO officials, and people who wanted to speak out against excision was not seen as a coincidence. Writing about post-Apartheid South Africa, Adam Ashforth notes that "Cases of premature death or untimely illness in Africa are almost always attributed to the action of invisible forces, frequently those described as 'witchcraft'" (2004:147). In a similar vein, most Senegalese would see a relationship between the two incidents and think about whose spiritual forces were stronger and who was better protected against evil.

In addition to the events of opposition to the law being about different conceptions of justice and authority, these incidents are obviously about power. Power struggles between the traditional and moral authorities of Fouta on the one hand and the secular state and NGO officials on the other do not just take place in realms of the profane. But, like other conflicts across Africa (Ashforth 2005; Evans-Pritchard 1976; Geschiere 2008; Gluckman 1956; Niehaus 2001), success and misfortune are immediately associated with the realms of the spiritual—people succeed because their prayers have been heard or they are well protected. Others encounter misfortune, injury, or death because they are not well enough protected—someone else is stronger or spiritually more powerful, or has evil inflicted on them.

Some glorify events like the Aere Lao incident as a defeat of the "white people's NGOs," putting them in their place and successfully chasing them out of Fouta. Others interpret them in a different way: although religious leaders condemned NGO officials, and ministers were threatened not to publicly discuss FGC, they were well protected and the infliction fell back on the religious leader who pronounced their condemnation. While many felt that the meeting didn't go very well and Tostan experienced a major backlash with social and political consequences in the realms of the profane, others see the NGO in a different light: the fact that Tostan centers have been consistently present in Fouta since those events and have not disappeared means that they are powerful in the spiritual realm and have not been defeated by the religious leaders.

However, so far we have not addressed the voices of women with regard to the abandonment of FGC. The next section therefore looks at the perspectives of two female activists on excision, social change, and the marabouts' power. Although both women are Senegalese, they are clearly outsiders in that they do not share Futanke views on the importance and cultural value of excision that I have described in previous chapters.

The Midwife and the Marabout of Dounga Wouro Alpha

October 2022. I rest in the new hotel on the outskirts of Ourosogui after meetings with various people for my research. There is a swimming pool with loud African hip hop blaring through the speakers. There was no swimming pool anywhere in Fouta when I was doing fieldwork fifteen years ago; if I wanted to go swimming it had to be in the river, perhaps less polluted by rubbish and plastic bags back then. The pool is empty except for a little boy. I get into the warm water and the boy starts chatting to me in perfect French with a Senegalese accent. He is eight years old. He wants to do diving and swimming competitions with me, complaining that there are no other children to play with. He tells me that his mum has the afternoon off so she has taken him to the pool. I eventually get out of the pool and greet his mother, Mariama. Mariama is a midwife originally from Dakar. She talks about her working conditions, about being on call, about seeing patients from rural areas, and about the gynecologist, who is currently on sick leave. I eventually tell her that I am doing research on excision.

> "Oh, that is a serious problem here in Fouta. Ninety percent of women have undergone excision here in Fouta. You see all types of excision here! All types. And they do it when they are very young."

I ask, "Have you noticed any change since you have been working here? As the law was passed such a long time ago now and there has been so much sensitization, do you think anything has changed?"

"No! Nothing has changed. Most women and girls are still excised. If anything, I have noticed that the girls are cut at an even younger age! They are already cut before their first postnatal appointment!"

Intrigued by this conversation with Mariama I ask her to put me in touch with other midwives in the area. The next day I meet Madame Lo at the health post in Ourosogui. Before being moved to Ourosogui she was posted at the health center in Dounga Wouro Alpha, a maraboutic village on the road between Ourosogui and Thilogne. Dounga Wouro Alpha is well-known among anti-FGM campaigners. Before I met Madame Lo, various activists had already told me that the great marabout of this village, Thierno Mamadou Lamine, was one of the key troublemakers opposing governmental and nongovernmental interventions against the abandonment of excision.

I also heard from others that when the exciser was arrested in Matam, Thierno Mamadou Lamine from Dounga Wouro Alpha was in the crowd with people protesting against the arrest. And various people told me that he said to the police, "Excision has to continue! You can arrest me, I do not mind spending the rest of my life behind bars because I know deep down that excision is the right thing to do and God's justice is on my side." I am intrigued that Madame Lo was posted in this village now known as one of the new hotspots of resistance.

That great marabout of Dounga Wouro Alpha, he doesn't want to hear a word about the abandonment of excision! When the exciser was arrested in Matam, he was heading the march of protesters demanding for the exciser to be released.

She tells me that she used to organize discussion groups on reproductive health with women in Dounga Wouro Alpha and she would also bring up excision and the health consequences. During the discussions the women would not ask any questions about excision, but afterward they would come and see her at the clinic and say to her that they were suffering from the problems she had spoken about and wanted to know more. However, when the maraboutic family found out that she addressed the subject of excision, they told her to stop:

"Once I was supposed to hold a session on excision on the community radio in Dounga Wouro Alpha. The night before it was supposed to take place an announcement was made on the radio of what the program was going to be for the next day. The marabout [*giggles*] sent his son to my house to tell me not to hold this radio program, otherwise he is going to force me to leave this village [*laughs*]. That was the day I stopped talking about excision in this village. That was the day I stopped! He sent his own son, all the way to my house! To tell me not to mention excision."

"He scared you?"

"He really scared me."

"As they have spiritual power . . ."

"That's it. He is very well respected in the village! From that day onward I stopped even mentioning the practice in that village."

"Mm."

"Perhaps one day the practice will disappear, but not right now. In Dounga Wouro Alpha, you cannot even get married if you are not excised. They say don't marry the daughter of so and so, she has not been cut. As long as you have a clitoris you are not clean! [. . .] I had a birth attendant who used to accompany me when I used to go and hold discussion groups against excision in the village. She used to help me raise awareness. But when her own daughter gave birth to a girl, she cut her [*laughs*]. She was a trained birth attendant! But she had her cut. When I examined the girl on the day of the postnatal appointment eight days after delivery, I saw that she was already cut."

Throughout this chapter we have seen examples of activists in fear of religious leaders' spiritual power and divine punishment. Madame Lo represents a recent example of an activist whose activities are terminated by members of a powerful religious family. Despite the sustained efforts of governmental and nongovernmental organizations to stop the excision in Fouta Toro over the last twenty years, the midwives tell us that there is little change; if anything, girls are cut at a younger age. On the other hand, we have the outraged accounts of marabouts who perceive NGO employees and activists as corrupt, fearing that their culture will die with the abandonment of excision. NGO interventions are perceived as neocolonial trickery developing intelligent ways to undermine their power and authority. We know that notions like culture and tradition are not unchanging, but they are often reinterpreted and may gain or lose importance depending on current political events. Traditions are a way of celebrating and reifying social identity. In a similar way, activist agendas may gain or lose popularity depending on economic factors, such as the available funding, the motivation of public health and development agents, and the efficiency of their interventions. Shweder (2013) shows how culturally embedded convictions around the harm or benefit of female and male circumcision practices can be. Shweder refers to the proscription of male circumcision in European countries as an example of how non-Jewish and non-Muslim populations may be biased against male circumcision, which is not seen as a cultural tradition in Europe. In a similar way, to those who are already convinced that FGC is a mutilation, no evidence regarding cut women's ability to experience pleasure and orgasm will be persuasive. Although the 2012 Hastings Center report entitled "Seven Things to Know About Female Genital Surgeries in Africa" published evidence showing that a lot of the reasons commonly cited against FGC by United Nations agencies were factually erroneous and inconsistent with other practices, like female genital cosmetic surgery and male circumcision, the evidence was violently dismissed by the press and ignored by the UN agencies (Shweder 2013:362). Despite the prestige of the Hastings Center in the United States and the academics authoring the report, there was little engagement with the arguments and the evidence presented.[12] In a similar way, those who endorse male or female circumcision as ancient and religious practices are not easily convinced by what NGOs and health professionals present as evidence on health consequences. Some health professionals parrot the health consequences in sensitization meetings but their personal opinions seem contradictory to public health recommendations (O'Neill 2018).

Conclusion

This chapter has shown that the opposition to the law is about more than women's bodies and personhood. It is tied to the conviction that holy law is superior to the state—a domain that the Tooroɓɓe religious leaders pride themselves to have authority over in Fouta Toro. It is clear that governmental and nongovernmental intervention on excision disturbs and unsettles

Futanke social, moral, and political order. The opposition to the law and the NGOs is an act of defense against changes in morality and leadership that challenge the Tooroɓɓe leaders' moral authority and political power. I have shown that they perceive Futanke way of life to be threatened and seriously challenged through these interventions and the associated social change. Whereas they fear the foreign influence of NGOs and believe the Senegalese state to be corrupt, local people—including NGO workers and state representatives and health professionals—fear the marabouts' spiritual power as well. We have seen that marabouts are not just spiritual guides but also the symbolic leaders of Futanke society.

If some Futanke perceive this social change as a sign of the demise of Futanke culture and values, governmental and nongovernmental intervention may be counterproductive. However, in the next chapter I show not only that many women and men feel that it is important to stop practicing excision, but also that the NGOs are providing them with information that helps them to take this decision. Human rights provide some people with tools and inspire them with ideologies that give them the courage to stand up against those who require them to obey a stagnant social and moral order. Even though the marabouts' outcry against governmental and nongovernmental intervention opposes the social and moral disintegration of a society that takes pride in its traditions and moral integrity, social change may be what many people aspire to: hence they support abandonment and seek the support of NGOs and health professionals.

CHAPTER 6

A Right to Health, Freedom of Speech, and Nondiscrimination

The Role of Human Rights in the Abandonment Movement in Fouta Toro

There are nearly always problems. Most women know that the problems Tostan is talking about exist but it is difficult to abandon. It's honor and their religion that stops them from leaving excision.

(Seynabou, Tostan facilitator, May 2007)

There are nineteen human rights. Among these nineteen, the right to health impressed us the most. We were 145 participants in Demba Diallo's classes. After the classes we felt like getting the message out there to others who had not participated and had not understood. We did some sketches. There were some people who were reticent about the activities we organized. We went from door to door to sensitize them and finally we came to an agreement for a public declaration. Sinthiou Sebbe had understood but that wasn't enough, we could not stop there so we went out to meet others who agreed to a public declaration.

(Kumba, president of the management committee of Sinthiou Sebbe in February 2008)

This chapter is about those who have stopped practicing excision and who collaborate with the NGOs to raise awareness about health problems and human rights. As the epigraphs above suggest, idioms pertaining to health and human rights are often mobilized to justify abandonment. I admit that I admired many of the female local activists I met in Fouta, because they were not afraid to speak out against social conventions and did not get easily discouraged in spite of the threats of religious leaders. The questions that continuously circulated in my head were, What was it that gave them the courage to do so? Why were they not afraid of the marabouts' power or of bringing shame over themselves or their families? After following—or teaching—Tostan's two-year development education program, many activists use Tostan's human rights language, social mobilization strategies, and resources to publicly renounce the practice. Although for many, the desire to stop excision in their family is genuine, there are other benefits to publicly abandoning the practice that will be explored in this chapter.

We have seen that the foundations of human rights were born in an era marked by colonialism and imperial domination. There were a lot of doubts about whether a universal declaration of human rights was in the interest of the hundreds of millions of people in the world who were colonial subjects with limited sovereignty (Goodale 2022). Initially the United Nations endorsed members to assume "responsibilities for the administration of territories whose peoples have not yet attained a full measure of self-government" (Article 73, Chapters XI–XIII of the UN charter). They were thus allowed to continue ruling invaded territories with the full blessing of the UN but with the obligation to report back on how colonial rule was being exercised for the "well-being" of the colonized peoples. Eventually, human rights language was deployed in anticolonial struggles for freedom and independence. Human rights were not adopted as a monolithic framework for resistance or to replace preexisting ideologies; rather, Goodale (2022) argues that human rights were appropriated strategically in the face of colonial and structural violence. Terretta (2012) suggests that human rights language and concepts became a powerful framework within which African anticolonial activists confronted the violence of colonial rule and created alliances with Pan-African social movements and transnational NGOs. Grassroots activists and political leaders used the rights discourse as a logic for collaborative political agency.

Engle Merry and Ferguson call intervention involving so-called global standards of human rights "transnational." These transnational standards of what human rights are and what constitutes their violation have been defined by international committees as issues of women's rights.[1] Engle Merry and Shell-Duncan have emphasized that these international agreements frequently need to be translated into the vernacular, with the aid of NGO education programs or through activist groups. This process of "translation" (Engle Merry 2006) takes place because many "indigenous women" do not perceive their problems or personal conflicts as "human rights violations." They are often assisted in formulating personal issues in human rights language by NGOs and activists in order to make their case viable and strong (Engle Merry 2006; Strathern 2004).

Ahmadu and Kamau (2022) recently argued that the prohibition to practice FGC in African countries actually takes rights away from women. Dr. Tatu Kamau contested the act prohibiting female genital mutilation at the High Court of Kenya. Based on her professional experience of caring for hundreds of patients from various ethnic groups throughout Kenya, she argues that the health complications listed by the WHO "were just hype, drama and racism." While working in a maternity unit in the 1990s where a lot of patients had undergone Type III FGC, she "woke up to the reality of the blatant distortion of facts about FC" (2022:31). Ahmadu and Kamau argue that in many communities across Africa (and for the Dawoodi Bohra of India), female circumcision "is a signifier of physical maturation of females from girlhood to womanhood" (2022:35) and represents the social creation of "wife," the vehicle of matriarchy, and "the ancestral authority to reproduce lineages" (2022:35). They contend that the FGM act discriminates against females: "while both female and male circumcision are primarily conducted for cultural reasons, men have access to the highest standard of healthcare for their circumcisions but health workers are prohibited from providing services to women wishing to be circumcised" (2022:32). Kamau finally argues that Kenya has "international obligations for the empowerment of women, a laudable goal that is achieved by increasing women's agency and autonomy, not by increasing government control over their lives" (Ahmadu and Kamau 2022:32). These arguments are incredibly important and interesting. Throughout this book I have pointed out the many ways in which FGC is important to women and men in Fouta Toro, and how it creates gender, womanhood, and the foundations for moral personhood. Yet, this chapter is about women who desire to stop practicing and who mobilize health and human rights in their arguments to justify their decisions.

Engle Merry's supposition—that it is mostly "middle-level women" and transnational elites who adhere to human rights ideology and who are more committed to using human rights approaches than indigenous women— seems misplaced in the case of the Futanke. Engle Merry says that so-called indigenous women are often pushed by NGOs to formulate their personal issues in terms of the violation of human rights. She argues that their orientation to human rights models is often temporary. Although some Futanke women and men feel pressured to publicly declare their abandonment of FGC, I show in this chapter that many Futanke women perceive the international human rights agreements as protecting their bodies and rights. The notion of harm has an interesting role to play in this process: although evidence of the negative health and psychosocial effects of FGC are controversial and experts disagree on the extent of the harm in relation to male circumcision or female genital cosmetic surgery, the negative health consequences are mobilized in arguments that justify the abandonment of excision. My interlocuters who rejected FGC and mobilized health and harm as reasons for abandonment did so in ways that often seem inconsistent with scientific evidence. Sometimes it is not clear what exactly they are referring to, and perhaps their subjective experiences of their health problems should not be scrutinized for scientific facts but merely taken as accounts of an experience that was their own in a specific context. In the argument I am making here, the fact that they mobilized these health problems as justifications to speak out against the practice are the most relevant, not whether these descriptions are realistic. Anthropological and psychological literature has shown that people may express their emotional or psychological suffering in parts of their body that are clinically or physiologically healthy from a biomedical perspective.

Those who have experienced sexual or reproductive health problems because of their own excision, but find it hard to stop practicing, see the rights framework provided by transnational institutions and the state as a way out of oppressive structures in their own society. It provides them with an ideology that gives courage (cuusal) to publicly discuss their health problems and speak out against excision. As we shall see, vernacular human rights discourses revolve around the idea that daughters have the right to nondiscrimination and the highest standards of health. The fact that many women in Senegal have declared their abandonment of excision before them and that they are supported by an international community has given them strength to challenge local leaders' opposition to the abandonment of excision.

The first part of the chapter explores the views and experiences of those who are against excision and shows how they perceive the opposition. Most of them have personally experienced reproductive health problems and have come to understand these as linked to excision through NGO education classes. They perceive the law as being in place to protect women's health and believe that those who oppose it either are not aware of the underlying cause of the problems most women experience or are socially constrained to adhere to a moral order that has been in place for a long time and is not normally challenged. I argue that the attribution of gynecological problems to excision, whatever the strength of the empirical evidence, leads women to perceive the opposition as "wrong" or to "have not understood" and that this motivates women to go out and raise awareness against excision. If the law is seen as being there to protect women from the health problems associated with excision, and an international community is perceived to be there to support them, it is possible for women to stop practicing and stand up against leaders who oppose the ban. In contrast to the anger and fear in discourses around the abandonment of excision explored in the previous chapters, the women below express hope and desperation for change.

The President of the Management Committee for the Public Declaration in Gulumadji

In May 2007, a public declaration of the abandonment of excision and early/ forced marriage was planned to take place in Daande Lao. Although the village chief was keen for this to happen, not all of the seventeen other villages on the list of declaring villages agreed. In the neighboring village of Gulumadji, for example, the village chief was outraged about the planned public declaration when I interviewed him on their motivations to publicly declare their abandonment to stop FGC. He did not want his village to be on an official list of villages that had abandoned the practice. The president of the management committee for the public declaration in Gulumadji, however, was very disappointed that this declaration had failed. After having interviewed the village chief of Gulumadji, my research assistant and I walked over to the other end of the village and were approached by a man who had been looking for us. He was one of the organizers of the public declaration and was aware of the village chief's opposition. However, he explained to us that "the young people" in the village had wanted a declaration anyway and he hoped that the village chief had not turned Tostan against the idea of Gulumadji participating in one.

The midday heat was becoming oppressive and it was approaching lunchtime. This man took us to a house to rest. We lay down on mattresses arranged in a cool, mud-brick room. The children brought us *ataaya*, the strong tea that helps to fight the lethargy that accompanies the heat. Hosting important guests (singular, koɗo; plural, hoɓɓe) is prestigious. Members of the management committees for public declarations are fairly used to having researchers, journalists, or volunteers sent to them by the NGO to discuss excision and declaring. Those villagers who want development go out of their way to present a certain image of the village in order to make guests believe that they are dynamic and worthy of funding. When people hear that a white person has come to the village, those who have something to say come to the hut where the white person is hosted. They are keen to talk about issues that are on their mind and tell stories of their struggles as they believe that they will be heard by people who will be able to help (also see Hodzic 2017).

Soon, various people, all part of the management committee for the failed declaration, came to greet us. As I am white, the president of the management committee of Gulumadji presumed that I was one of those volunteers or NGO workers who had come to ask questions about their decision to stop practicing excision. The presidents of management committees are often articulate women who are not afraid to express their opinions and are not easily intimidated by people who challenge their decisions. They are often the driving force behind the declarations and encourage other women to join their cause. While I try to stay awake in the midday heat and before I ask any questions, the president of the management committee begins to talk: "People are so keen on doing a public declaration! They really want to do a public declaration if the misunderstanding won't stop them [Tostan and the authorities who had planned to come to the declaration that failed to take place] from coming back here to organize a public declaration. We are for Tostan. We have understood the program well. We will always support Tostan and their work even if there are people here in the village who don't, we want Tostan!" At this point we are not sure why and what this declaration means to them. I asked, "What is it that makes you want to abandon?" The woman replies, "In fact we've had problems with many of our young girls' health. Upon marriage a lot of young girls have had problems with penetration. They often needed to be taken to the doctor to be opened. And we didn't know why they were having these difficulties. We asked why and it was said that it was because of the excision. Then Tostan came to the village and explained the same thing. That is why we want to abandon."

In previous chapters, I showed that girls tend to be cut during infancy. I explained that most women do not remember any pain and rarely have any medical problems due to excision until they are penetrated on marriage, or at pregnancy and childbirth. Throughout my fieldwork I often asked myself why some of my interlocutors, like my friends in Diawoury, never complained of health issues, whereas whenever I went to interview women about their decision to stop practicing, they spoke of their troubles. I was not sure whether only some women suffer from these medical problems or whether it was very common. Was the antiexcision movement guided only by those who had experienced health problems, or were more complex social and political factors involved? I ask, "The consequences you were talking about, do only some women suffer from them?" The woman replies, "It is very common! Because before, young girls who were cut used to be treated with 'traditional' products but this treatment is not done anymore.[2] The girls' excision is not treated anymore. One just expects them to be virgin upon marriage and then they are taken to the healthcare center to be opened. [. . .] Nowadays, the most important thing is that the girl is closed so that her vagina is closed and she cannot have sexual intercourse." In previous chapters, I presented the views of people who felt that excision was safe and does not cause harm by saying that it has been around "since the beginning of the universe and has never caused problems" (*gila dawaa-dawi kaddungal ina wadee kono cadeele meedaa heen wonnde*). Here, on the other hand, it is said that the problems have become more common with reference to "loss of tradition." The woman implies that there has been a shift in the way excision is practiced so that it causes more harm. The emphasis is on closure and control of desire. It is possible that there is an increasing concern with virginity before marriage and with making sure that the girl does not risk losing her honor. In that case, excision could be seen as a preventive measure against the threats of a changing society, where women need to wait for their husbands for longer periods than in the past, or where there are more pregnancies before marriage than in the past. The Futanke are losing their traditions and the values that have made them proud of who they are.

However, I also met many people who saw no relation between the way in which women are cut and any increase in the risk that girls will lose their virginity before marriage. These people did not perceive excision to be more harmful than in the past and said that the problems always existed. They said that they did not know that the problems were due to excision but thought that all women experience difficulties when in labor. In her ethnography on perceptions of FGC in Ghana, Hodzic shows that discourses on harm and the purpose and meaning of excision can change over time. Whereas during her research in the 1990s excision was not linked to control of desire and sexuality at all, more recent NGO discourses engage with notions around the loss of traditions and degrading sexual morals, for which women are often blamed. Perhaps this is a result of transnational discourses on the purposes of FGC that have imbued Ghanaian NGO workers' understanding of the practice and reshape—possibly even reinvent—local understandings of tradition and harm. In view of the village chief's disagreement with the organization of the public declaration, I asked the following question:

> *Sarah* Is it not possible to abandon without doing a public declaration?
>
> *Woman* Yes, that is possible. There are people here in the village who have already abandoned.
>
> *Sarah* If that's the case, why do you want to have a public declaration?
>
> *Woman* To prove to everyone that we have abandoned so that others can follow our movement as well.

Tostan developed its strategies in line with Gerry Mackie's concept of "organized diffusion."[3] Mackie (2000) argues that if a practice has become a social norm, it is impossible for individuals in a group to abandon a harmful practice alone. He compares the abandonment of FGC to the disappearance of Chinese foot-binding. He argues that, as with the abandonment of foot-binding in China, FGC needs to be abandoned collectively. Otherwise, individual members of the community remain ostracized. Mackie and Tostan therefore suggest that this abandonment process can happen only if a whole community decides to stop together and makes their decision public. The president of the management committee, however, asserts that it is possible for individuals to separately abandon the practice. For her, the declaration is important so that everyone in the region hears about it and can join their movement. This will raise awareness about the impact of the cutting. As we shall see, others disagreed with this. To find out more about their motivations, I ask,

> *Sarah* What are the most convincing reasons to abandon excision?
> (1) Health, (2) the harmful consequences of excision, (3) the law, (4) human rights, or (5) money.
> *Woman* I think it's health because if you are sick you can't choose to refuse anything that will make you feel better. The main reason to abandon is health. Every time a woman is in labor or has to have an operation because of it, she realizes. I think that is even why the law was voted in, in the interests of the population, for the health of the population.

I asked this question in many interviews with people who wanted to stop practicing and had organized public declarations in Fouta Toro and other areas.[4] The responses varied. Some authorities, such as the village chief Gulumadji, said that only the law can make them stop practicing, not the NGOs or anyone else. In Daande Lao, on the other hand, the village chief suggested that his village would become more important through a public declaration. He had aspirations for his village to be in the newspapers and on the radio, and to hear people say that it was a "progressive village" that wanted to develop. He seemed to believe that this would attract more funds. In the Diery, however, in a village called Sinthiou Wallube, a village chief we spoke to said that the law had no power and could not stop anyone from doing anything. If people decided to stop practicing "their customs," there had to be a well-founded reason that had been approved by the religious leaders.

In contrast to those who oppose the antiexcision movement and the law and see it as a form of cultural colonialism, and as a way of persuading people to abandon Islam, the interlocutor quoted above believes that the law was passed because of the health problems associated with excision. What she has learned from health professionals and in Tostan classes has given her courage

to speak out, despite the social importance of excision and the leaders' opposition, as I explore in greater detail through the case of Raki.

Raki in Daande Lao

Raki was one of the main organizers of the failed public declaration in
Daande Lao. Her father was a powerful Maabo marabout in the village who
supported her cause and was ready to speak out despite the Tooroɓɓe marabouts' disapproval. When we first arrived in Daande to discuss the failed
declaration, Raki accompanied us everywhere and tried to determine whom
we should speak to. She was evidently afraid that we would meet people who
were against the declaration. This was against her interests because, me being
white, she saw me as someone who had been sent by Tostan to inquire. Nevertheless, after a few days, she despaired and was frustrated that the declaration
would not take place. In a formal interview she told us that it was difficult
for those who wanted to stop excising to stop alone and that it was better if
everyone heard why they were abandoning and that they were supported
by the law and international organizations. She was afraid that because the
declaration had failed, Tostan might abandon them and focus on working
in other villages where there was a general consensus to stop excising.

My research assistant and I had come back to Raki's house after a few days
of visiting Gulumadji and other villages that were supposed to take part in
the public declaration of Daande Lao. Raki, whose husband was in the Democratic Republic of Congo, had prepared our bed under a mosquito net under
a tree in the compound. I slept there with her and her baby. Raki and I were
creeping under the mosquito net and settling into bed in the dark when she
asked me where we were going the next day. I told her. She asked me if it was
not going to turn Tostan against the declaration if we found information that
showed that not everyone was in favor. I said, no, not at all . . .

"Tostan needs to know what's going on in order to be able to organize
things better. In Gulumadji for example, the village chief and quite a few other
people are against the declaration. But there are also a lot of people who are
passionatcly for the abandonment of excision and I think it's going to help
them to organize a public declaration. I don't think they will change their
mind. And they support people who want to abandon excision and these
women are so convinced of the consequences themselves," I say hopefully.

"Mm," she replies.

To give her courage I continue: "Yes. I think it's amazing. One of the women in the *comité de pilotage* is so strongly against it, she says that everyone is aware of the consequences without exception. Because every woman needs to be opened upon the wedding night and most women have problems with their excision."

"Mm," she says, not sounding particularly surprised.

"Do you think that what she says is true? That most women have problems upon the wedding night and need to be opened?" I ask.

"Well, yes. There are problems with it and most women, I would say 90 percent of women experience it—the opening upon the wedding night. And then you have to be cut again when you give birth. My wound didn't heal for a whole month, it was so painful. I would say that most women know that these problems exist but many of them don't know where they come from. Because it's what they found with the ancestors.[5] They cannot imagine anything else. But most women know the problems," Raki says.

"That is so strange that they don't talk about it," I reply.

Raki "Mm."
Sarah "So strange."
Raki "It's their honor and the religion that stops them from
     abandoning."

Raki's descriptions of reproductive health problems and interventions during childbirth may or may not have been caused by excision. Episiotomy is just as common in countries where FGC is not practiced. As an ethnographer I am not in a position to evaluate or judge the veracity of Raki's statements, but that does not matter. What matters is that, based on Tostan's reproductive-health education classes, Raki believes that the problems many women experience are linked to FGC.

When Raki says that religion stops people from renouncing excision, she is referring to both the concept of religious purity explored in Chapter 4 and the religious leaders' opposition to abandoning a Prophetic recommendation. "Honor" could mean being able to control one's desires and being able to resist temptations. A number of marabouts said that a woman who loses her honor is devalued. This implies that a woman who cannot resist temptation is shameless. "Honor stops them from abandoning" may also mean that someone may be ashamed to be different from everyone else and being rejected or ostracized as a result.

My conversations with these two women raise a number of questions with regard to excision and "health" and women's desire to participate in public declarations. First of all, is excision a harmful practice or not? As we can see in the ethnography, women's views on whether FGC is harmful vary. Throughout the last few chapters, we have discussed women who do not perceive the practice as harmful and reason that it is a tradition that has existed for a long time, which must therefore be safe. However, the women we meet in this chapter do perceive excision as harmful. They argue that most women experience the problems associated with excision but are not aware that they are due to the cutting. Most women think that the gynecological problems they are suffering from are an inevitable side effect of childbirth. Others who do attribute their problems to excision continue cutting because they perceive the risk of not cutting their daughters to be worse. Whether someone stops practicing therefore does not seem to depend solely on whether they have experienced problems, but also on the extent to which it is possible for them to talk about their problems openly and admit that they are against excision. This is why both Raki and the president of the management committee find the public declarations useful. The president of the management committee said that it is possible to stop without declaring, but the declaration is useful so that everyone can hear about the cause of the problems most women experience. Raki, on the other hand, supports Mackie's theory (2000), saying that it is hard to stop practicing alone, and a public declaration where everyone hears that a group of women has stopped saves women from being ostracized. Where purity and honor are the social norm, everyone excises and those who do not are "different" and "repulsive." In these circumstances, however, health and human rights reasons justify collectively stopping the practice. If everyone understands and accepts that the problems most women experience are due to excision and people come to a consensus to stop in the name of women's health, then purity perhaps becomes less of a priority and honor becomes associated with taking pride in being one of the few who have given up the practice in the name of women's health and reproductive capacity.

Shell-Duncan (2008) argues that the antiexcision campaigns' arguments have shifted from discourses about health to discourses about human rights. This has been particularly the case since various biomedical studies have shown that the so-called medical facts of long-term and short-term risks of FGC were either trivial or based on small or poorly designed studies (Shell-Duncan 2008:226). In a 2006 WHO study on the health risks of FGC it was found that "for women with WHO III mutilations (the most severe) there was a relative risk of 1.3 for both caesarean section and infant resuscitation, and 1.6 for stillbirth or early neonatal death, and there was no increased risk for the 32 percent of women who had WHO type I mutilation" (Conroy 2006:106). Conroy (2006) further notes that this places the risk of FGC somewhere behind maternal smoking (in Shell-Duncan 2008:226).

Over the last fifteen years various systematic reviews of the different consequences of FGC have been published. For instance, Berg, Denison, and Fretheim (2010) conducted a systematic review examining the sexual consequences of FGM. All studies except two reviews showed that painful coitus, low satisfaction, and low desire were more likely with FGM. Painful coitus was 1.5 times more likely.[6]

In terms of birth outcomes Berg et al. (2014) suggest in a systematic review and meta-analysis that "there is clear evidence that FGM significantly increased the risk of childbirth complications" (Sarayloo, Latifnejad Roudsari, and Elhadi 2019). Yet others contest these analyses, arguing that the effects of FGC on sexual and obstetric outcomes are exaggerated, and frequently sexual problems are attributed to FGC instead of other health issues that uncut women also frequently suffer from (Ahmadu and Kamau 2022; Essen and Mosselmans 2021; Public Advisory Network on Female Genital Surgeries in Africa 2012; Johnsdotter 2020).

Perhaps the number of those who really do stop practicing is relatively low because the so-called health effects are exaggerated and human rights are perceived as an imposition by many and an "intelligent form of cultural colonialism," as suggested by the outraged marabouts after the arrest of the exciser of Matam. However, as we can see here, some women internalize the health information given to them, believe that their reproductive health problems were caused by excision, and want to stop practicing and declare their decision for the reasons discussed above. In the following we explore how women who raise awareness about the problems associated with excision are accepted despite the opposition.

Fatou Barry

Fatou Barry was a Tostan facilitator who came to work and live in Diawoury in October 2007. Diawoury, along with some other villages on the Ile Amorphile, was considered a difficult zone by Tostan coordination, as there had been fierce opposition from the neighboring villages in the past. When the idea of participating in the program was introduced during meetings with the village council in Diawoury, Tostan still had an extremely bad reputation. This was why initially I did not tell people what my research was about nor did I tell them that I was in touch with Tostan and occasionally went to the local headquarters to check my emails. Although the women would not have known much about Tostan as they were not involved in local politics nor particularly interested, influential men in Diawoury might have disapproved and poisoned others against me. However, by the time Tostan became active in Diawoury, I was already well-known to most Diawourynaaɓe, and they were proud that I had chosen to live in their village. I was in no way considered a threatening intruder but was more like a grown-up child learning to talk and live like them, constantly laughed at, ridiculed, and taught how to do things properly. When Tostan introduced themselves to the village council of Diawoury, my teacher informed the villagers of the benefits of the program, and the Diawourynaaɓe agreed to the implementation of Tostan classes. The Tostan coordinator picked Fatou Barry to teach in Diawoury because she had been teaching the Tostan program in Fouta for many years and had successfully handled some fierce opposition. Although she regularly complained about the fact that she was sent to the most remote villages where transport was extremely difficult, where there was no electricity and few other comforts, Tostan management reasoned that she would do a good job and prevent any polemics against Tostan, and since she was divorced, having a job with a regular income was better than sitting at home relying on her siblings' financial support. Fatou Barry was a round, sociable, and kind lady who liked to come over to my hosts' compound in the afternoons to have a chat with Fama Ly or Fatoumata. As Fama Ly's husband Samba Sarr had also worked for Tostan in the past, Fatou Barry felt welcome in their household. She got to know the household I had become part of well. At first, she refused to speak to me in French, and I did not know that she spoke any French at all, so she got to know me by speaking to me in Pulaar and observing me interacting with the family in Pulaar. After a few months we started speaking in French, with which I was more comfortable, and we had many long conversations during the sandstormy afternoons of January and February 2008.

For the first few months of the Tostan program, Fatou Barry had mainly focused on human rights. Having rights (*jojjanɗe*) meant having duties (*fotde*) toward one's community, as she explained. The classes were well attended and women were interested in these rights and duties, as well as the structure of the state and democracy. In January 2008 we spoke of To-stan's ambition to get communities to organize public declarations against excision on the veranda of Fama Ly's house. Until this point Fatou Barry had only expressed her opposition to excision in personal conversations with villagers, not during classes.

I say to Fatou, "You know what always surprises me? Some people have never had any problems with excision, how are they going to be convinced that they should stop if they've never had any problems? People like Fatou-mata for example, she has given birth to I don't know how many children? I think eight or so. And she doesn't seem to have any problems and all her girls are excised. Why would someone like that want to abandon?"

Fatou Barry replies, "Well, but often there are problems. I think in most cases there are problems. I've had many problems which is why I don't want any more children. When I was pregnant with my first child, the nurse looked at everything and said 'Oiooo, childbirth is going to be very difficult!' Because of the excision. Everything is very tight down there and I would have many problems so my first child was a caesarean."[7]

"Ah," I reply.

"There are nearly always problems."

I had known the views of the Diawourynaaɓe, and particularly the women in my household, on the benefits of excision since the beginning of my fieldwork and knew how their beliefs were associated with conceptions of purity, cleanliness, and ethnic identity. It was hard for me to believe that they could ever change their minds about practicing excision. As the women in my household never complained of any problems because of their excision, I believed that convincing them of the necessity to stop prac-ticing was an impossibility and Fatou's work was somewhat futile. However, Fatou did not see it the same way. Like Raki and the president of the man-agement committee, Fatou Barry was convinced that women think that complications are an inevitable side effect of childbirth and having many children.

Knowing that Fatou Barry did not hesitate to speak about reproductive health and the problems she had experienced because of her own excision, I asked Fatoumata again what she thought a few days before the end of my field-work in 2008. I said that I had understood that she had never experienced any problems and considered excision a good thing, as she had told me so many times before. However, this time, she replied that there are always many problems during childbirth (*ina heewi cadeele*) and that she was no longer sure whether excision was a good thing.

How was this change of view on excision possible? For a number of reasons, I suggest. Even if Fatoumata thought that her excision had never caused her any problems, Fatou Barry's personal stories of her pregnancy and childbirth are something Fatoumata can relate to. Perhaps she recognized some of the symptoms Fatou Barry talked of and came to the realization that she had also suffered from these problems during childbirth, but had not previously linked them to excision.

Even if there is hostility toward antiexcision campaigns in an area, because the facilitators are women who know how to communicate their personal experiences to others this makes them more difficult to disagree with. Personal witness accounts seemed to be more convincing than human rights rhetoric and threatening people with the law. Even if Fatoumata and other women were concerned about purity and their daughters' control of desire, a woman who speaks out against the practice cannot be ostracized if her reasons are based on personal experiences.

We can see that speaking out of personal conviction and courage can have a stronger effect than concerns with purity and the control of desire. In addition, Fatou Barry fitted into the community. She was well respected and knew how to defend her views with reference to the state and human rights. In contrast to those who oppose the law, she interpreted laws as being in place to defend women's health and interests. This was also persuasive for many Diawourynaaɓe.

Fatou Barry, as well as Raki and the president of the management committee, who could all be defined as grassroots activists,[8] are undermining the authority of those who oppose the law and the NGOs. They are not "middle-level women" of the educated classes who have been socialized into accepting human rights ideology and associated conceptions of violence against women, nor have they been taught to parrot human rights language to defend their personal agendas and issues for other purposes, as Engle Merry argues for women in China. These women dare to speak out against excision in an environment hostile to FGC sensitization and the political institutions associated with them because they have personally experienced what the NGOs and the state say to be true. For them, the law, therefore, does not represent a threat to their cultural integrity and gender identity, but is seen as a force protecting them and their reproductive health, as well as that of future generations.

Divorce

The following account of Khadija Diallo at the Tostan meeting with the marabouts of Fouta after the denunciation of the exciser in Matam gives an impression of the medical problems some women suffer from and the effect on their relationships with their husbands.

> I was excised at the age of seven. On the day my mother took me to an old woman who did it, I hemorrhaged. I was bleeding for three days and my family were afraid that I would not be able to walk. They used *borgo* (boiled sheep feces), which eventually stopped the hemorrhage, but afterward I was nearly completely closed. When I first had my period I could only see it for a day and there was only a small quantity of blood coming out. I was obliged to go to the health care assistant every month for him to get out a thick beige and black liquid by pressing on my abdomen. When I married for the first time I had to be opened and I was scared of having sex with my husband because it hurt so much. Three days later I was closed again and had to be cut open again. Since then I've been afraid of having sex. I am with my fourth husband now and all my divorces are because of that!
>
> (Khadija Diallo at a meeting with Tostan and marabouts of Fouta,
> May 2009)

Even for activists it is rare to speak of personal problems in this way and most women who speak of them in public do so in a less personal way. However, when women say that their divorce was due to excision, they are not implying that their husbands divorced them because they were excised but that fear of sexual intercourse or lack of mutual satisfaction eventually led to a breakdown in the relationship. We also have to bear in mind that most of these women married when they were very young, between the ages of ten and fifteen.

A lot of divorced activists I met had been through a series of marriages before the age of twenty, and possibly because of their young age, had not managed to establish a relationship with their husbands. In Diawoury I heard some people say that early marriage was a good thing; it taught a young girl responsibility and manners. If she did not get on with her first husband and they divorced, she was considered mature enough to choose her next husband but at least she did not get pregnant before marriage. Some of the activists I met decided not to get married anymore after a few divorces but enjoyed the freedom and independence work gave them. For these women, Tostan did not just represent an avenue to talk about issues they felt strongly about (excision and early/forced marriage) but also gave them financial independence from their kin. Furthermore, the facilitators emphasized on numerous occasions that Tostan let them travel, teach, and be listened to and respected by people in the communities they were working with.

Being a Working Woman and an Activist

During my first month in Diawoury, I met a facilitator at a wedding. Khadija was on leave for a few days. Her workplace was at least 250 kilometers away in Matam, but her four children stayed on her father's compound in Diawoury. I met her again in the coming months at preparatory meetings for the public declaration in Semme, at the Tostan coordination in Ourosogui, at home in Diawoury. Our get-togethers were always warmhearted and we became friends. She was then promoted and became a Tostan supervisor. When I interviewed her in December 2007 at the Tostan coordination, I found out that she had married her first husband at the age of ten, the second at the age of fifteen, the third a few years later. Since she had divorced her last husband, she had decided not to marry any more. Khadija wore the clothes of a respectable well-to-do woman. She could afford the most beautiful boubous made of Malian cloth. Other women admired and envied her whenever she came to Diawoury. Although she was not married and spent her time debating controversial issues, she had status because she had money and could do as she pleased. Khadija's behavior was not considered shameful as she acted in a very respectable way and justified her behavior with reference to human rights. She was listened to when she spoke. I admired her greatly for her courage and strength after her divorces. It was not easy for her to gain so much respect and independence after the difficult youth she had with her husbands.

How was it possible for Khadija to achieve this independence without losing her honor? How was it possible for her, as well as Fatou Barry and Bintou Sow (Chapter 2), to discuss controversial issues despite widespread opposition to the law and NGOs and to live as a single woman? Besides the financial independence gained through work, these women were convincing and persuasive for two reasons. Their life experiences and stories make the NGO's messages strong and credible. Their talk, while raising awareness, was not considered vulgar and shameful because they could relate what was said to their own lives. Furthermore, because they could justify their views with reference to the law and human rights, they were not easily intimidated by those who disagreed with what they said. The education they had received, and were actively passing on in the Tostan classes, had perhaps provided them with social mobility. However, in contrast to Engle Merry's example, they pass on the human rights message out of personal conviction after a deep learning process (Gillespie and Melching 2010). The following example will explore how arguments about human rights are mobilized to stop practicing excision.

Human Rights and the Public Declaration of Sinthiou Sebbe

Sinthiou Sebbe was the first place where a public declaration of the abandonment of excision took place in Fouta Toro. After many difficulties with the religious leaders and failed declarations, Sinthiou Sebbe declared with ten villages in 2003 and again in 2005 with seventy villages. Due to the many events of opposition and incidents where antiexcision activities were blocked by local authorities, Molly Melching and UNICEF officials did not believe that this declaration would succeed until it was actually over. Since then, the villagers of Sinthiou Sebbe have been frequently visited by journalists, filmmakers, ministers, UNICEF representatives, and other NGOs who want to speak about their courage in abandoning in this conservative region. Kumba, a member of the blacksmith caste and president of the management committee, is a representative of those who stopped practicing and the face of public declaration. I went to Sinthiou Sebbe to interview people in February 2008. A Tostan supervisor dropped me off at Kumba's house early in the morning. I greeted her politely and spoke to her in my broken Pulaar, which she was very pleased about as she said that she often had to receive visitors who pass by only for a couple of hours for some quick film shots and then disappear again. Often they showed little appreciation of Pulaar customs and hospitality and appear very impolite. She preferred people to stay for longer so that she got some pleasure out of conversing with them as well. I stayed in Sinthiou Sebbe for two nights. Kumba and I got on very well. She was a warm and charismatic woman who did not hesitate to say what she thought. On the second night of my stay in Sinthiou Sebbe, Kumba's co-wife gave birth to a baby. It was the last child of their late husband, who had died recently. They decided to name the girl after me. I had brought good fortune to their home, they explained. I had come to stay and she had had a good birth. This gesture was extremely honorable for me. It commemorated my visit and showed that they appreciated my presence.

The following interview with Kumba and another member of the management committee took place in Kumba's room. I was not allowed to record the interview because Kumba was in mourning and said she was not allowed to have her voice recorded during this forty-day period. I therefore noted everything they said carefully. I began by asking:

"Why organize a public declaration? If you want to abandon excision, why go as far as organizing a public declaration?"
"I welcome you to my home; everyone who is sent here by Tostan is welcome. There is a good relationship between us. We have done two public declarations. The first one was in 2003, the second in 2005. Before Tostan came to the village, the side effects of excision were ignored. We learned all the Tostan modules and there are nineteen human rights. Among these nineteen, the right to health impressed us the most. We were 145 participants in Demba Diallo's classes. After the classes we felt like getting the message out there to others who had not participated and had not understood. We asked the facilitator to show us how to go about raising awareness. Khalidou Sy came and watched some of the sketches. There were some people who were reticent about these activities. We went from door to door to sensitize them and finally we came to an agreement for a public declaration. Sinthiou Sebbe had understood but that was not enough, we could not stop there, so we went out to meet others who agreed to a public declaration. In 2003 we organized a declaration but there were only ten villages. We continued the sensitization activities until 2005 and declared again with seventy villages."

Like the president of the management committee of Gulumadji, Kumba expresses how much what they had learned in the Tostan classes affected them and encouraged them to change their lives. They became motivated to go out and spread the word among others who "had not understood." I found that people who declared their renunciation of excision often used metaphors like, "We were blind but now we can see" or "We were in the dark but now we have understood" to express what they had gained from the Tostan program. There is a slogan that is often used to express how people are encouraged to change their lives: *tiidtinde mbaawkaaji*. *Tiidtinde* means to reinforce or to make stronger, and *mbaawkaaji* means "what can be done" or capability. This phrase is also used when someone wants to improve their language skills. A similar expression I found widely used in Tostan circles was *renforcer les capacités*. Following the Tostan program was seen as helping people to improve their capabilities in everyday life—not just with regard to excision, but by giving them courage (*cuusal*, to dare; *pellital*, to be decisive) and strength to make decisions themselves rather than relying on "what has existed since the beginning of the universe" or what others decided for them. Kadia from Diawoury incessantly used the expression *renforcer les capacités* to explain how people had to take their lives into their own hands rather than complain and give in to other people's wishes. Although these expressions are originally from Tostan, inspired by Martha Nussbaum's capability approach, they have taken on meaning in people's personal lives.

What also comes across is Kumba's gratitude to Tostan when she says, "Everyone who is sent here by Tostan is welcome." Kumba knew that I was a researcher and that Tostan's work had nothing to do with me—she was not doing anyone any favors by complimenting their work to me. The connections between understanding, gratitude, and the motivation to go out and tell others about one's positive experience and new personal convictions are important to my argument. Kumba also emphasizes how much the role of human rights impressed them. "Fouta is a very conservative area," I say. "How was it possible for people to dare speak of customs that are normally taboo like that?" She responds:

> In the Tostan program it is taught that discrimination between people is not to be desired. We also learned the effects of excision. We wanted other communities to understand the same things we had understood. We wanted to let others know that Senegal is a democratic country, that we have the right to express ourselves openly without hiding our views and that we have the right to take decisions in public. So we worked incredibly hard for this public declaration. The path was hard but eventually we achieved what we wanted. After the first declaration the management committee had

become a bit weak. But they worked a lot, especially raising aware-ness, and eventually managed to declare again.

Kumba describes human rights not as abstract but basic rights like the right to nondiscrimination and the right to freedom of speech and the right to health, which she lists in her explanation of what gave them the courage to publicly declare their decision. It is important to bear in mind that as a member of the blacksmith caste (*hinnde*), Kumba cannot be a leader accord-ing to traditional Futanke social structure, where only noblemen are granted rights to leadership. However, the transnational human rights ideology and democratic election processes make it possible for her to be a leader on the basis of her personal conviction and drive to raise awareness among those who have not understood and who have not dared to break with the tradi-tion. Although the fact that the lower castes are organizing movements against a so-called Islamic recommendation, which some Tooroɓɓe strongly disagree with because their authority is being undermined, others draw hope and strength from it. These frequently repeated slogans during sensitization activities are not merely an adoption of NGO terminology; rather, they jus-tify speaking out against a matter that traditionally has not been theirs to decide. The slogans are an expression of hope for social change. Even if the abandonment of excision is not a priority for some of those attracted to the movement, the fact that it bypasses the usual hierarchy of decision-making processes lets people aspire to social change.

"Do people really have these problems because of excision?" I ask.

Kumba replies, "Here, people are really convinced of the harmfulness of the practice after what they have learned! That is even why we created an-other association. All the people present here in the room are here because they feel passionate about it."

"What is the origin and the aim of this association?"

"We personally never met Anna Lindh[9] but we know that she is very ac-tive over there for human rights and children's rights. That is why we called our association after that woman. Then we found out that this woman was very dynamic over there and that we are working toward the same goal. In the end we found out that she was killed and it made us very sad because we were fighting for the same cause—for human rights. Once Molly gave us an Anna Lindh prize and said it was because we were working for the same cause. We were so upset about her death that we named our association after her. The aims of the association are human rights, the abolition of excision, early

and forced marriage, and the education of children and vaccination of pregnant women. We want girls to go to school. Thirty-two villages are part of
the Anna Lindh association and here in this village we have 120 members.
Even the village chief is one of them."

Kumba, like many others, links the health problems discourse to the
human rights discourse. The fact that they decided to name the association
after a Swedish human rights activist may be partly motivated by the fact
that the name will attract funds from abroad, but it is clearly also motivated
by concern for gendered human rights. "Is there still forced marriage in this
village?" I ask. Kumba replies, "Haa?! No. Girls go to school here! They don't
leave their studies to get married like they used to. There has been no forced
marriage since 2003."

Among those who do not support Tostan activities, it is possible that
some still give their daughters in marriage at a young age. However, those
who are part of these human rights networks have come to an agreement
that girls should not get married before they have finished school. I suggest
that public declarations work in a similar way for excision. Those who have
come to a consensus to stop practicing adhere to the agreement, but nevertheless in most villages that have declared, some families do not join the
movement. During my two days of interviewing different families in Sinthiou Sebbe I spoke to a few who were not part of the movement. One was a
marabout living on the outskirts of the village, who endorsed excision as an
Islamic recommendation, rejected the abandonment movement, and was
afraid of the demise of Futanke society through Western influence. He perceived the NGO's influence in the village as a serious threat. Although he
knew that the village chief was behind the movement, he was not part of the
consensus.

I met another family that was not part of the movement. When we came
onto the compound we were greeted warmly by the family and were asked
to sit down. No one spoke any French. Engaging in friendly banter, we found
out that none of the four young women who were bringing us tea and water
had gone to school. They all learned the Qur'an instead. The family did not
value state school education, the women's movement, or any of the activities
going on in Sinthiou Sebbe. Nevertheless, they were friendly and I did not
notice any hostility toward me because I was white. However, I did dress according to local custom, my head was covered, and I communicated with
them in Pulaar.

Perhaps these families did not see a benefit in joining the movement because they were Tooroɓɓe, who occupy the highest rung of the social hierarchy and had nothing to gain from the democratization process going on in their village. It is interesting that whereas the abandonment and human rights movement is led by a Ñeeño blacksmith and Galluŋke (former slave), the religious noble families in the village seem to have withdrawn from the discussion and the social activities associated with the declaration and abandonment movement, which frequently attract media attention. In the official discourses claiming that "everyone has abandoned" and "all girls go to school now," the voices of those who were previously the leading social groups in the village are being pushed aside. In places like Sinthiou Sebbe, such families feel their culture and society are falling apart, first of all because the NGO's and the state's recommendations are more important than their interpretation of the Qur'an and religious way of life. Furthermore, they are no longer the leaders—instead the village is run, to a large extent, by a charismatic blacksmith woman, her followers, and the cooperating village chief, who has received plenty of gifts from the NGOs, the frequent visitors, celebrities, and the media throughout the years.

How Long-Lasting Is This Human Rights Movement? Revisiting Fifteen Years Later

I return to Sinthiou Sebbe in September 2022 to visit Kumba and see how things have changed. How do the inhabitants think about the abandonment of FGC now, almost twenty years later? And what kinds of marks has Tostan left many years after the program ended? A Tostan supervisor drops me off in Sinthiou Sebbe. He has not worked for Tostan for long and does not know the village very well. As I walk through the village toward where Kumba lives now, some women ask the supervisor who I am. He responds that I am Sarah and I have come to see my namesake and Kumba. They start shouting and singing: "*Ohhhhh ndeysaan. Sara artii, aan ka moyyo* [Ohh, Sarah has come back! You are kind]." I am amazed to receive this reaction after fifteen years. They would not remember me, but the fact that the girl was named after me has left an imprint.

Kumba has moved further away from the center of the village; she no longer lives on the compound she used to share with her co-wife. Her two-bedroom house is made of banco mud brick and has a large compound with grass everywhere. She has a bull, some sheep, chickens, a horse, and a little vegetable garden. It is beautifully calm. Kumba cannot believe that I have come back to Sinthiou Sebbe after fifteen years.

"*A wayrii doo Saara*! [You have been away for a long time]. I did not think I would see you again, you have stayed away for so long."

"You are right, it has been a long time! You thought that you would never see me again?!"

"No," she laughs, holding my hand and leading me slowly into her hut. "Have you seen your Tokara [Saara]?"

"No not yet. We came straight here."

"She has grown up! She will come later."

We sit down and the Tostan supervisor who has brought me here greets them. The beginning of the meeting is formal; they think that I have come with a purpose and want me to introduce my mission. I tell them that I came back to Fouta to go to the public declaration in Velingara Ferlo, which took place the weekend before, and as I was already in Ourosogui I decided to come here, too, to greet them and to meet my Tokara and see how they are and what they have been doing—that is the main purpose of my visit. Kumba responds, "Sarah, you are so kind, Tostan has left us, no one has come here since you left fifteen years ago. No one has spent time here and now you are coming to meet your Tokara, that is truly kind."

"I am so sorry I've stayed away for so long."

"At least you have come back."

"Did you expect to see me after so many years?"

"Mm. I did not think that I would ever see you again. Even your *homonyme* keeps asking, who is my Tokara? Who is Sara? And we told her it's a tuubako [white person]. Now she will finally know whom she has been named after."

Kumba and the former members of the management committee regret that Tostan has not involved them in any activities recently. Although the NGO has stopped organizing activities in the area, human rights are still important to them, I am told. Especially the right to education, the right to marry whom you choose, the right to health, and the right to freedom of speech and nondiscrimination are incredibly important, especially for the young generation.

I eventually meet Sara; she looks at me curiously, finally meeting her namesake after fifteen years. Kumba's husband died fifteen years ago, and Sara's mother has a lot of children to feed and get through school. Life is not easy. They don't even have smartphones, which means connecting on WhatsApp has been impossible—one of the reasons I have not been able to keep in touch over the last couple of years.

We spend the rest of the afternoon eating and drinking tea until Sara and lots of children from the neighborhood take me for a long walk along the outskirts of the village. In the evening, I lie under the stars drinking tea, listening to the radio, talking to Kumba and another friend. There is no television here, no electric light, just the sky, the radio, and the company of old friends. Kumba prepares a bed for me under the awnings of her banco house. Although the days are hot and humid, the nights are cool, but I still prefer to sleep under the stars as I always have. She reassures me that she will stay next to me all night. We are covered with thick blankets.

In the morning, we have breakfast on a mat in front of the house. The birds are singing and there is a light breeze. While Kumba pours me a cup of coffee, her son comes around the corner with a couple of kids. I do not remember him, but he greets me as if I was very familiar. Kumba tells her son that I went to the declaration in Velingara Ferlo. "Ahh! We didn't know that there was a declaration. Why were we not invited? We would have gone," he says disappointedly.

I explain that they were having lots of difficulties organizing this declaration, especially with transportation. Velingara is far from Ourosogui, 200 kilometers. "So what!?" he says. "We would have gone anyway. We would have found a way of getting there. When we had our declaration here in Sinthiou Sebbe people came from all over the country to participate. A lot of people came all the way from Kolda to support us! We would have gone to support them!"

Remembering the chaos caused by the rain and the swarm of unpleasant insects, I say, "well, accommodation was also difficult. They did not know where to lodge everyone and it was rainy, it was very difficult. Everything was wet and many guests did not find a dry place to sleep."

"Ah, right," he says.

I show the son photos and videos of the declaration. He loves the photos of women dressed in traditional dress, the Lawɓe women. "Ohh, that is fantastic, the cosaan. Ohh, look at that, haa! Truly wonderful! Beautiful, all those traditions. Why were we not invited? I would have gone! I wanted to go." Looking at the performance of teenagers dancing, he says, "Ahh, hôtesse! Look at all these girls dancing. Yeee! So nice! They should have received a diploma for this."

When I ask them what they did for their declaration, he replies, "Ahh, our declaration was the best ever! We had sooo many animals! We had so many cows walking through the declaration, we had horses, and goats and everything! It was wonderful! Lots of people came from all over, it was fantastic. We had cosaan and everything."

I am amazed to see what fond memories they have of their declaration and how much they want to continue to support this movement. It is more than the abandonment of excision. It is a desire to connect with other people who share similar values and the display and celebration of Futanke traditions they are proud of. These people's interpretation of human rights anchors Pulaar traditions and ethnic identity in an ideology according to which everyone is equal, has the right to the highest standards of health and to freedom of speech and nondiscrimination. For them, tradition is not linked to social hierarchy and status within the caste system but to pride in the customs and identity of the individual status groups without giving preference to any particular rank. The abandonment of excision and early marriage comes in a package with an ideology of social justice that also provides social mobility and economic opportunities. I argue that these benefits to the abandonment of excision are almost more attractive and convincing than the risk of health complications linked to FGC. The support of international NGOs and their funding to end FGC have made grassroots activists who have become local leaders using the rights discourse as a tool for collaborative political agency. Whether excision is abandoned or not, the desire for social justice, the highest standards of health, and education remains. The abandonment of excision is an opportunity to meet and connect with others who share similar political aspirations to those promised by the human rights discourse provided by international NGOs.

Conclusion

Both Engle Merry and Shell-Duncan argued that international human rights are a top-down process whereby international agreements are "translated," transferred and in some ways imposed onto local populations. Kumba's case has shown us, however, that in Fouta Toro some people come to perceive human rights as assurances of their personal integrity and rights as individuals. The case of the villagers of Sinthiou Sebbe shows that human rights were understood as a transnational ideology that advocated values such as equality before the law, the right to nondiscrimination and freedom of speech, and the right to the highest standards of health. I have shown that these principles, and the idea that they were universal and backed by an international community, helped people to speak out against structures and authorities that they found oppressive. Although local women felt that this transnational ideology had come from somewhere else, it gave them strength and courage to stop practicing excision despite religious leaders' opposition to the ban, and to speak up for ideals that they believe many communities have come to an agreement to abide by. As we can see, Kumba and her followers in Sinthiou Sebbe do not just feel part of a network of communities in Senegal that have decided to publicly declare their decision to abandon excision, but feel united with women who fight for human rights across cultures—as their solidarity for the Swedish human rights activist shows. I therefore argue that human rights ideologies are not just necessarily top-down and prescribed by "middle-level women" and "transnational elites" (Engle Merry 2006) but, in this case, represent a lever that can alter the social structure, allowing those who have traditionally had no say in Fouta Toro due to their social status (*ñeeñɓe*) to make decisions without their noble patrons' approval and allowing them to become leaders of local development movements.

I have shown that women who are against excision for health reasons are convincing to others because they can relate the law and human rights to their personal stories. Due to the fact that their behavior is respectable and decent, they are tolerated and respected by those who have concerns about purity and control of sexual desire. In addition to this, they are backed by the local authorities, the state, and NGOs that are seeking to develop the area according to local discourses.

I suggest that because those who want to stop practicing are supported by the state, the NGOs, and a growing number of locals who agree to leaving the practice, the authority of those who have concerns for religious reasons or control of desire is undermined. The local discourses are changing to some extent through the social changes that are instigated by Tostan's human rights teachings. The fact that lower-status groups are provided with possibilities for leadership and social mobility through this movement means that those Tooroɓɓe who feel threatened by the changing society and who are concerned about women's chastity are sidelined.

Epilogue

I t is around 8:30 in the morning in October 2022 and I am waiting for my old friend Samba Sarr at the bus station in Ourosogui. He should arrive any minute. I rushed to get here, afraid that he might get on the next bus toward Tambacounda if I don't catch him. We've agreed to an interview on his work for Tostan around the time of the trials of Matam. I haven't had breakfast yet and am walking around the food stalls, searching for coffee and beans. It has been raining a lot. The muddy ground is drying. I finally see my old friend, the poet, after so many years. He makes fun of me for searching for beans for breakfast, and we laugh heartily. He was very tempted to catch the next car down to Tambacounda, but I persuade him to stay with me for a few hours. We go to a quieter place to do the interview. He explains what happened at the meeting with the marabouts as follows:

> So, after the exciser was arrested in Matam the religious leaders
> were closing down one Tostan education center after the other; [. . .]
> it was necessary to assemble this meeting of religious leaders
> around the marabout of Ndioum to try and rectify the situation.
> But there were some marabouts who did not want to understand.
> First of all, the Tostan coordinator explained the objectives of their
> program and also that the incident in Matam was not linked to
> Tostan. It was a political affair that led to the judgment. But some
> marabouts didn't believe a word we said! They said, "let them leave!
> They are nonbelievers, they are here to destroy the religion!" It was
> really difficult. They said, "Those people were bought by the
> toubabs, they are here to destroy our community and our culture." I
> was supposed to take notes, but I could not write down a single

word. But I was not allowed to speak out either. I had to wait until we were invited to speak. So, when we were finally given a chance to speak, I exploded. I told them, "I believe in a perfect God. If the God I believe in is perfect, he cannot make something imperfect. If the part that is cut off does not have an important role to play in the body, if it is imperfect, then I don't think that God would have put it there. It is us, the ones who are doing the cutting, who are making the mistake. God has created the human body to perfection. He cannot have made mistakes. You cannot justify the practice by saying that you cut away an imperfection, because God does not create things that are imperfect. You can only justify it as a custom or something like that."

He continues:

"We respected these marabouts. We did not appreciate that these marabouts were knocked about by soldiers, that the marabouts were running around the streets of Matam, that their hats fell off their heads, that their prayer beads fell to the ground, because they are our kin! They are our leaders! We believe in those marabouts, we respect them! We do not support the state's violence. No one should think that we were pleased to see the marabouts beaten and tear gassed. We don't accept that because they are our kin, they are our religious leaders! They are the ones that baptize us and who pray for us."

"You told them that?" I ask.

"I told them that. And even my colleagues thought that I had said too much! They were sweating, they were scared. 'Nooo, he is crazy,' they thought. [We both laugh.] Especially when I talked about imperfection."

*   *   *

These are the images that stay with me after all this time and with which I would like to end this ethnography: From the female body as compromised by the threat of "too much pleasure" destroying Futanke civilization to the female body created to perfection by God. My old friend changed his mind! From women having great sexual desire because they can get aroused so quickly that they risk jeopardizing the honor of the family and bringing debauchery to Futanke civilization to the embodiment of human perfection. Sherry Ortner argued that "the intentionalities of actors evolve through praxis, and the meanings of the acts change, both for the actor and for the analyst." I have shown how gender is made through excision and how the larger sociopolitical structures are embodied. The need to control sexual desire through excision is naturalized and justified by referring to religious doctrines. Yet, Samba dared to speak out against powerful religious leaders, feared and respected all over Fouta. In *Politics of Piety*, Saba Mahmood shows how even the most pious Muslim women, who from a Western perspective may be considered oppressed and disadvantaged, find agency in their interpretations of the religious doctrines. Samba Sarr deeply reflected on this so-called Prophetic recommendation of excision, comparing it to different interpretations of the Qur'an and Islamic practice, concluding that God must have created the female body perfectly. His convictions gave him courage to speak out against the leaders despite their spiritual power and political influence. Even though culture and political economy is embodied, and we may view things according to the structures of feeling that constitute our habitus, there is always a potential for agency within the framework of possibilities in a social environment (Mahmood 2011; Ortner 1995, 1996).

The second image I would like to invoke is that of great men falling by the hand of the state. Men who represent the spiritual bedrock of the Futanke civilization. In their view, these men were defending their right to practice their religion. To these marabouts, whose prayer beads were falling to the ground, the law criminalizing female genital cutting felt like it could not be the result of a consensus among Senegalese parliamentarians. It could not have emerged from within. It felt exogenous, like an imposition from an external power, an act of cultural imperialism, an attempt to destroy their culture and their way of life.

These great(ly respected) men were falling in the name of women, to protect them from their own uncontrollable desire, from sexual libertarianism, from fornication and debauchery. They were protecting their society from social and moral degradation, from sadness and loss; they were fighting to maintain order, they were concerned that the pillars of civilization might collapse if women lose their senses due to sexual pleasure. These men's mission is also compromised by a changing society where individuals change their minds and make decisions about their bodies (and their daughters' bodies) that appear to be based on values that have come from the outside but are the result of long processes of reflection and social change. Anthropological scholarship has shown that exogenous ideologies that appear to have been adopted, such as human rights, are often rather different to the Western universal claims of rights and personhood (Adams 1998). In internationalist human rights terms, the individual body is "the indivisible unit of symbolic currency" (Adams 1998:83). Strathern (1988), Adams (1998), Lambek and Strathern (1998), Wardlow (2006), and others have shown that in many places the body is not seen as an individualized unit belonging to an autonomous individual ideologically detached from society. In Fouta Toro, too, the physical body is not thought to belong to one individual: the body is social. Decisions regarding the modification of the physical body are taken by those who have authority over it. That does not mean that women and men do not like the notion of having rights over their individualized physical body. However, this is merely an ideology; the larger social body has more impact on what happens to women's and men's physical bodies.

I revealed a glimpse of the multiplicity of ways in which female body is at the center of tensions between the secular and the religious, human rights and customary law, new elites and intercaste relations, international politics and sectarianism. It is objectified and appropriated, *compromised* and redefined by different interest groups who imagine the body to be violated by larger political forces and power struggles at play within their social body. It is subject to injustice in the eyes of those who want to save it from health problems, gender violence, and human rights. But in the same way, I have shown, it is seen as being subject to injustice by those who believe that their cultural and religious traditions have been violated by international policies. It is perceived to be under threat, vulnerable and in need of protection by those who defy the law as much as by those who defy tradition and embrace their own interpretation of human rights. The story I have told is not monolithic—there are not one dominant and one resistant party to the conflict. Again, Ortner's words exemplify the argument I am making: "If we are to recognize that resistors are doing more than simply opposing domination, more than simply producing a virtually mechanical re-action, then we must go the whole way. They have their own politics—not just between chiefs and commoners or landlords and peasants but within the local categories of friction and tension: men and women, parents and children, seniors and juniors; inheritance conflicts among brothers; struggles of succession and wars of conquest between chiefs; struggles for primacy between religious sects; and on and on" (Ortner 1995:177). Where is the agency in all of this? The female body I write about is not merely an object, reified by different ideologies, appropriated by different interest groups. I have shown the many ways in which larger discourses are embodied, the ways in which they make people angry and sad, the ways in which this "violation of rights" is experienced physically and how these emotions produce action.

Csordas (1994) and Lambek and Strathern (1998) and others have shown that our understanding of embodiment can be confused by a distinction between the imagined body and the "embodied body." I have looked at both: the female body as conceived of in human rights debates and Fulani discourses on the one hand, and how these discourses are viscerally embodied, lived, and felt on the other. I argue that discourses on the body and viscerally lived experiences of the body are often contradictory and seem paradoxical (O'Neill 2018). These paradoxical views and emotions can elicit the desire to change things, to look for solutions and do things that may or may not break with social conventions. Theoretically held views on the body and its rights and seemingly disparate embodied responses of the body can be lived at the same time. I argue that this makes human rights changes regarding gender and sexuality challenging to implement. Human rights can be perceived as ideologies of change, removed from their intended meaning within the international human rights framework, and appropriated and adapted to local discourses (Merry Engle 2006; Turner 1997; Goodale 2022). Different discourses can sit alongside each other fomenting political tension and conflict between agents and affecting the ways in which women's bodies are perceived, appropriated, and surveilled to protect society against the Other (Islam, or cultural colonialism) threatening to compromise its physical or moral integrity.

GLOSSARY OF PULAAR TERMS

Almaamy: derived from Arabic: al-Imam; rulers who succeeded the Deniyanke Fulɓe herders in the sixteenth century

Anasara: religions of the book other than Islam

Awluɓe: praise singers (status group)

baawaado ngoraagu: someone who cannot control him/herself

bandiraabe: relatives

bannde: relative

banndi am: my relative

banndu: body

Baylo: member of blacksmiths (status group; singular)

besngu: extended family

biɓɓe: children

bileejo: healer/witch hunter

binbin: chains of beads women wear around the stomach to excite men

biyam: my child

bonnitde: to spoil

ɓoorde: to strip off (e.g., bark of a branch)

ɓoornaade: to dress up, but also male circumcision

borgo: boiled sheep feces (traditional remedy to stop bleeding after excision)

boubou: gown/dress (French/Wolof)

Buurnaaɓe: potters (status group)

cadeele: problems

cagataagal: bravery/courage

ceemeedo: nonvirgin/married woman

cefi: incantation

Cubballo: member of fishermen (status group)

cuuray: aphrodisiac incense

cuusal: to dare

debbo: woman

debbo yid, kono woto hoolo: love a woman but never trust her (proverb)

dendiraabe: cousin, joking cousin

Deniyanke: Fulɓe herders who were the rulers of Fouta Toro from the sixteenth to the eighteenth century

dewgal: marriage

dewgal bonngal buri innde bonnde: a bad marriage is better than a bad reputation (proverb)

diery: grasslands where herders take their cattle

diine: religion/Islam

dimo: noble person (singular)

duhaade: male circumcision, to knot up (e.g., a pair of trousers)
dulndu: forest
endam: extended family
fadde: to wait
feccere: piece
fedde: age group
fonngi: speaking at meal times
foonde: the forest
fotde: duties
gacce: modesty/shame
galle: house
gandal: knowledge (spiritual)
gandal balewal: "black knowledge"—spiritual practices of occupational groups used for healing
    or craftsmanship; passed on in families
gandal danewal: "white knowledge"—spiritual practices of Islamic clerics
gawde: powder that is put on fresh circumcision wound
Gawlo (singular of Awlube): member of praise singers (status group)
gila: since
gila dawaa dawi: since the beginning of the universe
Gila dawaa-dawi kaddungal ina wadee kono cadeele medaa heen wonnde = since the beginning
    of the universe excision has been practiced but it has never caused problems
giyiraaɓe: age mates (plural)
giyiraaɗo: age mate (singular)
gorko: man
griot: praise singer (French)
Haalpulaar'en: those who speak the Pulaar language/Fulani people
haddaade: circumcision (vulgar term used by adolescents)
haddinde: to excise
hadith: recommendation/saying/imitation of the prophet Mohammed
hakkille: intelligence/forethought
hannde: today
haram: forbidden
hersude: to feel ashamed
hinnde: status group or "caste" (singular)
hirjino: to raise awareness
hoɓɓe: guests (plural)
hoore am: my head/myself
ina heewi cadeele: there are lots of problems
innde: name
ittude: take off
ittude ñaande paaka: take off the leftovers of the knife
Jaawamɓe: councilors of the Almaamies (status group)
Jeeri/Diery: grasslands where herders take their cattle
jeyaaɓe: the owned (slaves)
jeyi: belong
jinnaaɓe: parents
jinne: spirits
jiwo: unexcised woman
jogaade hoore mum: to control oneself/keep control of the body
jojjande: rights

jokkondiral endam: solidarity

jombaajo: newly married man/woman

jontaado: respected man/knowledgeable man

kaddingol: excision

kaddinowo: exciser

kala ko woni am hannde oo ko aan jeyi: all that I am belongs to you today

kinde: status groups, "caste" (plural)

kodo: guest (singular)

laabde: to be clean/pure

labaani: to be dirty/impure

Lawbe: woodworkers (status group)

leñol: ethnicity

leydi: land

lootaade: to wash oneself

lootngal janaaba: big ablutions washing the whole body

Maabube: weavers (status group)

Maccube/Galluŋkoobe: slaves (plural)

Maccudo/Galluŋke: slave (singular)

marabout: spiritual guide or Islamic leader

maraboutage: French term for spiritual afflictions performed by a marabout/ witchcraft

mawnam: older sibling

mbaawkaaji: what can be done

mbada yidi yettade ma: I want you/desire you

mbada yid maa: I love/want you

Mbalax: Wolof dance

Mbaroodi: dangerous animal—crocodile or lion

mbayyungu: boiled maize or millet

mbelemma: pleasure

mboomri: unmarried girl/virgin

miñam: younger sibling

min tawrii ko taaniraabe amen: we have inherited it from the ancestors

mi rokkiima hoore am: I give myself to you

mo haddaaki: the one who was not excised

mo haddinaaka: unexcised woman (literally, the one who is not excised)

mo waawaa jaggude hoore mum: he/she cannot control themselves; also used when talking about sensuality

muñal: endurance/self-discipline

muum: mute (adjective)

Muumo: mute person

Muumiraado: woman whose vagina is closed (cannot have sexual intercourse before marriage)

ñaagunde alla jabaande: divine prayer accepted—God's protection of a village against colonialism

ñaande: leftovers when millet is ground in a mortar

ñebbe: beans

ñeeñbe: men or woman of skill status groups (not noble; plural)

ñeeño: man/woman of skill (singular)

ñengi: magic

ngende: to have sex

njodom: erotic underskirt worn by married women during sex

njulli: circumcised boy

o waasi teddungal makko: he/she lost his/her honor
o waawa fadde gorko makko: she cannot wait for her husband
paaka: knife
pagne: skirt/sarong (French word)
pellital: decision
Pulaaku: way of life of the Fulani/Fulaniness
Pullo: herder (singular of Fulɓe)
rewɓe: women
rewiraaɓe: succeeding age sets
rimɓe: noble status groups
rokkude: to give
saali: forgetting something/leaving something behind because of distraction or lack of
    self-control
Sakkeeɓe: leather workers (status group)
sallige: purifying washings/small ablutions
sandar: small marabout—not well known
satalla: watering can/jug (to wash)
Seɓɓe: warriors (status group)
selbe: circumcised boy who instructs *njulli*
sernaaɓe: scholars of Islam
soɓe: dirty/impure
solima: uncircumcised boy
Subalɓe: fishermen (status group)
sukuñaaɓe: soul eaters
sunna: recommendation of the Prophet
sunninde: female circumcision—term derived from *sunna*
suturo: secret
taarorde: toilet area
taawirde: to inherit
talibe: students of the Qur'an (Wolof)
tawde: to find
tergal: member/sex—neutral term for either male or female sex organs
tiidtinde: reinforce
tinnaade: be brave/courageous
Tokara: namesake
Toorobbe: status group of Islamic clerics/leaders of Fouta Toro (plural)
Tooroodo: member of status group of Islamic clerics (singular)
toubab/tuubaako: white person
ulama: those "who lay down the canons of Islam and interpret them" (Willis 1978:195)
waalo: river land
waawde: to be able/capable
wadde: to do
wad ko welmaa e am: do what you like with me
Wambaaɓe: bards who specialize in playing *hoddu* guitar (status group)
Wayilɓe/Waylube: blacksmiths, silversmiths (status group)
wayrude: to go a long time without seeing someone or going somewhere
weleede: to like
weltinde: to satisfy/please
wittooji: research
wonnde: to be

woppu am: let go (of my gown)
woppude: to leave/abandon something
woppude adaa amen: to leave behind our customs
wutte: gown/dress
yah lootoyo a ronkii jogaade hoore ma: go and wash yourself, you can't control yourself
yettade: to arrive
yettoode: family name
yiɗɗe: to want/love

NOTES

Introduction

1. 'L'évaluation a permis de mettre en relief la pertinence de l'approche intégrée éducation communautaire et mobilisation sociale ainsi que l'impact important qu'elle a eu sur l'abandon de la pratique de l'excision dans plusieurs régions du Sénégal. L'évaluation a aussi révélée que Tostan était aujourd'hui la seul ONG à intervenir sur le terrain de manière large avec un potentiel et une capacité technique importante avec mise en point d'un paquet d'éducation communautaire fondée sur l'approche droits' (République du Sénégal 2008).

2. My translation. The original says, "les opérations rituelles . . . résultant de conceptions sociales et culturelles" (Abu-Salieh 2001: 398).

3. These WHO classifications were updated in 2016 particularly in response to research on the anatomy and size of the clitoris, and the new classification now refers to the partial or total removal of the clitoral glans.

4. For instance, GAMS (Groupe pour l'abolition des mutilations sexuelles), IAC (Inter African Committee), CAMS (Commission d'abolitions des mutilations sexuelles), COSEPRAT, and others.

5. Article 111 du code la famille: "Le mariage ne peut être contracté qu'entre un homme âgé de plus de 18 ans et une femme âgée de plus de 16 ans, sauf dispense d'âge accordé pour motif grave par le président du tribunal régional après enquête" (loi n° 99–82 du 02 septembre 1999).

6. *Muum* means mute. A mute person is called *muumo*. Although the root of the word refers to being mute, muumiraaɗo is exclusively used for women whose vulvas are closed to prevent sexual intercourse before marriage.

7. See also Ginio (2002) on French colonial anthropologists and their influence on policy.

8. The use of the term *caste* is controversial in local and academic discourses on Africa and beyond. Dumont (1980) argued against the use of the term outside India. Goody (1980) shows that concepts derived from European feudalism are not appropriate when describing the centralized polities of West Africa. Schmitz (1986, 1994) uses the term *groupe statutaire* in French. He suggests that many terms used for the analysis of the social and historical stratification of particular status groups are subject to etymological transformations (Schmitz 1986: 351). Terms like caste, feudalism, and segment should therefore be reassessed (Schmitz 1994). I do not at any point attempt to compare concepts of social stratification such as caste in other places to kinɗe/hinnde among the Haalpulaar.

9. Also see Newman (2020).

10. *Kitab al mughrib fi dhikri bilad Ifriqiata wa-l Maghrib [of] al Masalik wa-l-Mamalik* (1911), translation (1913) edited by Baron De Slane (see Al-Naqar 1969: 367).

11. Inhabitants of Fouta Toro.

12. Clerical tribes.

13. *Gacce* is the noun and *hersude* is the verb.

14. The connotations are what the Fulɓe found when they were born and reproduce with pride.

Chapter 1

1. President Abdou Diouf's speech at the Congress of the International Federation for Human Rights in Senegal on November 21, 1997. Published in the governmental newspaper *Le Soleil.*

2. Dr. Camara (a Senegalese sociologist), personal communication; Molly Melching (executive director of Tostan), interview; COSEPRAT, interview.

3. Besides Dr. Camara, I also discussed conditions that favored the law with Molly Melching (originally American), who was executive director and founder of Tostan and has been involved in development, governmental, and UN politics in Senegal since the 1970s, and with Madame Sidibe Ndiaye (Wolof), head of COSEPRAT, who has been involved in activism against FGC in Senegal since 1984.

4. The hadith can be defined as a collection of Islamic traditions containing sayings of the Prophet Mohammed with accounts of his daily practices (the Sunna) and customs he observed and tacitly approved of. The hadith constitute a major source of guidance for Muslims besides the Qur'an. Regarding excision, the relevant hadith can be found in *Al- Kabir de Dahhak b Qays . . . : al-Fawakih ad Dawani ala Risala b ibn Abi Zeyd al-Qayrawani* and in *Bulghat as-salik* as well as in the *Fatawi* of Cheikh Ibn Taymiyya, vol. 21, and in *ad-Dahhak b Qays'.*

5. The French word *sensibilisation* is used in NGO and activist circles to describe activities whereby often uneducated and/or illiterate people are made aware of threats to their health through behavior that they are not conscious of—such as drinking polluted water or feeding food to infants that they cannot digest and that may cause sickness or death (to reduce child mortality—one of the UN's targets since the 1980s), as well as the benefits of vaccination and information about reproductive health and fertility. The verb *sensibiliser*—to sensitize—is thought of as making a person sensitive to recognising potential threats to their health and prevent sickness. In Pulaar the word *hirjino* is used, which has much the same connotations.

6. Awareness of at least two consequences of FGC increased significantly for both men (from 11 percent to 83 percent) and women (from 7 percent to 83 percent) immediately after participating in the program (Diop et al. 2004: 19).

7. "Between baseline and post-intervention survey, the proportion of women who approved of FGC decreased by 50% among participating women, and by 40% among non-participating women" (Diop et al. 2004: 20).

8. Malicounda Bambara is a village near the cities of Mbour and Thiès. It is about 400 kilometers from Fouta Toro by road, and the ethnic and sociocultural context is very different from Fouta Toro.

9. Part of the social mobilization method of the program is that women are instructed to tell another person, an "adopted sister," about what they have learned in class.

10. In 2007, most international Tostan volunteers were taken to Malicounda at the beginning of their contract. However, I never officially worked for Tostan, so I was not taken there nor did I ask to go. Malicounda is Tostan's showcase village for funders and journalists. The village is situated between the cities of Mbour and Thiès around 600 kilometers from my field sites in Fouta Toro. At the time of my fieldwork, it did not occur to me that it might be important to visit Malicounda and, as the village is used to a lot of visitors, I am not sure that I would have received responses different from the ones published in national and international newspaper articles and reports.

11. The titles of the newspaper articles in the following text boxes are translated by me from French and the content was summarized by me.

12. Translated from French: "Malicounda Bambara: les femmes renoncent à l'excision."

13. The original says, "Le Serment de Malicounda 'Plus d'excision!' Les femmes de Malicounda, un village situé à quelques kilomètres de Mbour, ont décidé de mettre fin aux mutilations sexuelles des filles. Soutenues par l'Unicef et Tostan, une Ong qui s'intéresse aux droits de la femme, elles ont levé un tabou. Reportage."

14. "The end of excision in Malicounda."

15. "Malicounda Bambara—Des descendants de maliens bien intégrés."

16. "Le monde s'effondre," in *Le Soleil*, August 28.

17. For example, Madame Sidibe Ndiaye of COSEPRAT interviewed by me in 2005.

18. "Mutilations genitales feminines au Senegal. La face cachée du drame féminine."

19. "Le point de vue religieux: 'L'excision est recommandable, pas obligatoire.'"

20. My own translation.

21. "Il faut une loi. Elle est plus forte que la tradition."

22. Derrida also writes about the future anterior that puts in place a "lace of obligation" that binds and unbinds the ethical actor. The possibility of pursuing justice beyond the determinations of law is one important effect (Derrida 1990: 329). Lacan (1977) writes about retroaction and discourse: the analyst and advocate (Fortun 2001) rework the past so that the future is anteriorized differently. I argue that these analyses of discourses of the past and the future relate to how events are represented in different ways for particular purposes.

23. "Les exciseuses n'ont pas déposé les lames."

24. "120 filles excises, en attendant.... Dans ce département ou une centaine de filles ont été excises il y a une dizaine de jours, on accueille la pénalisation des mutilations génitales féminines sans grande illusion. Car le travail préalable de sensibilisation a été bâclé, voire inexistant."

25. "Interdiction et pénalisation. On veut nous humilier."

26. Kedougou is called an "isolated" (*enclavé* in French) region by most development agents because there are hardly any roads, and in the rainy season it is virtually impossible to get to some places due to flooding. I found when traveling to Salemata in Kedougou that health care assistants and teachers complained about the failure of the state to provide infrastructure and access to resources. They vividly described their difficulties trying to assist people in desperate need of health care, who ended up dying on the way to the health care center.

27. Négritude was a literary and ideological movement led by francophone black intellectuals, writers, and politicians. The founders were African and Afro-Caribbean intellectuals (Césaire, Damas, Senghor) who lived in Paris in the 1930s. One of them, Leopold Sedar Senghor, became the first Senegalese president after independence in 1960. According to Senghor, the Négritude movement would enable black people under French rule to meet the colonial racism as equals. Négritude was a political and intellectual tool reinforcing solidarity among black people across the world against racism. The term Négritude is closely related to Pan-Africanism in Anglophone colonial and postcolonial African/Black literature.

28. According to my knowledge, Senegambia does not have a particularly high record of pedophilia or commercial exploitation of children for sexual purposes. Sex tourism of white women with Senegalese men, however, does occur in the tourist areas.

29. "Après avoir souligné que la pratique de l'éxcision ne semble pas avoir un fondement coranique, rapporte des propos attribués au Prophète (psl) s'adressant à l'exciseuse des femmes esclaves de Medine (". . . excisez légèrement et ne coupez pas complètement le clitoris; vous permettez de ce fait à la femme d'éprouver du plaisir, d'avoir un visage radieux et de donner du plaisir à son mari")."

30. "La charia classe l'éxcision parmi les pratiques dites de bienséance (sunna, fitria) qui concourent à la perfection de la nature humaine comme la circoncision, le fait de se couper les ongles, de s'épiler, de se raser les pubis etc."

31. *Rissala* is often used as another word for Islam or Islamic tradition. *Ar-Risāla* means the word of God revealed through a messenger to the people. The messengers bring law and humanity, guiding people on a straight path toward God (social laws, state laws, etc.).

32. According to Abusharaf, the term *khifad* literally means decreasing the height of the clitoris. It is propagated by those who support female circumcision as an Islamic practice but not identical to male circumcision. As the other authors mentioned above describe, the notion of khifad is based on a hadith where the Prophet Mohammed advised an exciser to lower the clitoris but not cut so much (Abusharaf 2007: 107).

33. While Niang refers to the intellectual tradition of Négritude in his defense of excision, the Senegalese scholar Cheikh Anta Diop knew Molly Melching and suggested the name Tostan, meaning "breakthrough" in Wolof, for her NGO. I do not want to imply that the Négritude movement is against the abandonment of excision, although the author of the article seems to argue that it is.

34. The legendary Islamic leader El Hadj Oumar Tall (Al Hajj Umar according to Robinson [1985] and Willis [1989]) is celebrated for having introduced the Tijaniyya order (*tariqa*) to Senegal in the nineteenth century as well as for having defended Islam and the interests of the Futanke against French colonialism. Islamic practice is said to have been present in the Tekrur empire, the region called Fouta Toro today, since at least the Mana dynasty in the ninth century (Wane 1969). Wane (1969) suggests that the Maninka ruler of Tekrur, War-Jabi, introduced Sharia law between 1030 and 1040. From here, Islam slowly spread further south into Djolof, Kayor, Baol, and Sine Saloum, areas that are Senegal today. However, the predominant tariqa until El Hadj Oumar's reforms was the Qadiriyya (founder, Iranian Abdul-Qadir Gilani, 1077–1166) mixed with local religious beliefs and indigenous spiritual practices. Although El Hadj Oumar Tall, born around 1797 in Halwar, Fouta Toro, started his religious life as a member of the Qadiriyya, he later converted to the Tijaniyya and was declared a khalifa of the order (Dilley 2004: 102). His mission was to proselytize the way of the Tijaniyya, to fight against religious syncretizm or mixing (*ikhtilât*), and to "reinstate a purified form of Islam" (Dilley 2004: 102). Robinson suggests that he even considered the Muslim inhabitants of upper Senegal and upper and middle Niger valleys "pagan," one of the reasons why he launched a Jihad against them (Robinson 1987: 249). Besides being known as a warrior in the name of Islam and the founder of the "Umarian state" (Robinson 1987, 1988), he is admired by locals for contesting the French expansion in the upper and middle valleys of the Senegal River. Robinson suggests that, for the first time, the French had to seriously justify and defend a strong European presence in the region, an ideological challenge for Governor Faidherbe (Robinson 1988: 418). Locals interpret El Hadj Omar Tall's success in establishing an Islamic state in spite of the French antagonism as due to his spiritual strength and the guidance of Allah. For many Futanke and Senegalese I met, Thierno Mountaga Tall's kinship ties to this legendary figure were of great importance. His recommendations were far more influential than a politician's.

35. *Preuves éclatantes au sujet de la pratique recommandable de l'éxcision des jeunes filles* (1999).

36. "*Al-Fawz Wa An-Najah; Hadith* of Tabarani called *Al-Awsa*; according to Abou Hurayra excision is *Fitra* (bringing the human being to perfection); Nawawi Tome; Abu Abdallah, Ibn Dawud a *Hadith* of the Prophet's wife Aicha; Buhayqi; the Prophet's companion Ibn Abbass. These *Hadith* can be found in *Al- Kabir de Dahhak b Qays . . . : al-Fawakih ad Dawani ala Risala b ibn Abi Zeyd al-Qayrawani* and in *Bulghat as-salik* as well as in the *Fatawi* of Cheikh Ibn Taymiyya vol. 21 Tome, and in *ad-Dahhak b Qays*" (Tall 1999).

37. "Nous avons compris maintenant que l'intérêt de l'excision est de protéger la femme contre l'excès de sensualité qui pourrait la pousser à commettre des bassesses ou (simplement) à s'en approcher" (Tall 1999: 15). There is not a commonly used term for "sensuality" in Pulaar except

mo waawaa jaggude hoore mum,—"she cannot control herself," or *baawaado ngoraagu,* "he cannot control himself."

38. Also see Gottlieb (2002:177), who shows that the idea that women have greater sexual urges than men is common among Muslims (without specifying groups or places), which is why women need to be protected from their own desire for sex and unacceptable transgressions.

39. LES VOTES A L'ASSEMBLEE NATIONALE. L'excision est est interdite. Fin de la première session de l'assemblée nationale. Les exciseuses risquent désormais 6 mois à 5 ans de prison.

40. According to witness accounts of activists, NGOs, and the governmental newspaper *Le Soleil.*

Interlude

1. Literally, "divine prayer accepted/heard."

2. Haalpulaar'en society is hierarchically ranked according to status/occupational groups. Each group is called *hinnde* (plural *kinɗe*), which is translated into French as *caste.* Among all groups there are three broad categories: the noble, Rimɓe; the men of skill, Ñeeñɓe; and slaves, Jeyaaɓe. Paradoxically, even though in Pulaar all members of these categories are referred to as belonging to kinɗe, in French the Ñeeñɓe and Jeyaaɓe are referred to as *casté* and the noble as *non-casté*—literally, "without caste." This conforms to the Pulaar distinction between Rimɓe, the noble, and Rimayɓe, the bondsmen/women. I use the local French terminology here because it was used by NGO staff when speaking of opposition to their awareness-raising activities. The above conflict therefore takes place between the noble and the bondsmen (men of skill and former slaves).

Chapter 2

1. *Hadinaaki* is the negation of the verb *haddinde,* "to excise," in its past tense

2. In 2007, a state schoolteacher's salary was approximately CFA150,000. A goat cost about CFA8,000–15,000 during my fieldwork. This price has not changed, except in urban areas.

3. The naming ceremony is done seven days after the birth of the child. During this religious ceremony, called *innde* in Pullar, the marabout or imam whispers a prayer into the baby's ear and gives it a name from the Qur'an, which was previously chosen by the parents. From that day onward the baby can be taken out of the room where it has been kept for protection from evil spirits and sickness. Also see O'Neill et al. 2016.

4. The expression that "one-third" is cut is very common in Fouta Toro, indicating less severe forms of cutting. To use the WHO FGM classification, this can mean Type I, II, or IV.

5. The expression for a woman whose vagina is closed and cannot be penetrated before marriage is *muumiraaɗo.* Here, the exciser implies that this is achieved through the incantation. Some women undergo a more severe form of cutting referred to as *muumiraaɗo* where the blood coagulates to form scar tissue that closes the vulva, resembling a Type III infibulation.

6. Among the Diola there is a conception of the "sacred forest" where circumcision takes place and boys learn their duties and responsibilities as men and toward the elders. It is forbidden to speak of what one has learned, seen, or experienced to uninitiated members of the community among the Diola (see Dellenborg 2004). Although coming-of-age rites involving circumcision are not uncommon among some Fulani communities in West Africa, to my knowledge there is no concept of a "secret society."

7. *Ñaande* is also what is left over when millet is ground in the mortar. If these leftovers are put on the skin, they cause an itching, burning sensation similar to the discomfort experienced after circumcision before the glans gets used to exposure.

8. Prepubescent boys are not expected to have sex to "take off the leftovers of the knife," and circumcised boys roaming villages at the age of five certainly do not understand what is meant by that phrase. Adults joke about this.

9. This powder is made of the dried fruits of a tree.

Chapter 3

1. "These operations are a systematic surgical attack on the essence of our female sexual being and on the vitality and superiority of the female personhood which men seek to control at any price—even the price of our lives" (Hosken 1982: 47); also, "In order to effectively deal with the abolition of these mutilations, it is necessary to recognise that we are concerned here with a basic power issue: the issue of control by all males over all females—or the ordering of society along patriarchal lines" (Hosken 1982:48).

2. Although the local ideal is that men support the family and act as producers in contrast to women, who are reproducers bearing and looking after the children and the household, anthropological literature has described the ingenious ways in which women make up for lack of financial support from their husbands (Guyer 1984; Davidson 2019, 2020).

3. Mahmood (2005) illustrates her argument by describing discussions on women leading other women in prayer or the requirement of modesty and how to do things that require women to mix with the opposite sex.

4. Also see Hernlund on the origin of the word for female circumcision in Mandinke, *nyiaka*, which is a contraction of *nyiama* (grass or weed) and *kaa* (to cut clean). The excised genitals resemble farmland that must be weeded and cleared according to people's conceptions, as Hernlund points out (2000:238). Bledsoe (1984) and Ahmadu (2005, 2009) argue that clitoridectomy during ritual initiation is thought to "invest" women with fertility (Bledsoe 1984:457).

5. Mauss (1985) discusses conceptions of personhood and "the self" as developing differently in different societies. Morris (1985, 1991) argues that the idea of the development of "the self" as socially separate from others is rooted in humanistic philosophical ideas of the seventeenth, eighteenth, and nineteenth centuries.

6. By "elder," I mean an older person (*mawɓe*), not necessarily a blood relative.

7. *Jokkere* means "connecting," *endam* means "relation" but also "breast."

8. Although there are no longer any crocodiles in the river today, there are many stories of brave fishermen and their successful defeat of the beasts of the river (*mbaroodi*). These stories point to the idea that these are dangerous places.

9. Many boys wanted me to acknowledge their bravery by taking photos of them undertaking dangerous activities like standing on top of the roof, whereas girls often wanted their pictures taken in their most beautiful clothes or when their hair was beautifully plaited.

10. In this case the community is the neighborhood, the village, relatives, and acquaintances.

11. Coumba Kane for *Le Monde* on April 29, 2022; Allyn Gaestel and Ricci Shryock, "In Senegal, the Tragedy of the Anti-Abortion Crusade," *New Yorker*, October 1, 2017; Sabine Panet, "The Price of Senegal's Strict Anti-Abortion Laws," *Axelle Magazine* January–February 2024, "Exilée pour avortement."

12. Also see Whitehouse (2023), *Enduring Polygamy: Plural Marriage) and Social Change in an African Metropolis.*

13. The Wolof are 90 percent Islamic as well, but many Futanke perceive their own practice of Islam as "the real" way.

14. In Pulaar the neutral third-person singular is used: *o waasi teddungal makko.*

Chapter 4

1. The local term used is *weltinde*, which locals translate as *satisfaire* in French. It could also be translated, however, as *to please*, or *rendre content* in French. There is no distinction between *to please* and *to satisfy* in Pulaar.

2. Unmarried men make themselves desirable by being economically productive and displaying generosity by buying presents for girlfriends or fiancées. Men who do not manage to support their families well are not considered good husbands and are said not to satisfy their wives' or girlfriends' needs. Men can also be desirable to women if they are socially successful—e.g., politically or as religious leaders.

3. In 2002, a third (33 percent) of the population of the region of Saint-Louis had access to electricity for light, in contrast to 16 percent of the population in the region of Matam. However, these figures are no longer representative of Fouta Toro as the city of Saint-Louis and urban agglomerations bring up the rate for that region (Senegal—Troisième Recensement Général de la Population et de l'Habitat, 2002).

4. Either because electricity from solar panels runs out quickly or because the cost of electricity is high. Electricity is mostly paid in advance and turns off when money runs out.

5. Also see Riesman (1971) on courtship among Fulani in Djibo, Upper Volta. Riesman discusses notions of beauty and desire and how men seek out married women. What Riesman describes, however, is different from what I observed among sedentary Haalpulaar'en in Fouta Toro.

6. When people talk about genitals, they often refer to them using the neutral Pulaar expression *tergal*—member. This can refer to a man's penis or a woman's vagina. I have translated this Pulaar expression that locals consider unoffensive with the English gender-neutral term *sex*.

7. Fama Ly and I had a game, in which one person puts down and reduces what the other person likes. Fama Ly knew that I liked ñebbe (beans) and she would keep saying that ñebbe are not nice and good but I liked them, which makes me a bean eater. I knew that Fama Ly liked sugar and called her Sucar Ly, and insisted that sugar was not good and not nice, so she likes things that are not nice. Many people in Fouta jokingly reduce what a person loves to make the relationship between them stronger. People say, for example, "Your husband is not good, he is a bad person," or "He doesn't look after you" and "He is ugly," even though the person knows that none of this is true. This tightens bonds of solidarity between people, as among friends of the same age group or between *dendiraabe* (joking cousins).

8. *Dey* is an affirmative sound very common throughout Senegal.

9. Also see a discussion of literature on the role of women's reproductive and sexual capacity in the construction of boundaries of group identity in Chapter 5 (e.g., Pitt-Rivers 1965; Davis 1977; Okeley 1983; Caplan 1987; Goddard 1987; Yuval-Davis and Anthias 1989; Kandiyoti 1991; Hawley 1994; Wilson and Frederiksen 1995).

Chapter 5

1. Translation through Deeple, December 2022. Original title in *Jeune Afrique*: " Sénégal: une exciseuse condamnée à six mois de prison ferme."

2. Original:

DECLARATION DE PRESSE

Après la guère froide, la disparition de l'Union Sophiatique exce URSS les occidentaux à leur tête les Etats-Unis d'Amérique combattent l'Islam par des méthodes intelligentes qui consiste à combattre certaines pratiques recommandées par l'Islam pour effacer la culture musulmane car une société sans culture va disparaître.

Cette lutte généralisee se mène par plusieurs formes ambigues. Des ONG ont été crée soit disant pour aider des citoyens pour mieux comprendre leurs droits et devoir, mais en réalité c'est pour faire disparaître l'Islam. **Ils ne pourront jamais**.

Aujourd'hui au Sénégal (Pays musulman de 95%), on se permet d'interdire des pratiques recommandées par l'Islam telle que:

- L'excision qui était pratiquée par les Arabes depuis le temps du **Prophète Paix et Salut** sur lui qui nous est venu par l'Islam, car les sociétés Africaines non musulmanes ne le pratique pas. Nos illustres ancêtres le pratiquer sans problème. Honte à tout ceux qui ont voté cette Loi satanique. Honte à tout ceux qui ont voté cette Loi impratiquable au Sénégal.

3. The marabout uses the word *embargo*, meaning the UN agreement among African countries that FGM is a form of violence against women (VAW). Also see Shell-Duncan (2008).

4. In Pulaar, the word *diine* is used for religion, generally referring to Islam and not different religions. Other religions are referred to as *anasara*—which are other religions of the book, i.e., Christianity or Judaism but not animism. When people are speaking about the destruction of religion, they exclusively refer to their religion—Islam.

5. My translation from French.

6. The spelling varies across sources: *Toorodo, Torodbe, Turudiyya*.

7. Those "who lay down the canons of Islam and interpret them" (Willis 1978: 195).

8. See Dilley (2006) or Jean Schmitz for more details on status groups or castes among Haalpulaar'en.

9. Gillespie and Melching (2010) explain that reproductive health and human rights modules were introduced after a survey of 10,000 former participants, undertaken in 1995, showed that this was what rural women were interested in learning more about.

10. Also see Johnson (2020) and D'Alisera (2013) on fear and respect for spiritual forces in West Africa and its diaspora.

11. There are rumors that in the past some people have tried to do Tostan harm through corruption or by stealing money. However, according to these stories, whenever the NGO's survival was seriously threatened by an adversary's actions, the adversary ended up dying or getting seriously injured. Most people I know believe that such incidents are not coincidental but conclude that the NGO is protected against evil inflictions.

12. Some of the arguments put forward in the Hastings Report are the following: "Research by gynecologists and others has demonstrated that a high percentage of women who have had genital surgery have rich sexual lives, including desire, arousal, orgasm, and satisfaction"; "Female genital surgeries in Africa are viewed by many insiders as aesthetic enhancements of the body and are not judged to be 'mutilations'"; "Female genital surgery in Africa is typically controlled and managed by women"; "The findings of the WHO Study Group on Female Genital Mutilation and Obstetric Outcome is the subject of criticism that has not been adequately publicized. The reported evidence does not support sensational media claims about female genital surgery as a cause of perinatal and maternal mortality during birth." Source: Public Policy Advisory Network on Female Genital Surgeries in Africa, "Seven Things to Know About Female Genital Surgeries in Africa," *Hastings Center Report* 6 (2012):19–27.

Chapter 6

1. At the Vienna World Conference on Human Rights in 1993, female genital mutilation became classified as a form of VAW. At this conference VAW was for the first time acknowledged to fall under the purview of international human rights law (Shell-Duncan 2008: 227). In 2008, the WHO published a policy statement on FGM representing the views of UN agencies (UNAIDS, UNDP, UNECA, UNFPA, UNHCHR, UNIFEM, etc.) to highlight the wide recognition of human rights and the legal dimensions to the problem of FGM (Shell-Duncan 2008:229; WHO 2008:3).

2. The "traditional" products applied by some excisers during excision are discussed in interviews with excisers in Chapter 2.

3. Organized diffusion means that if a person has learned something and is convinced, they go and tell others about their conviction. At every public declaration, there are villages that have participated in the Tostan program and organized diffusion villages that apparently joined the movement because they were convinced by the others. Mackie (2000) argues that if a social norm changes for the dominant intermarrying group, the others feel obliged to adapt. In practice, however, I have found that only a few inhabitants in the organized diffusion villages are actually convinced of the importance of stopping excision. Other inhabitants are not even informed that their village had officially declared their abandonment.

4. We designed this question for the Sigrid Rausing project. It was phrased in this particular way because these were the responses given by people in interviews we had done in previous research in Casamance and Salemata. As some were slow replying to this question, we thought that providing them with possible answers to choose from would make the interviewee think of possibilities they may not have thought of before. This seemed to work, so I sometimes asked the same question in my own research.

5. I translated this interview into English from the French translation, where it was said, "C'est ce qu'on a trouvé avec les ancêtres." In Pulaar, the common expression is "to inherit from the ancestors"—*min tawrii ko taaniraabe amen*. The verb *taawirde*, to inherit, similar to *taawde*, to find, is used when people talk about practices that are believed to have been practiced by the ancestors and passed down from generation to generation. In *Freedom in Fulani Social Life*, Riesman discusses the meaning of *tawaangal*—the Jelgoɓe Fulɓe's word for custom—literally translating as "that which is found." Riesman explains that the meaning of tawaangal "concerns the manner in which one acquires the possibility of accomplishing this activity, notably by the passage 'from hand to hand,' from generation to generation, of culture" (Riesman 1977: 9).

6. Relative risk [RR] = 1.52, 95% confidence interval [CI] = 1.15, 2.0) and no sexual desire was twice as likely with FGM (RR = 2.15, 95% CI = 1.37, 3.36.

7. Again, we are in no position to know or judge whether the description of the medical facts, i.e., "being very tight down there," were actually linked to the health care professional's decision to do a caesarean section and whether this was linked to FGC or a different biomedical condition. However, this was my interlocutor's understanding of the health problems she experienced and the causes.

8. According to the criteria of Engle Merry (2006).

9. Anna Lindh was the Swedish minister of foreign affairs from 1998 to 2003. Before her death in 2003 she criticized the invasion of Iraq without the support of the UN as a major failure and advocated greater respect for international law and human rights in the Israeli-Palestinian conflict. In 2003 she was murdered by a Swede of Serbian origin who was suffering from mental illness at the time of the killing. He was sentenced to life imprisonment but was moved from prison to a psychiatric ward.

BIBLIOGRAPHY

Abu-Lughod, L. (1990). "The romance of resistance: Tracing transformations of power through Bedouin women." *American Ethnologist* 17(1): 41–55.

———. (1999). *Veiled Sentiments: Honor and Poetry in a Bedouin Society.* Berkeley: University of California Press.

———. (2002). "So Muslim women really need saving? Anthropological Reflections on Cultural Relativism." *American Anthropologist* 104(3): 783–790.

———. (2008). *Writing Women's Worlds: Bedouin Stories.* Berkeley: University of California Press.

Abu-Salieh, S. A. A. (2001). *Circoncision masculine, circoncision féminine: débat religieux, médical, social et juridique.* Paris: L'Harmattan.

Abusharaf, R. M. (2000). "Revisiting feminist discourses on infibulation responses from Sudanese feminists." *Female "Circumcision" in Africa: Culture, Controversy, and Change.* Ed. B. Shell-Duncan and Y. Hernlund. London: Lynne Rienner.

———. (2007). *Female Circumcision: Multicultural Perspectives.* Philadelphia: University of Pennsylvania Press.

Adams, V. (1998). "Suffering the winds of Lhasa: Politicized bodies, human rights, cultural difference, and humanism in Tibet." *Medical Anthropology Quarterly* 12: 74–102.

Agarwal, B. (1994). *A Field of One's Own: Gender and Land Rights in South Asia.* Cambridge: Cambridge University Press.

Ahlberg, B. M., Krantz, I., Lindmark, G., and Warsame, M. (2004). "'It's only a tradition': Making sense of eradication interventions and the persistence of female circumcision within a Swedish context." *Critical Social Policy* 24: 50–78.

Ahmadu, F. (2000). "Rites and wrongs: An insider/outsider reflects on power and excision." *Female "Circumcision" in Africa: Culture, Controversy, and Change.* Ed. B. Shell-Duncan and Y. Hernlund. London: Lynne Rienner.

———. (2005). *Cutting the Anthill: The Symbolic Foundations of Female and Male Circumcision Rituals Among the Mandinka of Brikama, the Gambia.* PhD thesis. London: London School of Economics.

———. (2007). "'Ain't I A Woman Too?' Challenging myths of sexual dysfunction in circumcised women." *Transcultural Bodies: Female Genital Cutting in Global Context.* Ed. Y. Hernlund and B. Shell-Duncan. New Brunswick: Rutgers University Press.

Ahmadu, F., and Shweder, R. (2009). "Disputing the myth of the sexual dysfunction of circumcised women." *Anthropology Today* 25(6): 14–17.

Ahmadu, F. S., and Kamau, T. (2022). "Dr Tatu Kamau vs The Attorney General and Others: Problems and prospects in Kenya's 2021 High Court ruling to uphold the Prohibition of Female Genital Mutilation Act 2011—a reply to 'The prosecution of Dawoodi Bohra women' by Richard Shweder." *Global Discourse* 12(1): 29–46. https://doi.org/10.1332/204378921X16388161357195.

Al-Naqar, U. (1969). "Trakrur: The history of a name." *Journal of African History* X(3): 365–374.

Amadiume, I. (1987). *Male Daughters, Female Husbands*. London: Zed Books.

———. (1997). *Re-inventing Africa: Matriarchy, Religion and Culture*. London: Zed Books.

Amalgor, U. (1987). "The cycle and stagnation of smells: Pastoralists-fishermen relationships in East African societies." *RES* 14: 106–121.

Apffel-Marglin, F., and Simon, S. (1994). "Feminist orientalism and development." *Feminist Perspectives in Sustainable Development*. Ed. W. Harcourt. London: Zed Books.

Asad, T. (1986). "The idea of an anthropology of Islam." *Occasional Papers Series*. Washington DC.: Center for Contemporary Arab Studies, Georgetown University.

——— (2003). *Formations of the Secular: Christianity, Islam, Modernity*. Stanford, CA: Stanford University Press.

Ashforth, A. (2004). "AIDS and witchcraft in post-apartheid South-Africa." *Anthropology in the Margins of the State*. Ed. V. Das and D. Poole. Santa Fe, NM: SAR Press.

Azarya, V. (1978). *Aristocrats Facing Change: The Fulbe in Guinea, Nigeria and Cameroon*. Chicago: University of Chicago Press.

Ba, A. H. (1993). *Contes Initiatiques Peuls*. Abijan: Nouvelles Editions Ivoriennes.

Barth, R. (1969). *Ethnic Groups and Boundaries: The Social Organization of Cultural Difference*. London: Unwin.

Berg, R. C., Denison, E. M., and Fretheim, A. (2010). *Psychological, Social and Sexual Consequences of Female Genital Mutilation/Cutting (FGM/C): A Systematic Review of Quantitative Studies*. Oslo: Norwegian Knowledge Centre for the Health Services.

Berg, R. C., Odgaard-Jensen, J., Fretheim, A., Underland, V., and Vist, G. (2014). "An updated systematic review and meta-analysis of the obstetric consequences of female genital mutilation/cutting." *Obstetrics and Gynecology International*. doi: 10.1155/2014/542859.

Bensa, A., and E. Fassin. (2002). "Les sciences sociales face à l'événement." *Terrain* 38.

Berliner, D. (2018). *Perdre sa Culture*. Brussels: Zones sensibles.

———. (2020). *Losing Culture: Nostalgia, Heritage, and Our Accelerated Times*. New Brunswick: Rutgers University Press.

Bledsoe, C. (1984). "The political use of Sande ideology and symbolism." *Man* 21: 202–226.

Boddy, J. (1989). *Wombs and Alien Spirits: Women, Men, and the Zār Cult in Northern Sudan*. Madison: University of Wisconsin Press.

———. (1991). "Body politics: Continuing the anticircumcision crusade." *Medical Anthropology Quarterly* 5: 15–17.

———. (1996). "Violence embodied? Circumcision, gender politics, and cultural aesthetics." *Rethinking Violence Against Women*. Ed. R. E. Dobash and R. B. Dobash. Thousand Oaks, CA: Sage.

———. (2007). "Gender crusades: The female circumcision controversy in cultural perspective." *Transcultural Bodies: Female Genital Cutting in Global Context*. Ed. J. Boddy. New Brunswick: Rutgers University Press.

———. (2007). *Civilizing Women: British Crusades in Colonial Sudan*. Princeton: Princeton University Press.

Bordo, S. (1993). *The Unbearable Weight. Feminism Western Culture and the Body*. Berkeley: University of California Press.

Borofsky, R. (1987). *Making History: Pukapukan and Anthropological Constructions of Knowledge*. Cambridge: Cambridge University Press.

Bourdieu, P. (1977). *Outline of a Theory of Practice*. Cambridge: Cambridge University Press.

———. (1984). *Distinction: A Social Critique of the Judgement of Taste*. London: Routledge & Kegan Paul.

Brenner, L. (1988). "Concepts of Tariqa in West Africa." *Charisma and Brotherhood in African Islam*. Ed. D. B. Cruise O'Brien and C. Coulon. Oxford: Clarendon Press.

———. (2001). *Controlling Knowledge: Religion, Power, and Schooling in a West African Muslim Society*. Bloomington: Indiana University Press.

Butler, J. (1993). *Bodies that Matter: On the Discursive Limits of "Sex."* London: Routledge.

Caplan, P. (1987). *The Cultural Construction of Sexuality*. London: Tavistock.

Carsten, J. (2004). *After Kinship*. Cambridge, UK: Cambridge University Press.

Clark, A. (1996). "The Fulbe of Bundu (Senegambia): From theocracy to secularization." *International Journal of African Historical Studies* 29(1).

Classen, C. (1992). "The odor of the other: Olfactory symbolism and cultural categories." *Ethos* 20(2): 133–166.

Comaroff, Jean, and Comaroff, John. (1991). *On Revelation and Revolution*. Cambridge: Cambridge University Press.

——— (2006). *Law and Disorder in the Postcolony*. Chicago: University of Chicago Press.

Comaroff, John. (1995). "Ethnicity, nationalism and the politics of difference in the age of revolution." *Perspectives on Nationalism and War*. Ed. J. Comaroff, J. and P. Stern. Amsterdam: OPA.

Comaroff, John and Comaroff, Jean. (2009). *Ethnicity, Inc.* Chicago: University of Chicago Press.

Connerton, P. (1989). *How Societies Remember*. Cambridge: Cambridge University Press.

———. (2011). *The Spirit of Mourning: History, Memory and the Body*. Cambridge: Cambridge University Press.

Conroy, R. (2006). "Female genital mutilation: Whose problem, whose solution." *BMJ* 333: 106–107.

Courbin, A. (1986). *The Foul and the Fragrant: Odor and the French Social Imagination*. Cambridge, MA: Harvard University Press.

Cruise O'Brien, D., and C. Coulon. (1988). *Charisma and Brotherhood in African Isla*. Oxford: Clarendon Press.

Csordas, T. (1990). "Embodiment as a paradigm for anthropology." *Ethos* 18: 5–47.

———. (1994). *Embodiment and Experience: The existential Ground of Culture and Self*. Cambridge: Cambridge University Press.

———. (1999). "Embodiment and cultural phenomenology." *Perspectives on Embodiment*. Ed. G. Weiss and H. Haber. New York: Routledge.

Curtin, P. D. (1971). "Jihad in West Africa: Early phases and inter-relations in Mauritania and Senegal." *Journal of African History* 12(1): 11–24.

———. (1974). "The chronology of events and reigns in the Upper Senegal Valley." *Bulletin de l'IFAN* 16: 525–558.

D'Alisera, J. (2013). *An Imagined Geography: Sierra Leonean Muslims in America*. Philadelphia: University of Pennsylvania Press.

Das, V. (1996). *Critical Events: An Anthropological Perspective on Contemporary India*. Oxford: Oxford University Press.

———. (2001). *Remaking a World: Violence, Social Suffering, and Recovery*. Berkeley: University of California Press.

———. (2004). "State and its margins. Comparative ethnography." *Anthropology in the Margins of the State*. Ed. V. Das. Oxford: James Currey.

———. (2007). *Life and Words: Violence and the Descent into the Ordinary*. Berkeley: University of California Press.

Davidheiser, M. (2006). "Joking for peace: Social organization, tradition, and change in conflict prevention and resolution." *Cahiers d'Etudes Africaines*. 184: 835–859.

Davidson, J. (2020). "The problem of widows," *American Ethnologist* 47(1): 43–57.

Davidson, J., and Hannaford, D. (2022). *Opting Out: Women Messing with Marriage Around the World*. New Brunswick: Rutgers University Press.

Davis, J. (1977). *People of the Mediterranean. An Essay in Comparative Anthropology.* London: Routledge & Kegan Paul.

de Bruijn, M. (1995). *Arid Ways: Cultural Understanding of Insecurity in Fulbe Society, Central Mali.* Amsterdam: Thela.

Delaney, C. (2001). "Cutting the ties that bind: The sacrifice of Abraham and patriarchal kinship." *Relative Values: Reconfiguring Kinship Studies.* Ed. S. Franklin and S. McKinnon. Durham: Duke University Press.

Dellenborg, L. (2004). "A reflection on the cultural meanings of circumcision. Experiences from fieldwork in Casamance, Southern Senegal." *Rethinking Sexualities in Africa.* Ed. S. Arnfred. Stockholm: Nordiska Afrikainstitutet.

Derrida, J. (1990). *Glas.* Lincoln: University of Nebraska Press.

Diallo, A. (2004). "Paradoxes of female sexuality in Mali. On practices of Magnonmaka and Bolokoli-kela." *Rethinking Sexualities in Africa.* Ed. S. Arnfred. Stockholm: Nordiska Afrikainstitutet.

Di Leonardo, M. (1991). *Gender at the Crossroads of Knowledge: Feminist Anthropology in the Postmodern Era.* Berkeley: University of California Press.

Diabate, N. (2020). *Naked Agency. Genital Cursing and Biopolitics in Africa.* Durham: Duke University Press.

Dilley, R. M. (1989). "Secrets and skills: Apprenticeship among Tukolor weavers." *Apprenticeship: from theory to method.* Ed. M. Coy. New York: SUNY Press.

———. (1999). "Ways of knowing, forms of power: aspects of apprenticeship among Tukulor Mabuße weavers." *Cultural Dynamics* 11(1): 33–55.

———. (2000). "The question of caste in West Africa with special reference to Tukulor craftsmen." *Anthropos* 95(1): 149–165.

———. (2004). *Islamic and caste knowledge practices among Haalpulaar'en in Senegal.* Edinburgh: Edinburgh University Press.

———. (2009). "Specialist knowledge practice of craftsmen and clerics in Senegal." *Africa: Journal of the International African Institute* 79(1): 53–70.

Diop, C. A. (1979). *Nations nègres et culture: de l'Antiquité nègre égyptienne aux problèmes culturels de l'Afrique noire d'aujourd'hui.* Paris: Présence africaine.

Dopico, M. (2007). "Infibulation and the orgasm puzzle: Sexual experiences of infibulated Eritrean women in rural Eritrea and Melbourne, Australia." *Transcultural Bodies: Female Genital Cutting in Global Context.* Ed. Y. Hernlund and B. Shell-Duncan. London: Rutgers University Press.

Douglas, M. (1966). *Purity and Danger.* New York: Routledge Classics.

———. (1968). "Social control of cognition. Factors in joke perception." *Man* 3(3).

Dumont, L. (1980). *Homo Hierarchicus.* Chicago: University of Chicago Press.

Dupire, M. (1970). *Organisation Social des Peul.* Paris: Librairie Plon.

Durkheim, E. (1951). *Suicide: A Study in Sociology.* New York: The Free Press.

Dwyer, D. (1978). *Images and Self-Images: Male and Female in Morocco.* New York: Colombia University Press.

Ekeh, P. (1990). "Social anthropology and two contrasting uses of tribalism in Africa." *Comparative Studies in Society and History* 32(4): 660–700.

El Dareer, A. (1982). *Women, Why Do You Weep.* London: Zed Books.

Elias, N. (1997). *Über den Prozess der Ziviliation.* Frankfurt: Suhrkamp.

Elwert, G. (1989). "Nationalismus und Ethnizität. Über die Bildung von Wir-Gruppen." *Kölner Zeitschrift für Soziologie uns Sozialpsychologie* 3: 440–464.

Engle Merry, S. (2006). *Human Rights and Gender Violence: Translating International Law into Local Justice.* Chicago: University of Chicago Press.

Epstein, A. (1958). *Politics in an Urban African Community.* Manchester: Manchester University Press.

Escobar, A. (1995). *Encountering Development: The Making and Unmaking of the Third World.* Princeton: Princeton University Press.

Essén, B. (2020). "One genital, two judgments: Why do 'expert witnesses' draw different conclusions in suspected cases of illegal cutting of girls' genitals?" *Female Genital Cutting: The Global North and South.* Ed. S. Johnsdotter. Centre for Sexology and Sexuality Studies, Malmö University.

Essén, B., and Mosselmans, L. (2021). "How to ensure policies and interventions rely on strong supporting facts to improve women's health: The case of female genital cutting, using Rosling's factfulness approach." *Acta Obstetricia et Gynecologica Scandinavica.* 100(4): 579–586.

Evans-Pritchard, E. (1937). *Witchcraft, Oracles, and Magic Among the Azande.* Oxford: Oxford University Press.

Fardon, R. (1996). "Ethnicity, the Person and the 'Problem of Identity' in West Africa." *African Crossroads. Intersections Between History and Anthropology in Cameroon.* Ed. I. Fowler and D. Zeitlyn. Oxford: Berghahn Books.

Farge, A. (2002). "Qu'est-ce qu'un événement?" *Terrain revue d'ethnologie de l'Europe* 38.

Farnell, B. (1999). "Moving bodies, acting selves." *Annual Review in Anthropology* 28: 341–373.

Fenton, S. (2010). *Ethnicity.* Cambridge: Polity Press.

Ferguson, J. (2006). *Global Shadows: Africa in the Neoliberal World Order.* Durham: Duke University Press.

Ferrandiz, F. (2004). "The body as Wound. Possession, Malandros and everyday violence in Venezuela." *Critique of Anthropology* 24(2): 107–133.

Fortes, M. (1945). *The Dynamics of Clanship Among the Tallensi.* London: Oxford University Press.

Fortes, M., and Evans-Pritchard, E. (1940). *African Political Systems.* London: Oxford University Press.

Fortun, K. (2001). *Advocacy After Bhopal: Environmentalism, Disaster, New Global Orders.* Chicago: University of Chicago Press.

Foucault, M. (1975). *Discipline and Punish.* New York: Vintage.

——. (1978). *The History of Sexuality. Volume 1: An Introduction.* New York: Vintage.

——. (2007). "Governmentality." *The Anthropology of the State.* Ed. A. Sharma and A. Gupta. Oxford: Blackwell.

Fowler, D., and Hardesty, D. (1994). *Others Knowing Others: Perspectives on Ethnographic Careers.* Washington, DC: Smithsonian Institution Press.

Fraser, M., and Greco, M. (2005). *The Body: A Reader.* London: Routledge.

Galvan, D. (2006). "Joking kinship as a syncretic institution." *Cahiers d'études africaines* 184: 809–834.

Geertz, C. (1973). "The integrative revolution: Primordial sentiments and civil politics in the new states." *The Interpretation of Cultures.* Ed. C. Geertz, New York: Basic Books.

Geisler, G. (2000). "Women are women and how to please your husband: Initiation ceremonies and the politics of 'tradition' in Southern Africa." *Gender, Agency and Change.* Ed. V. Goddard. London: Routledge.

Geschiere, P. (1997). *The Modernity of Witchcraft. Politics of the Occult in Postcolonial Africa.* Charlottesville: University of Virginia Press.

Gillespie, D., and Melching, M. (2010). "The transformative power of democracy and human rights in nonformal education." *Adult Education Quarterly.* 60(5): 477–498.

Gilroy, P. (2002). *"There Ain't No Black in the Union Jack": The Cultural Politics of Race and Nation.* London: Routledge Classics.

——. (2007). *Black Britain: A Photographic History.* London: Saqi.

Ginio, R. (2002). "French colonial reading of ethnographic research." *Cahiers d'études africaines* 166: 337–358.

Gluckman, M. (1956). *Custom and Conflict in Africa*. Oxford: Blackwell.

———. (1960). "Tribalism in modern British Central Africa." *Cahiers d'études africaines* 1: 55–70.

Goddard, V. (1987). "Honour and shame: The control of women's sexuality and group identity in Naples." *The Cultural Construction of Sexuality*. Ed. P. Caplan. London: Tavistock.

———. (1994). "From the Mediterranean to Europe: Honour, kinship and gender." *The Anthropology of Europe. Identities and Boundaries in Conflict*. Ed. V. Goddard, J. R. Llobera, and C. Shore. Oxford: Berg.

———. (2000). *Gender, Agency and Change*. London: Routledge.

———. (2000). "'The virgin and the state': Gender and politics in Argentina." *Gender, Agency and Change*. Ed. V. Goddard. London: Routledge.

Goodale, M. (2022). *Reinventing Human Rights*. Stanford: Stanford University Press.

Goody, J. (1956). *The Social Organisation of the LoWiili*. Oxford: International African Institute.

———. (1980). *Technology, Tradition and the State in Africa*. London: Hutchinson.

Gosselin, C. (2000). "Handing over the knife: Numu women and the campaign against excision in Mali." *Female "Circumcision" in Africa: Culture, Controversy, and Change*. Ed. B. Shell-Duncan and Y. Hernlund. London: Lynne Rienner.

Gottlieb, A. (2002). "Interpreting gender and sexuality: approaches from cultural anthropology." *Exotic no more. Anthropology on the Front Lines*. Ed. J. MacClancy. Chicago: University of Chicago Press.

Green, M. (2000). "Globalizing development in Tanzania policy franchising through participatory project management." *Critique of Anthropology* 23(2): 123–143.

———. (2000). "Participatory development and the appropriation of agency in Southern Tanzania." *Critique of Anthropology* 20 (1): 67–89.

———. (2003). "Globalizing development in Tanzania: Policy franchising through participatory project management." *Critique of Anthropology* 23(2): 123–143.

Griaule, M. (1970). *Conversations with Ogotemmeli*. Oxford: Oxford University Press.

Grosz, E. (1994). *Volatile Bodies: Towards a Corporeal Feminism*. Bloomington: Indiana University Press.

Gruenbaum, E. (1982). "The movement against clitoridectomy and infibulation in Sudan: Public health policy and the women's movement." *Medical Anthropology Newsletter* 13: 4–12.

———. (1996). "The cultural debate over female circumcision: The Sudanese are arguing this one out for themselves." *Medical Anthropology Quarterly* 10: 455–475.

———. (2001). *The Female Circumcision Controversy: An Anthropological Perspective*. Philadelphia: University of Pennsylvania Press.

Gupta, A. (2001). "Governing population: The integrated child development services program in India." *States of Imagination*. Ed. T. B. Hansen and F. Stepputat. Durham: Duke University Press.

Gupta, C. (2002). *Sexuality, Obscenity, Community*. New York: Palgrave.

Guyer, J. (1984). *Family and Farm in Southern Cameroon*. Boston: Boston University Libraries.

Handelman, D. (1990). *Models and Mirrors: Towards an Anthropology of Public Events*. Cambridge: Cambridge University Press.

Hannaford, D. R. (2017). *Marriage Without Borders: Transnational Spouses in Neoliberal Senegal*. Philadelphia: University of Pennsylvania Press.

Hansen, T. B., and Stepputat, F. (2001). *States of Imagination*. Durham: Duke University Press.

Hardin, K. (1993). *The Aesthetics of Action: Continuity and Change in a West African Town*. Washington, DC: Smithsonian Institution Press.

Harrison, C. (1988). *France and Islam in West Africa, 1860–1960*. Cambridge: Cambridge University Press.

Herzfeld, M. (2016). *Cultural Intimacy: Social Poetics in the Nation-State*. London: Routledge.

Hecquart, H. (1853). *Voyage sur la Côte et dans l'Intérieur de l'Afrique Occidentale*. Paris: Imprimerie de Bénard et Compagnie.

Hernlund, Y. (2000). "Cutting without ritual and ritual without cutting: Female circumcision and re-ritualization of initiation in the Gambia." *Female "Circumcision" in Africa: Culture, Controversy, and Change*. Ed. B. Shell-Duncan and Y. Hernlund. London: Lynne Rienner.

———. (2003). *Winnowing Culture: Negotiating Female "Circumcision" in The Gambia*. PhD thesis. University of Washington.

Hobbes, T. (2002). *Leviathan*, London: Penguin Classics.

Hodzic, S. (2016). *The Twilight of Cutting African Activism and Life After NGOs*. Berkeley: University of California Press.

Holmes, D., and Marcus, G. (2005). "Cultures of expertise and management of globalisation: Toward the re-functioning of ethnography." *Global Assemblages*. Ed. A. Ong and S. Collier. Malden, UK: Blackwell.

Hosken, F. (1982). *The Hosken Report: Genital and Sexual Mutilation of Females*. 3rd rev. ed. Lexington, MA: Women's International Network News.

Howell, S., and Talle, A. (2012). *Returns to the Field: Multitemporal Research and Contemporary Anthropology*. Bloomington: Indiana University Press.

Johnsdotter, S. (2002). *Created by God: How Somalis in Swedish Exile Reassess the Practice of Female Circumcision*. PhD thesis. Lund University.

———. (2020). *Female Genital Cutting: The Global North and South*. Malmö: Centre for Sexology and Sexuality Studies.

Johnsdotter, S., and Essen, B. (2005). "'It is only a tradition': Making sense of Swedish Somalis' narratives of female circumcision and avoiding submission to hegemonic political discourses." *Critical Social Policy* 25: 578–596.

Johnson, J. P. (1974). *The Almamate of Futa Toro 1770–1836: A Political History*. PhD thesis. University of Wisconsin.

Johnson, M. C. (2000). "Becoming a Muslim, becoming a person: Female 'circumcision', religious identity and personhood in Guinea-Bissau." *Female "Circumcision" in Africa: Culture, Controversy, and Change*. Ed. B. Shell-Duncan and Y. Hernlund. London: Lynne Rienner.

———. (2020). *Remaking Islam in African Portugal: Lisbon, Mecca, Bissau*. Bloomington: Indiana University Press.

Journet, O. (1983). "La quête de l'enfant, représentation de la maternité et rituels de sterilité dans la société Diola, Basse Casamance." *Journal des Africanistes* 51(1–2): 97–115.

———. (1985). "Les Hyper-Mères n'ont plus d'enfants, maternité et ordre social chez les Joola de Basse-Casamance." *L'Arraisonnement des Femmes, Essais en Anthropologie des Sexes*. Ed. N. Claude-Mathieu. Cahier de l'Homme Nouvel Série 24. Paris: Editons de l'Ecole des Hautes Etudes en Sciences Sociales.

Kandiyoti, D. (1988). "Bargaining with patriarchy." *Gender and Society* 2(3): 274–290.

———. (1991). *Women, Islam and the State*. Philadelphia: Temple University Press.

———. (1998). "Gender, power and contestation: Rethinking bargaining with patriarchy." *Feminist Visions of Development*. Ed. C. Jackson and R. Pearson. London: Routledge.

Kane, O. (1974). "Les Maures et le Fouta Toro au XVIIIème siècle." *Cahiers d'études africaines* 14(2): 237–252.

Kapur, R. (2002). "The tragedy of victimization rhetoric: Resurrecting the 'native' subject in international/post-colonial feminist legal politics." *Harvard Human Rights Journal* 15: 1–37.

Kleinman, A. (1988). *The Illness Narratives. Suffering, Healing and the Human Condition*. New York: Basic Books.

Kopytoff, I. (1987). "The internal African frontier: The making of African political culture." *The African Frontier: The Reproduction of Traditional African Societies*. Ed. I. Kopytoff. Bloomington: Indiana University Press.

Kratz, C. (2007). "Seeking asylum, debating values, and setting precedents in the 1990s: The cases of Kassindja and Abankwah in the United States." *Transcultural Bodies: Female Genital Cutting in Global Context*. Ed. Y. Hernlund and B. Shell-Duncan. New Brunswick: Rutgers University Press.

Lacan, J. (1977). *Ecrits*. London: Tavistock.

Lambek, M. and Strathern, A. (1998). *Bodies and Persons: Comparative Perspectives from Africa and Melanesia*. Cambridge University Press.

Latour, B. (2005). *Reassembling the Social: An Introduction to Actor-Network-Theory*. Oxford: Oxford University Press.

Launay, R. (2006). "Joking kinship." *Cahiers d'études africaines* 184: 795–808.

Lentz, C. (1995). "'Tribalism' and ethnicity in Africa. A review of four decades of anglophone research." *Cahier Science Humaine* 31(2): 303–328.

Leve, L. (2011). "Identity." *Current Anthropology* 52(4): 513–535.

Lightfoot-Klein, H. (1989). *Prisoners of Ritual: An Odyssey into Female Genital Circumcision in Africa*. New York: Haworth Press.

Linares, O. (1992). "From tidal swamp to inland valley: On the social organization of wet rice cultivation among the Diola of Senegal." *Africa* 51(2): 557–595.

Lindenbaum, S., and Lock, M. (1993). *Knowledge, Power and Practice: The Anthropology of Medicine and Everyday Life*. Berkeley: University of California Press.

Lukes, S. (1971). "The meanings of 'individualism.'" *Journal of the History of Ideas* 32(1): 45–66.

Ly, D. (1938). "Coutumes et Contes de Toucouleurs du Fouta Toro." *Bulletin du Comité des etudes historiques et scientifiques de Afrique occidentale francaise* 21.

Lock, M. (1991). "Contesting meanings of the menopause." *Lancet* 337: 1270–1291.

———. (1993). "Cultivating the body: Anthropology and epistemologies of bodily practice and knowledge." *Annual Review of Anthropology* 22: 133–155.

Lock, M., and Scheper-Hughes, N. (1990). "A critical interpretive approach in medical anthropology: Rituals and routines of discipline and dissent." *Medical Anthropology: A Handbook of Theory and Method*. Ed. T. Johnson and C. Sargent. New York: Greenwood.

Mackie, G. (2000). "Female genital cutting: The beginning of the end." *Female "Circumcision" in Africa: Culture, Controversy, and Change*. Ed. Y. Hernlund and B. Shell-Duncan. London: Lynne Rienner.

Mahmood, S. (2005). *Politics of Piety: The Islamic Revival and the Feminist Subject*. Princeton, NJ: Princeton University Press.

Mamdani, M. (1996). *Citizen and Subject: Contemporary Africa and the Legacy of Late Colonialism*. Princeton, NJ: Princeton University Press.

———. (2012). *Define and Rule: Native as Political Identity*. Cambridge, MA: Harvard University Press.

Marcus, G. (2007). "Ethnography two decades after writing culture: From experimental to baroque." *Anthropological Quarterly* 80(4): 1127–1145.

Mark, P. (1978). "Urban migration, cash cropping and calamity: The spread of Islam among the Diola of Boulouf (Senegal) 1900–1940." *African Studies Review* 21(2).

Martin, E. (1987). *The Woman in the Body: A Cultural Analysis of Reproduction*. Boston: Beacon Press.

———. (1990). "Toward an anthropology of immunology: The body as nation state." *Medical Anthropology Quarterly* 4(4): 410–426.

———. (1991). "The egg and the sperm: How science has constructed romance based on stereotypical male-female roles." *Signs* 16: 485–501.

Mauss, M. (1973). "Techniques of the body." *Economy and Society* 2(1): 70–88.

———. (1985). "A category of the human mind: The notion of person; the notion of self." *The Category of the Person: Anthropology, Philosophy, History*. Ed. M. Carrithers, S. Collins, and S. Lukes. Cambridge, UK: Cambridge University Press.

Meinert, L., and Kapferer, B. (2015). *In the Event: Toward an Anthropology of Generic Moments*. New York: Berghahn.

Merleau-Ponty, M. (1962). *Phenomenology of Perception*. London: Routledge.

Mitchell, C. (1956). *The Kalela Dance: Aspects of Social Relations Among Urban Africans in Northern Rhodesia*. Manchester, UK: Manchester University Press.

Mody, P. (2009). *The Intimate State: Love-Marriage and the Law in Delhi*. Delhi: Routledge.

Moghadam, V. (1994). *Gender and National Identity*. Oxford: Oxford University Press.

Morris, B. (1985). "The Rise and Fall of the Human Subject." *Man* 20(4).

———. (1991). *Western Conceptions of the Individual*. Oxford: Berg.

Morsy, S. A. (1980). "Body concepts and healthcare: Illustrations from an Egyptian village." *Human Organ* 39: 92–96.

Mosse, D. (2005). *Cultivating Development: An Ethnography of Aid Policy and Practice*. London: Pluto Press.

Murphy, R. (1987). *The Body Silent*. New York: Holt.

Narayan, K. (1993). "How native is a 'native' anthropologist?" *American Anthropologist*, 95(3), 671–686.

Nelson, N., and Wright, S. (1994). *Power and Participatory Development: Theory and Practice*. London: Intermediate Technology Publications.

Newman, A. (2020). "Honour, respectability and 'noble' work: Descent and gender-based obstacles to the education and employment of young Haalpulaar women in northern Senegal." *Children's Geographies* 18(6): 654–666.

Niehaus, I. (2001). *Witchcraft, Power and Politics: Exploring the Occult in the South African Lowvelt*. Claremont: David Phillip.

Njambi, W. N. (2004). "Dualisms and Female Bodies in Representations of African Female Circumcision: A Feminist Critique." *Feminist Theory*. 5(3): 281–303.

Nnaemeka, O. (2005). *Female Circumcision and the Politics of Knowledge: African Women in Imperialist Discourses*. Westport, CT: Praeger.

Obermeyer, C. M. (1999). "Female Genital Surgeries: The Known, the Unknown, and the Unknowable." *Medical Anthropology Quarterly* 13(1): 79–106.

Obiora, A. (2007). "A refuge from tradition and the refuge of tradition: On anti-circumcision paradigms." *Transcultural Bodies: Female Genital Cutting in Global Context*. Ed. Y. Hernlund and B. Shell-Duncan. New Brunswick: Rutgers University Press.

O'Brien, C. D. (1971). *The Mourides of Senegal: The Political and Economic Organization of an Islamic Brotherhood*. Oxford: Clarendon Press.

Okely, J. (1983). *The Traveller-Gypsies*. Cambridge, UK: Cambridge University Press.

O'Neill, S. (2018). "Purity, cleanliness and smell—female circumcision, embodiment and discourses among midwives and excisers in Fouta Toro, Senegal." *Journal of the Royal Anthropological Institute* 24 (4) https://doi.org/10.1111/1467-9655.1291

O'Neill, S., Richard, F., Vanderhoven, C., and Caillet, M. (2021). "Pleasure, womanhood and the desire for reconstructive surgery after female genital cutting in Belgium." *Anthropology & Medicine* 29(3): 237–254.

Ortner, S. B. (1995). "Resistance and the problem of ethnographic refusal." *Comparative Studies in Society and History* 37: 173–193.

———. (1996). *Making Gender: The Politics and Erotics of Culture*. Boston: Beacon Press.

———. (2001). "Specifying agency: The Comaroffs and their critics." *Interventions: International Journal of Postcolonial Studies* 3: 76–84.

Ortner, S., and Whitehead, H. (1981). *Sexual Meanings, the Cultural Construction of Gender and Sexuality.* Cambridge, UK: Cambridge University Press.

Panet, S. (2009). "C'est comme ca que ca germe. Changement social au Senegal: le cas de l'ONG Tostan." *Repenser l'action collective: une approche par les capabilités.* Ed. J.-L. Dubois, P. Bakhshi, A.-S. Brouillet, and C. Duray-Soundrou. Paris: l'Harmattan.

Peel, J. (1989). "The cultural work of Yoruba ethnogenesis." *History and Ethnicity.* Ed. E. Tolkien, M. McDonald, and M. Chapman. London: Routledge.

Perry, D. (2004). "Muslim child disciples, global civil society and children's rights in Senegal: The discourses of strategic structuralism." *Anthropological Quarterly* 77: 47–86.

Piot, C. (2007). "Representing Africa in the Kasinga asylum case." *Transcultural Bodies: Female Genital Cutting in the Global Context.* Ed. Y. Hernlund and B. Shell-Duncan. New Brunswick: Rutgers University Press.

Pitt-Rivers, J. (1965). "Honour and social status." *Honour and Shame: The Values of Mediterranean Society.* Ed. J. G. Peristiany. London: Weidenfeld & Nicolson.

Public Policy Advisory Network on Female Genital Surgeries in Africa. (2012). "Seven things to know about female genital surgeries in Africa." *Hastings Center Report* 42(6): 19–27.

Raffenel, A. (1856). *Nouveau Voyage dans le Pays des Nègres.* Paris: Imprimerie et Librairie Central des chemins de Fer.

Riesman, P. (1971). "Defying official morality: The example of man's quest for woman among the Fulani." *Cahiers d'étude africaines* 11(44): 602–613.

———. (1974). *Freedom in Fulani Social Life.* Chicago: University of Chicago Press.

———. (1992). *First Find Your Child a Good Mother: The Construction of Self in Two African Communities.* New Brunswick: Rutgers University Press.

Robinson, D. (1975a). *Chiefs and Clerics: Abdul Bokar Kan and Futa Toro 1853–1801.* Oxford: Clarendon Press.

———. (1975b). "The Islamic revolution of Futa Toro." *International Journal of African Historical Studies* 8(2): 185–221.

———. (1985). *The Holy War of Umar Tall: The Western Sudan in the Mid-Nineteenth Century.* Oxford: Clarendon Press.

Rosaldo, M. Z. (1980). "The use and abuse of anthropology: Reflections on feminism and cross-cultural understanding." *Signs: Journal of Women in Culture and Society* 5(3).

Rosen, L. (1978). "The negotiation of reality: Male-female relations in Sefrou, Morocco." *Women in the Muslim World.* Ed. L. Beck and N. Keddie. Cambridge, MA: Harvard University Press.

Sarayloo, K., Latifnejad Roudsari, R., and Elhadi, A. (2019). "Health consequences of the female genital mutilation: A systematic review." *Galen Medical Journal* 1(8): e1336.

Scheper-Hughes, N. (1992). *Death Without Weeping: The Violence of Everyday Life in Brazil.* Berkeley: University of California Press.

Scheper-Hughes, N., and Lock, M. (1991). "The message in the bottle: Illness and micropolitics of resistance." *Journal of Psychohistory* 18: 409–452.

Schmitz, J. (1985). "Autour d'al- Hajj Umar Taal. Guerre sainte et Tijaniyya en Afrique de l'ouest." *Cahiers d'études africaines* 15(4): 555–565.

———. (1986). "L'État géomètre: les leydi des Peul du Fuuta Tooro (Sénégal) et du Maasina (Mali)." *Cahiers d'études africaines* 26 (103): 349–394.

———. (1994). "Cités noires: les républiques villageoises du Fuuta Tooro (Vallée du Fleuve, Sénégal)." *Cahiers d'études africaines* 19(1-3): 419–460.

———. (1998). *Florilège au jardin de l'histoire des noirs. Zuhur al Basatin. L'aristocratie peule et la révolution des clercs musulmans de la vallée du Sénégal.* Paris: CNRS Editions.

Schneider, D. M. (1968). *American Kinship: A Cultural Account.* New York: Prentice-Hall.

Searles, E., and Johnson, M. C. (2021). *Reciprocity Rules: Friendship and Compensation in Fieldwork Encounters.* Lanham, MD: Lexington Books.

Sen, A. K. (1990). "Gender and cooperative conflicts." *Persistent Inequalities. Women and World Development*. Ed. I. Tinker. New York: Oxford University Press.

Sharpe, B. (1986). "Ethnography and a regional system: Mental maps and the myth of states of tribes in north-central Nigeria." *Critique of Anthropology* 6(3): 33–65.

Shaw, R. (1997). "The production of witchcraft/witchcraft as production: memory, modernity and the slave trade in Sierra Leone." *American Ethnologist* 24(4): 856–876.

Shell-Duncan, B. (2008). "From health to human rights: Female genital cutting and the politics of intervention." *American Anthropological Association* 110(2): 225–236.

Shell-Duncan, B., and Hernlund, Y. (2000). "Female 'circumcision' in Africa: Dimensions of the practice and debates." *Female "Circumcision" in Africa: Culture, Controversy, and Change*. Ed. B. Shell-Duncan and Y. Hernlund. London: Lynne Rienner.

———. (2007). "Transcultural positions: Negotiating rights and culture." *Transcultural Bodies: Female Genital Cutting in Global Context*. Ed. Y. Hernlund and B. Shell-Duncan. New Brunswick: Rutgers University Press.

Shweder, R. (2002). "What about female genital mutilation? And why understanding culture matters in the first place." *Engaging Cultural Differences*. Ed. R. Shweder, M. Minow, and H. R. Markus. New York: Russell Sage Foundation.

———. (2013). "The goose and the gander: The genital wars." *Global Discourse* 3(2): 348–366.

Silverman, E. (2004). "Anthropology and circumcision." *Annual Review of Anthropology* 33: 419–445.

Simmel, G. (1997). *Simmel on Culture*. Ed. M. Featherstone and D. Frisby. London: SAGE.

Skramstad, H. (1990). *The Fluid Meaning of Female Circumcision in a Multiethnic Context in Gambia: Distribution of Knowledge and Linkages to Sexuality*. Working Paper D 1990:12. Bergen: Chr. Michelsen Institute.

Smith, E. (2006). "La nation 'par le côté': Le récit des cousinages au Sénégal." *Cahiers d'études africaines* 184: 907–965.

Smith, E., and Canut, C. (2006). "Pactes, alliances et plaisanteries." *Cahiers d'études africaines* 184(4): 687–754.

Smith, G. G. (2009). *Medina Gounass: Challenges to Village Sufism in Senegal*. Books on Demand.

Southall, A. (1970). "The illusion of the tribe" *Perspectives on Africa*. Ed. R. Grinker, S. Lubkeman, and C. Steiner. London: Blackwell.

Stenning, D. (1959). *Savannah Nomads: A Study of the Wodaabe Pastoral Fulani of Western Bornu*. Oxford: Oxford University Press.

Stern, P., and P. V. Hall. (2010). "The proposal economy." *Critique of Anthropology* 30(3): 243–264.

Strathern, M. (1990). *The Gender of the Gift*. Berkeley: University of California Press.

———. (1999). *Property, Substance, and Effect: Anthropological Essays on Persons and Things*. London: Athlone Press.

———. (2004). "Losing (out on) intellectual resources." *Law, Anthropology, and the Constitution of the Social: Making Persons and Things*. Ed. A. Pottage and M. Mundy. Cambridge, UK: Cambridge University Press.

Tall, T. M. (1999). *Preuves Eclatantes au Sujet de la Pratique Recommandable de l'Excision des Jeunes Filles*. Dakar.

Tamari, T. (1991). "The development of caste systems in West Africa." *Journal of African History* 32(2): 221–250.

Tarlo, E. (2003). *Unsettling Memories. Narratives of the Emergency in Delhi*. London: C. Hurst.

Taussing, M. (1987). *Shamanism, Colonialism and the Wildman: A Study in Terror and Healing*. Chicago: University of Chicago Press.

Terretta, M. (2012). "'We had been fooled into thinking that the UN watches over the entire world': Human rights, UN trust territories, and Africa's decolonization." *Human Rights Quarterly* 34(2): 329–360.

Thomas, L. (2000). "'Ngaitana (I will circumcise myself)': Lessons from colonial campaigns to ban excision in Meru, Kenya." *Female "Circumcision" in Africa. Culture, Controversy and Change.* Ed. B. Shell-Duncan and Y. Hernlund. London: Lynne Rienner.

———. (2003). *Politics of the Womb: Women, Reproduction, and the State in Kenya.* Los Angeles: University of California Press.

Trouillot, M.-R. (1995). *Silencing the Past: Power and the Production of History.* Boston: Beacon Press.

Turner, T. (1997). "Human rights, human difference: anthropology's contribution to an emancipatory cultural politics." *Journal of Anthropological Research* 53: 273–291.

Turner, V. (1967). *The Drums of Affliction: A Study of Religious Processes Among the Ndembu of Zambia.* London: Routledge.

———. (1986). *The Forest of Symbols.* Ithaca: Cornell University Press.

Wane, Y. (1969). *Les Toucouleur du Fouta Tooro (Sénégal): stratification sociale et structure familiale.* Dakar: IFAN.

Wardlow, H. (2006). *Wayward Women. Sexuality and Agency in a New Guinean Society.* Berkeley: University of California Press.

Whitehouse, B. (2023). *Enduring Polygamy: Plural Marriage and Social Change in an African Metropolis.* New Brunswick: Rutgers University Press.

Wickström, A. (2010). "Virginity testing as a local public health initiative: A 'preventive ritual' more than a diagnostic measure." *Journal of the Royal Anthropological Institute* 16: 532–550.

Willis, J. R. (1978). "The Torodbe clerisy: A social view." *Journal of African History* 19(2): 195–212.

———. (1979). *Studies in West African Islamic History: The Cultivators of Islam.* London: Frank Cass.

———. (1989). *In the Path of Allah: The Passion of Al-Hajj Umar. An Essay into the Nature of Charisma in Islam.* London: Frank Cass.

Wilson, F., and Frederiksen, B. (1995). *Ethnicity, Gender and the Subversion of Nationalism.* London: Frank Cass.

Yanagisako, S., and Delaney, C. (1995). *Naturalizing Power: Essays in Feminist Cultural Analysis.* New York: Routledge.

Yuval-Davis, A., et al. (1989). *Woman, Nation, State.* New York: Macmillan.

Newspaper Articles/Local Pamphlets/Personal Communications

Camara, A. (2008). Email to S. O'Neill.

Diouf, A. (1997). "Restons fidèles au génie de nos ancêtres." *Le Soleil.* Dakar.

Gaestel, A., and Shryock, R. (October 2017). "The price of Senegal's strict anti-abortion laws." *New Yorker.*

Kane, C. (April 29, 2022). "In Senegal, the tragedy of the anti-abortion crusade." *Le Monde.*

Ndiaye, P. (June 14, 2009). *Opposed to the Prosecution of Excisers, the Religious Leaders of Matam Rebel.*

Niang, B. (1999). "Criminaliser la pédophilie, non l'excision." *Walfadjiri.* Dakar.

Niang, S. (2009). Notes from recording of meeting of Tostan and the Marabouts of Podor in Ndioum to discuss Tostan's involvement in the "Trials of Matam."

Panet, S. (January-February 2024). "Exilée pour avortement." *Axelle Magazine.*

Religious leaders of Matam. (May 28, 2009). "Press Declaration" document created by the Ulamas, Imams and religious leaders of the Ferlo and the Bundu to inform media and NGOs of their stance on the "Trials of Matam" following the arrest of an exciser.

Tall, T. M. (1999). *Preuves Eclatantes au Sujet de la Pratique Recommandable de l'Excision des Jeunes Filles*. Dakar: Imprimerie Ecaricom.

UNICEF Senegal. (1999). *l'Abandon de l'Excision*.

Unknown author. (1997). "Il faut une loi. Elle est plus forte que la tradition." *Point de Vue*. Dakar.

Unknown author. (1997). "La fin de l'excision a Malicounda." *Nouvel Horizon*. Dakar.

Unknown author. (1997). "Le monde s'effondre." *Le Soleil*. Dakar.

Unknown author. (1997). "Le point de vue religieux "L'excision est recommandable, pas obligatoire." *Le Matin*. Dakar.

Unknown author. (1997). "Le serment de Malicounda." *Le Matin*. Dakar.

Unknown author. (1997). "Les femme demystifient l'excision." *Dakar Soir*. Dakar.

Unknown author. (1997). "Mutilations génitales féminines au Sénégal. La face cachée du drame feminine." *Le Matin*. Dakar.

Unknown author. (1997). "Mutilations Sexuelles Féminines." *Nouvel Horizon*. Dakar.

Unknown author. (1997). "Malicounda Bambara—Des descendants des maliens bien integrés." *Le Soleil*. Dakar.

Unknown author. (1997). "Malicounda Bambara: le femmes renoncent á l'excision." *Le Soleil*. Dakar.

Unknown author. (1998). "Interdiction et Pénalisation. Ils veulent nous humilies." *Walfadjiri*. Dakar.

Unknown author. (1998). "Kedougou: 120 filles excises, en attendant. Dans ce département ou une centaine de filles ont été excise il y a ne dizaines de jours, on accueille la pénalisation des mutilations génitales féminines sans grande illusion. Car le travail préalable a été bâclé, voire inexistant." *Walfadjiri*. Dakar.

Unknown author. (1998). "Les excisieuses n'ont pas déposé les lames." *Walfadjiri*. Dakar.

Unknown author. (2009). "Sénégal: une exciseuse condamnée à six mois de prison ferme." Jeune Afrique.

Nongovernmental Organization Documents/ Public Health Research Papers

CRDH. (2010). *Evaluation de l'Impact du Programme de Renforcement des Capacités des Communautés sur le Changement de Comportements en Milieu Rural: PRCC-TOSTAN, Régions de Tambacounda et Kolda*. M. d. l. Santé, d. O. F. Ministère de la Famille and e. d. l. P. d. l'Enfance. Dakar, Centre de Recherche pour le Développement Humain (CRDH).

Demographic Health Survey Mali. (2001). Calverton, MD: Centre de Recherche pour le Developpement Humain et ORC Macro.

Demographic Health Survey Mauritania. (2001). Calverton, MD: Centre de Recherche pour le Developpement Humain et ORC Macro.

Demographic Health Survey Senegal. (2005). Calverton, MD: Centre de Recherche pour le Developpement Humain et ORC Macro.

Demographic Health Survey Guinea. (2005). Calverton, MD: Centre de Recherche pour le Developpement Humain et ORC Macro.

Demographic Health Survey Gambia. (2008). Calverton, MD: Centre de Recherche pour le Developpement Humain et ORC Macro.

Diop, N., Badge, E. et al. (2003). *Replication of the Tostan Progamme in Burkina Faso: How 23 Villages Participated in a Human Rights Based Education Programme and Abandoned the Practice of Female Genital Cutting in Burkina Faso*. Frontiers Report. Dakar: Population Council.

Diop, N., Mbacke Faye, M., et al. (2004). *The Tostan Program: Evaluation of a Community-Based Education Program in Senegal*. Frontiers Final Report. Washington, DC: Population Council.

Diop, N., Moreau, A. et al. (2008). *Evaluation of the Long-Term Impact of the Tostan Programme on the Abandonment of FGM/C and Early Marriage: Results from a Qualitative Study in Senegal.* Washington, DC: Population Council.

Ndiaye, S. a. M. A. (2006). *Enquête Démographique et de Sante au Senegal 2005.* Calverton, MD: Centre de Recherche pour le Développement Humain [Senegal] et ORC Macro.

Tostan. (1999). *Breakthrough in Senegal: Ending Female Genital Cutting.* Africa Operation Research & Technical Assistance/Project II Population Council.

———. (2007). *Etude sur les pratiques d'excision dans les regions Ziguinchor, Kolda, Tambacounda, Matam. Abandons et résistances.* Unpublished report financed by Sigrid Rausing.

UNICEF. (2008). *L'Excision au Sénégal: Sens, portée et enseignements tirés de la réponse nationale.* Dakar: UNICEF.

US Department of State. (2010). *2009 Human Rights Report: Senegal.* Available at http://www.state.gov/j/drl/rls/hrrpt/2009/af/135973.htm.

Official Governmental Documents

Agence Nationale de la Statistique et de la Démographie (ANSD) [Sénégal], and ICF. 2019. *Sénégal: Enquête Démographique et de Santé Continue (EDS-Continue 2019)—Tableaux.* Rockville, MD: ANSD and ICF.

République du Sénégal. (2008). *Évaluation du Plan d'action national pour l'abandon de la pratique des mutilations génitales féminines.*

Sénégal—Troisième Recensement Général de la Population et de l'Habitat (2002), Ministère de l'Économie et des Finances Agence National de la Statistique et de la Démographie. République du Sénégal.

INDEX

ACKNOWLEDGMENTS

Bringing this book to completion feels like coming to the end of a long journey that started more than fifteen years ago, and so many people have helped me get to this point. I would first of all like to thank my Futanke interlocutors for their kind hospitality, for opening up to me and accompanying me on my ethnographic journey. I owe immense gratitude to Ceerno Gaynaako Pulaar, his wife and children, and the larger family. I am incredibly grateful for their hospitality and patience and all the fun we had together. I would also like to thank Nene Jonké and family. Their doors were always open to me. I am also immensely grateful to all my friends in other villages where I stayed to do research. Thanks and greetings also go to my in-laws. One dear friend and in-law, Lego Niang, died in a tragic car accident and is dearly missed. He contributed to this book with Pulaar expressions and explanations of Pulaar traditions. He was incredibly supportive and kind.

I would also like to extend my gratitude to Tostan Fouta especially, but also the national staff. This research would not have been possible without Tostan's support and I appreciate them letting me come and go as I pleased, for their trust and free lodging when needed. Special thanks go to Abou Camara, Abou Diack, Alassane Boly, Khalidou Sy, Aissata Dia, and Molly Melching.

This book is partly the fruit of the guidance of my PhD supervisors Nici Nelson and Sophie Day at Goldsmiths College, University of London. I feel immensely grateful and indebted to them for their kind but firm support throughout my PhD. Victoria Goddard, Frances Pine, David Graeber, and my PhD cohort also provided stimulating comments on chapters.

I feel indebted to the African Studies Association of the UK for awarding me the Audrey Richards Prize. Before I received this prize, I believed that this work would end up as a dusty PhD thesis on the shelf that nobody would be interested in reading. However, the praise and enthusiasm for my work was incredibly encouraging to rewrite this into a book. I also feel indebted to John

Peel, who was so enthusiastic about the book project before he passed away and who connected me to David Pratten at the University of Oxford. I am grateful to David for his support and affiliation to the School of Anthropology and Museum of Ethnography, although unfortunately I was not ready to finish the project in 2015, and the birth of my daughter meant that my focus was elsewhere.

Perhaps I would have never chosen to work on female genital cutting if I had not read Janice Boddy's *Wombs and Alien Spirits* as an undergraduate student. I feel profoundly lucky and honored to have received the support and mentorship of Janice Boddy over the last couple of years. Thank you, Janice, for lending me your office at the University of Toronto, for reading through chapters, and for the many invigorating conversations we've had in Europe and Canada. I am also immensely grateful to Katie Kilroy-Marac for feedback, for rereading chapters, and for her enthusiasm about my work. I thank Holly Wardlow and the University of Toronto anthropology department for administrative support during my visiting professorship in 2022.

This work would not be the same without the inspiration of other anthropologists working on FGC whom I cite throughout this book: Ellen Gruenbaum, Bettina Shell-Duncan, Sara Johnsdotter, Elise Johansen, Fuambai Ahmadu, Saida Hodzic and Rick Shweder (and nonanthropologists Birgitta Essen, Jasmine Abdulcadir, and Brian Earp). Their writing has shaped my thinking immensely and I cherish the collegial and friendly ties that have developed over the years. Working on FGC in Brussels would not be the same without my wonderful colleagues at the School of Public Health, Isabelle Godin, Fabienne Richard, and Sophie Alexander, who have all helped me enormously, and I am thankful.

My recent academic and intellectual home has been the Laboratoire Anthropologique des Mondes Contemporains at the Free University of Brussels (ULB), and I would like to thank my dear colleagues Asuncion Freznosa, Joel Noret, Maité Maskens, Oliva Angé, and Pierre Petit for their support, good sense of humor, advice, and comments. Particular thanks go to David Berliner and Sasha Newell for advice and for rereading parts of the book. Anneke Newman and I have had many conversations about our shared field site region, Fouta Toro, over the years, which I thoroughly appreciate.

I thank my FEDtWIN advisor Jacky Maniacky at the Royal Museum of Central Africa. Nicolas Nikis of the Royal Museum of Central Africa/ULB helped me with the maps, for which I am very grateful.

I would like to thank Elisabeth Maselli and Alma Gottlieb, editor of the contemporary ethnography series, for their continuous support and the two anonymous reviewers for their helpful constructive feedback.

I would also like to acknowledge Sabine Panet, who is like family to me now in Brussels, but my journey researching FGC in Senegal started with her twenty years ago. It's been great to share that fun part of our lives in Senegal. I also thank my dear friend Nick Dobbson in London for always being there, across the channel. Shanon Brincat reread a chapter shortly before submission. I am also grateful to Kathy and Peter for sharing their home with me in Toronto and for all those incredible stories of their travels through Africa in the 1990s.

I am indebted to my parents David and Sigrid and my sister Theresa. My dad has actively contributed to this by rereading chapters and editing, and my mum with encouraging words. I thank you for your unconditional love and support wherever my journey has taken me. My aunt and uncle Sue and Mike Lofthouse and my grandparents John and Irene O'Neill were always there for me throughout my studies in the UK, for which I am immensely grateful. I am not sure I would have achieved this without their support earlier on in my life.

This book would not be the same without my dear husband, Seydou. As I have said before, I could not have physically, emotionally, or psychologically done this without you. I am also grateful for comments throughout the writing process and help with Pulaar spelling. And for looking after the children when I was away writing.

The research was funded by the Economic and Social Research Council (1 + 3) for my PhD at Goldsmiths College, University of London. The final writing of the book was funded by an ULB-ERC encouragement grant, a CCCI grant, and an FNRS mobility grant for my research stay at the University of Toronto in 2022.